Tata's Leadership Experiment

Tata's Leadership Experiment

THE STORY OF THE TATA ADMINISTRATIVE SERVICE

BHARAT WAKHLU | MUKUND RAJAN | SONU BHASIN

HARPER BUSINESS

An Imprint of HarperCollins *Publishers*

First published in India in 2022 by Harper Businesss
An imprint of HarperCollins *Publishers*
4th Floor, Tower A, Building No. 10, Phase II, DLF Cyber City,
Gurugram, Haryana – 122002
www.harpercollins.co.in

2 4 6 8 10 9 7 5 3

P-ISBN: 978-93-5629-326-7
E-ISBN: 978-93-5629-334-2

Typeset in 11/14.7 Arno Pro at
Manipal Technologies Limited, Manipal

Printed and bound at
Thomson Press (India) Ltd

MIX
Paper | Supporting responsible forestry
FSC® C010615

This book is produced from independently certified FSC® paper to ensure responsible forest management.

Dedicated to the memory of JRD and his vision of leadership

Contents

Part II
The Post-JRD Era

Part III
Leaders for the Future

About This Book

THE TATAS, ALSO KNOWN AS THE TATA GROUP, IS INDIA'S LARGEST corporate house—by revenue, number of employees, and percentage of stock market capitalization. The Group has a unique ownership structure, which has been in place for almost a century; charities own the majority stake in the Group's holding company, Tata Sons. Equally distinctive is the Group's purpose orientation instilled by the Founder, Jamsetji Nusserwanji Tata. His inclusive view of business found its way into the work of the charities, as well as that of the Tata companies.

In 1938, a very young JRD Tata took on the chairmanship of the Group. He was only thirty-four years old when he inherited the position in what was the largest industrial group of India at that time. Under his leadership, the company assets grew manifold—from USD 100 million to over USD five billion over the next five decades. He started with fourteen ventures in the Group and when he retired, after fifty-three years, the Tata Group was a conglomerate of over ninety-five enterprises.

JRD realized fairly early in his role that he needed people with calibre and intelligence who could help him grow the Group. He was not even a college graduate but understood the importance and need for all-round leaders in the overall leadership structure of the Tata Group. In the mid-1950s, there were no management schools in India that JRD, and the Tata Group could visit to select the right people who could be groomed as future leaders. The key focus, according to JRD, needed to be on the process of developing leaders. He was mindful that the development of leaders within an organization is a journey, not an event.

Leadership development takes time. On-the-job training and application of skills enables leaders to gain insights and experience that no academic course can ever deliver. Furthermore, the journey of development within an organization helps leaders to grow within the prevalent culture. With this as one of the core themes in his quest for talent, JRD envisioned the creation of an exclusive management cadre for the Group, christened as the Tata Administrative Service (TAS); this was created in the same vein as the Indian Administrative Service (IAS) of the Government of India. A TAS Committee, tasked with the responsibility of recruiting the finest brains for the Tata Group, was set up. JRD was clear in his directions to the Committee. He was looking for future leaders—people who would not only grow with the Group, to later take on leadership positions, but also perpetuate Tata values, including integrity, excellence, unity, responsibility and a pioneering spirit that spoke to nation-building. He also envisaged that the members of the cadre would be encouraged to move between different Tata companies and functional areas before settling down in one company. The first TAS officer was selected in 1956.

JRD conceived the idea behind TAS, ensured its birth and nurtured the cadre in its initial years. Early batches of the TAS clearly remember, with great fondness, many conversations with JRD, during which he shared his vision for the cadre. Like any indulgent parent, he wanted only the best for the cadre and those who would be its 'legionnaires'. The TAS was expected to become the Group's general cadre management team and a critical source of leadership talent for diverse Tata companies.

It is also a fact that JRD did not have any children to carry his and the Tata Group's legacy forward. He did look upon his brother-in-law, Leslie Sawhney, as his successor; but it was not to be, as Sawhney died of a heart attack in the 1960s. His death may have strengthened JRD's desire to nurture a cadre which would take the Group's legacy forward. In fact, within the Tata Group, the TAS was colloquially referred to as 'Tata's Adopted Sons'!

In this book, we have explored the concept of the TAS and its various facets—both positive and negative—as it developed over sixty-five years. Since the TAS is an intrinsic part of the Tata Group, we have also examined and analysed various events in the life of the Group as it strode confidently to become bigger each year. Because we have ourselves been a part of the TAS, we are well placed to present an 'inside view'. While there have been many books written about the Tatas and the Tata Group, this is the first time that the TAS and its officers are the protagonists; the Group is seen here through the eyes of a cadre.

A book about the TAS cannot be written, however, without a broader focus on the Tata Group as well. Thus, the various changes that the Tata Group experienced, coupled with those related to the Indian business environment, more generally, especially after 1991, have been narrated and analysed in this book. Since there is very little written about the TAS and its people, we have relied on interviews and conversations with many of the cadre's officers.

While we were always aware of the sterling professional qualities of TAS officers, the writing of this book sharpened the awareness that the TAS was, and continues to be, a very special cadre. The quality of people recruited, especially in the last century, was commendable. It is not a coincidence that almost all the officers, both past and present, are eclectic and humane—reflecting the effort and the thoughtfulness that went into their selection. They were selected through a meticulous and uncompromising selection procedure—the final stage of which, for many years, lasted as long as three days. The candidates were assessed on a host of exacting dimensions of management and leadership to assure the selectors that the officers chosen would be able to handle power and authority without losing their heads and, more importantly, that they would take decisions and actions that would be ethical, always—even in difficult times—remaining upright and upholding the values that were critical to the Tatas.

As you will see in the following pages, the recruitment strategy used was different from other typical selection processes for managerial positions. Senior Directors at Tata, including Chairman JRD thereafter, spent considerable time getting to know the candidates before making well-deliberated selections after almost two or three days of intense interaction.

With such a thorough filtering process in the initial stages of recruitment, it would have been natural to assume that everyone who was part of the TAS would have stayed on and gone on to lead a Tata company (or two). This book presents evidence that this did not happen, though quite a number made a name for themselves within the Group and also outside of it. We have examined the reasons that prevented the TAS from delivering its full promise—both to the officers and to the Group—as candidly as we could. We present accounts of TAS officers, and hope that the leadership lessons from their careers will be instructive to other managers.The book concludes with a look into the future, and the manner in which managers and leaders will create, and deliver value, in the decades to come. We believe that the commitment to values and community-orientation of the House of Tata will serve as valuable guides for other organizations.

Part I

The Genesis of the Tata Administrative Service (TAS)

1

Tata Values and the Founder

'I REMEMBER THAT RIGHT FROM THE BEGINNING, EVEN DURING OUR interviews, we were told about the Tata values,' says Bharat Wakhlu (co-author of this book and TAS officer from the batch of 1985). The Tata values—the intangible glue that binds the Group and its people within and creates a unique culture—were crucial to the formation of the TAS. The Group's values are not a product of the JRD Tata or the Ratan Tata eras; they go back to the founder, Jamsetji Nusserwanji Tata (1839–1904). Jamsetji was barely eighteen years old when the First War of Indian Independence broke out in 1857, affecting a number of major cities and towns in north and central India. In Bombay at the time, Jamsetji was due to graduate from the Elphinstone College; the developments around what the British termed a 'sepoy mutiny' would definitely have made an impression on the young man.

The East India Company, an organization with its own armed militia, was waging a brutal war to subdue the native Indian infantrymen and their allies. Although listed simply as a joint stock corporation in London, the company was actually behaving as a quasi-government entity and 'managing'—while simultaneously exploiting—a whole nation.

Jamsetji came to believe that it was the relentless drive for surpluses and profits—without any humane consideration—that spurred companies to abuse their power and exploit the disadvantaged.

Breaking free from the prevalent ethos and milieu of his times, he thus envisioned a new and pioneering approach to business—creating an enterprise based on the trust of all the stakeholders. He was a visionary businessman, no doubt, but he was also clear that making money was not his only motivation. In his early travels overseas, he had been struck by the miserable working conditions of women and children in the cloth mills in Lancashire and Manchester. It was there that he made a list of the many unjust and inappropriate practices that other businesses seemed to care little about and almost considered 'normal'. Jamsetji vowed that such practices would never be a part of any of his businesses. The values that he envisioned then have formed the bedrock of the Tata Group since.

'Jamsetji had a sensitive side to him that was stirred each time he saw a business practice that he found abhorrent, or an injustice being meted out to hapless employees,' says Bharat. 'The Principles of the Zoroastrian faith, namely persisting with Humata, Hukhta, Hvarashta—Good Thoughts, Good Words, Good Deeds—were fundamental to his approach to business. Being deceitful in one's personal and professional life was revolting to him, and he found it especially repulsive to think that his enterprises would be based on anything but a sound set of principles that were both inclusive and non-exploitative. He wanted his businesses to be led by humane leaders who had a broad vision that went beyond making more money for a small handful of people. Nation-building was an important part of this vision,' he opines.

In sync with this, one of the early entrants to the TAS, Arun Maira (TAS 1965) confirms, 'I joined the TAS because of the Group's focus on nation-building. I had no intention of joining a business house after my graduation and had instead wanted to join the government because I believed that businesses were exploitative. But the two days at Bombay House during the selection interview process changed my mind.' He continues, 'I was told to look at steel-making as a part of the nation-building exercise, for example. And then the senior Tata Directors named other businesses and told me how each was contributing towards building a better India.'

Dr Mukund Rajan (co-author of this book and TAS officer from the batch of 1995) joined the TAS three decades after Arun and agrees that the focus on nation-building was a proud and continuing commitment. He says, 'We would be constantly reminded during our induction about the many institutions of national importance that the Tatas had created, including the Tata Memorial Hospital for cancer research, the Tata Institute for Fundamental Research and the National Centre for the Performing Arts, and the role that the Tata Trusts were playing in supporting some of India's best-known social causes and non-profits.'

Jamsetji was a man of extraordinary ideas, many of which were far ahead of his times. Knowing that he would need the help of others to enhance his businesses and scale up his own efforts, he was always on the lookout for talented people with whom he could work. The people he chose were not always experts in the businesses he recruited them for; instead, many were individuals with good character, and had the ability to get things done with integrity, commitment, and a high degree of attention to detail.

There was one other reason, however, for Jamsetji wanting to focus on excellent and dependable people in his enterprises. He valued his personal leisure time, and that was why he wanted to have reliable individuals whom he wouldn't have to supervise much within his businesses! He would thus also look for the qualities of leadership and enterprise and invite only those who possessed them to be a part of his endeavours. In 1887, almost two decades after he had started his business ventures, Jamsetji inducted his elder son, Dorabji Tata, at that time about twenty-five years old, and the young man's cousin, R.D. Tata, who was then about thirty years of age, into his new company, Tata and Sons. RD had shown considerable acumen in managing the trading operations of his own father's business out of Hong Kong earlier, and that had been appreciated by Jamsetji. After their formal induction into the business, Jamsetji was pleased to note that the two new inductees demonstrated good judgement, sensitivity and suitable value orientation. Jamsetji's partners in Tata and Sons were also mindful of the people-friendly policies of the patriarch. Jamsetji was emphatic that not only were his employees eligible for the support and benevolence of the organization, but even the communities that depended on the businesses they ran had to be cared for. These ideas were reinforced through letters exchanged and during intimate conversations among themselves, thereby ensuring that Jamsetji's progressive ideas were transferred to the younger leaders involved in managing Tata and Sons.

'Evidence that Jamsetji's values and commitment to employee welfare, along with his sterling vision for the Tata Group, were honoured and strengthened in the years after him, comes from the fact that the Tata Iron and Steel Company (TISCO) introduced a slew of enlightened labour welfare measures from 1912 through 1956,' Bharat emphasizes, 'And this was well before any such schemes were introduced in the West!'

Jamsetji Tata breathed his last in May 1904. By the time he was no more, his vision and values, and the manner in which his businesses were to engage with their diverse stakeholders, were etched firmly in the minds of those at the helm of Tata and Sons. These became the guiding principles and shared values that would be embedded in the warp and weft of the Tata Group.

2
Passing the Baton

DORABJI TATA WAS MADE THE CHAIRMAN OF TATA AND SONS UPON THE passing of his father. The last words of Jamsetji Tata to his partners and successors were, 'If you cannot make it greater, at least preserve it. Do not let things slide.' Despite having views that were often divergent from those of his cousin, R.D. Tata, Dorabji worked closely with him, ensuring that those words were honoured.

RD, in the same manner as Jamsetji before him, had a keen eye for talented people who could be helpful in the running of the Tata empire. One of the people that RD took a liking towards was a young British Imperial Civil Service (ICS) officer, a Scotsman named John Peterson, who served as the Director of Munitions in India during World War I. RD noticed that unlike other ICS officers, Peterson was sensitive and helpful towards Indians, ensured that their problems were addressed with alacrity, and was also unpretentious, and down to earth, yet, effective.

After the war, RD approached Peterson and invited him to join TISCO (now Tata Steel) to help turn the company around. Peterson accepted, joining as TISCO's Director-in-Charge, and got down to work immediately. 'It was fortuitous that Peterson left the ICS and joined Tata Steel. The Scotsman understood the strategic importance of the company to the Group,' says Bharat Wakhlu (TAS 1985) as he narrates the story of John Peterson. 'He realized that the decline in prices in the Indian market was largely due to the unrestrained imports of steel from Britain into India. He was a Britisher and maybe understood better than anyone else how the wheels of the Imperial government in India functioned.' Peterson petitioned the Steel Tariff Board in India and sought protection from British imports. Whether it was the forceful petition or due to Peterson being British, the petition was acknowledged by the steel body. Furthermore, it recommended to the Central Legislative Assembly the introduction of a Steel Industry Protection Bill. 'I find it extremely interesting that the Indian Steel Industry at that time had only a single member—the Tata Iron and Steel Company!' laughs Bharat. 'I am sure that this fact was not lost on the Members of the Central Legislative Assembly either.'

The Bill was tabled and there were heated discussions among the members of the Assembly. Pointing out a little-known fact, Bharat says, 'It was Mohammed Ali Jinnah who, as a member of the Assembly, argued passionately for the Bill to be passed.' Jinnah's arguments, along with the arguments of some other members, won the day and the Bill was passed. 'This was the first time in the history of the British government in India that an Indian industry was being protected from imports from Britain!' exclaims Bharat with glee. 'It also was a precursor to the realization within the Tatas that interactions with the central government were necessary for the smooth flow of business.' Eventually, the Tata Sons liaison office was set up in Delhi in 1946 to enable the Group to communicate with various arms of the government. Years later, from 2008 to 2014, Bharat himself would take charge as the Tatas' Resident Director in Delhi.

Working alongside Peterson, RD realized that the seasoned officer could serve as an excellent mentor to his son, Jehangir or Jeh, as he would affectionately call JRD Tata. In 1925, RD requested Peterson to 'look after his boy'. The 'boy', JRD Tata, went on to become the iconic Chairman of the Tata Group and was responsible for its growth, not only in terms of revenues, but also in stature. He was also responsible for setting up the TAS.

3
JRD

JRD TATA, POPULARLY KNOWN AS JRD, WAS BORN IN FRANCE, IN 1904, TO R.D. Tata and his French wife, Suzanne or 'Sooni'. This was a mere two and a half months after the passing of Jamsetji Tata. JRD was schooled in France, England and Japan. After a twelve-month period of conscription in the French army, JRD wanted to study at Cambridge. However, his father decided against it and brought him back to India to join the family business—the Tata Group. A French citizen by birth, JRD gave up his French citizenship and took on the Indian one in 1929. By the time JRD joined the Tata Group, TISCO, which had been established in 1908, was a running concern in Jamshedpur. The company had prospered during the war years from 1914 to 1918, having supplied a variety of steel products—such as steel rails, artillery shells and steel plates—to the British government in India.

Given the high regard that R.D. Tata had for John Peterson, it was natural that the Englishman was asked to take the young JRD under his wing. Peterson took on the responsibility with enthusiasm and insisted that the young man should sit at a table next to him in the very same room at Bombay House.

'Just being with John Peterson was a great learning for JRD,' says Bharat Wakhlu (TAS 1985). 'Every letter or note that needed a decision from Peterson had to be first read and understood by JRD as the young trainee had to be ready to answer any question that his mentor might ask him. I think that the practice of young TAS officers being positioned as Executive Assistants to Senior Directors/Managing Directors of the Tatas started from there. After all, JRD was an Executive Assistant to Peterson, and he often acknowledged that it was that training—understanding the nuances of complex matters, and the myriad factors that had to be considered before taking a decision—that stood him in good stead when he took control of the Group.' Peterson left the Tata Group and went back to England in 1931. Seven years later, JRD took over as the Chairman of Tata Sons—three days before his thirty-fourth birthday.

JRD inherited a business group that had started as a trading company in 1868. The company traded in textiles and other commodities. Continuing the tradition of building new businesses—such as the creation of the Taj Hotel in 1903, the TISCO in 1907, Tata Hydro Electric Power Supply in 1910, the Tata Oil Mills Company in 1917 and Tata Power in 1919—JRD oversaw the establishment of Tata Chemicals in 1939 and the Tata Engineering and Locomotive Company (TELCO) in 1945. In an important development, he also set up Tata Industries in 1945 as the managing agency arm of the holding company, Tata Sons.

4

The Managing Agency System

In India, the managing agency system had evolved in the second quarter of the nineteenth century. The system was adopted by the British colonizers as an efficient way to manage joint stock companies operating in the Indian subcontinent, especially when the shareholders had no first hand knowledge of the businesses they were invested in. The system worked as follows: operating essentially as an entrepreneur, the managing agency would identify a business opportunity, for example a cotton mill, and then raise venture capital from friends and associates of the managing agent or promoter. The shortfall in funding, if any, was borrowed from a bank. With the funds in hand, the managing agency bought the mill and set up its operations. Once the mill and the business were running successfully, the managing agency sold the majority of its shareholding in the company to the public. However, it signed a long-term management contract with the company which gave it the right to continue to manage the business. The proceeds it derived from its sale of equity were then invested in some other business—say, a coffee plantation.

The managing agency, despite its small residual shareholding, continued to manage the cotton mill and the business thereof, under its long-term management contract. The managing agency would make key decisions on behalf of its operating businesses, on matters such as which products to manufacture, which markets to target and where to source raw materials.

The advantage of this system was that it enabled the agency to control and run a number of business enterprises with a relatively small financial stake in each. A managing agency's ability to raise capital from the bank and the public depended on its track record and reputation. The Tatas scored high on these parameters and were thus able to operate large businesses. The agency earned generous commissions, either as a percentage of sales or profits plus other fees. The partners of the agency, or the Directors in the case of Tata Sons and Tata Industries, had a high appetite for entrepreneurship.

The managing agency system was hugely popular in pre-Independent India as the British had adopted it with enthusiasm. By World War I, managing agencies controlled 75 per cent of industrial capital of India and almost half of industrial employment. And by 1954, managing agencies accounted for 51 per cent of the share capital of all companies.

Often, a single managing agency controlled a large number of operating companies—some of them completely unrelated. This led to a limit being placed, through the Companies Act 1956, on the number of companies that could be controlled by a managing agent. Now, it had become quite clear to JRD Tata, even before the introduction of the Companies Act of 1956, that there was a challenge in running companies across a diverse set of industrial domains—textiles, hotels, steel, automobiles, chemicals, and more. He looked at a number of personnel (there was no Human Resources (HR) in those days, only a Department of Personnel) management solutions with a focus on introducing greater professionalism in a coordinated manner.

When agency contracts were transferred from Tata Sons to Tata Industries, JRD brought in new Board members based on their professional expertise. The Directors of most major Tata companies were inducted into the Board of Tata Industries. But concerns remained about the development of talent within current managers as well as a steady supply of future managers to the growing number of Tata companies.

The Tata Industries Board was envisioned as a harmonizing body that would reconcile competing demands, ensuring that all Tata entities would grow together. They would leverage each other's strengths and capabilities rather than competing with each other for resources, talent or access to government contracts and orders. This was an idea that was far ahead of its time. While the cohesion within the Tata Group was considerably high in the early fifties, JRD foresaw that the Tata empire would continue to grow larger and needed an acceptable method to reconcile disparate goals and aspirations within its individual companies.

The experiment with Tata Industries inculcated a sense of collective ownership in the leadership teams of different Tata companies. The leaders, and especially the Chief Executives of the different Tata companies, viewed their roles as custodians of the well-being of the House of Tata, as much as of their own firms. This is what JRD wanted, and he was glad that the 'superglue'—that unique blend of Tata values and superordinate goals, which could only arise and get reinforced within the thinking and the decisions of the senior management teams of the respective companies—would serve to bind the whole of the Tata empire together.

JRD was conscious that with increasing profits and market shares, the leaders of the individual Tata companies could wish to forge a centrifugal trajectory that might deviate from the larger vision and values of the Tatas. The creation of the Tata Industries Board assured him that not only would the respective boards of the different Tata companies be there to assist and guide the Chief Executives, but even peers heading different Group companies would be able to weigh in with ideas and suggestions for their colleagues, in a non-threatening, collegial manner.

Tata Industries also became a vehicle for the creation of new enterprises for the Tata Group. At the same time, JRD realized that the concept of 'thinking for the whole' needed to be extended to a wider set of executives and managers. While the Tata Industries Board comprised of Directors and the heads of the Tata companies, the ideas they discussed would have to percolate down further and deeper within each Tata enterprise. The decision-makers at all levels had to resonate with the values and the 'mutuality' that had been a part of the Tata Group since its inception. To enable this, JRD instituted a system wherein an Inter-Departmental Conference would be held on a monthly basis, and the top thirty or so executives from different Tata companies would have a chance to interact. They deliberated on ways to resolve issues confronting the Group as a whole.

However, JRD was conscious that such a harmonizing influence would have to be made much more widespread. His mentoring by John Peterson had provided him with compelling evidence that talented employees, with the right qualities, aptitude, character and administrative judgement, when made an integral part of each of the Tata companies, could function as 'gyroscopes' to ensure that these companies remained on an even keel, well-aligned with the Tata values and the overarching goals of the Tata Group.

5
Focus on Leadership

THE FOCUS ON THE 'RIGHT' TALENT FOR THE TATA GROUP OF COMPANIES had started from the time Jamsetji Tata had set up his first textile mill in the 1870s. In the early days, even TISCO had relied largely on trained project engineers, brought in from firms in the US and Germany, for setting up the complex infrastructure in the factories, including the blast furnaces.

'But the Tata managers soon realized that it was difficult for them to find able-bodied and somewhat skilled workers to work in the steel factory,' says Bharat Wakhlu (TAS 1985).

It was difficult because of two reasons. One, people had no idea about the work to be done in a steel factory. Two, most were unwilling to work in the tough and hot environment in the factory, especially around the blast furnace.

'The managers found an interesting way to solve this problem. They sent their junior colleagues to the Kalimati train station at Jugsalai (now known as Tatanagar station). These employees waited for the slow trains of the Bengal–Nagpur Railway Company that would halt at Kalimati. When the trains stopped, the employees would quiz travelling young men on board about their interest in a job at TISCO, their education and their literacy levels, and would simultaneously gauge their fitness—sometimes even asking them to lift a few heavy objects. Those who were found willing, and with the aptitude for working in the steel mills, were offered jobs then and there,' chuckles Bharat as he thinks of those early Tata men lying in wait for potential employees.

By the 1950s, recruitment had become more scientific. The number of foreigners in key positions reduced. Each Tata company now developed its own methods for the recruitment of specialized workmen. These workmen who were brought in at entry levels would typically grow into larger roles with additional responsibilities, even as their domain focus and areas of expertise remained the same. A number of brilliant specialists were moved into higher administrative positions when there was a need.

This search for the right kind of talent for the Tata empire was an important driver of action for JRD. His key concern was: As the Tatas expanded, with different companies pursuing their best interests, how would the Tata values and the collective interests be safeguarded? This was a legitimate concern, since JRD was privy to many divergent requests for funds from expanding companies. He anticipated the need for something that would ensure that even as these companies continued to grow, the managers and executives would retain their Tata ethos and work for the expansion of the fortunes of Tata Sons with equal zeal.

JRD looked at the problem of talent acquisition and training with an open mind and undertook various initiatives. One such was to send select groups of his executives overseas, to learn more about best practices for the development of managers. These learnings were brought back to the Tata Group, and JRD used this knowledge to supplement his own approach.

He aspired to create a foundation for a common and distinctive Tata culture in management. He wanted this culture to be characterized by a spirit of consensus, and authority based on technical knowledge along with individual leadership. It was a tall task for any organization, and not all his experiments were successful.

One such initiative that failed was the establishment of the 'Superior Staff Recruitment Committee' in 1948. JRD had realized that a robust process was a prerequisite for acquiring the right talent. He created a small team of senior executives—the Superior Staff Recruitment Committee that would assess and recruit people. The term 'superior' was meant to establish that the personnel selected would be not only highly qualified, but would also bring a dash of energy and the right competencies. The Committee comprised senior executives from the Tata Group, including Homi Modi, Ardershir Dalal, John Matthai and JRD. They recruited three young men on the basis of their educational qualifications and an interview. However, all three new recruits left within a space of a few months. Apparently, the lack of guidance and attention given to the young men contributed to their lack of integration within the Tata companies to which they were assigned. JRD would admit, 'While they were not selected with proper preparations and study, and they did not last very long, I was still satisfied that this was the right thing to do and that we must do it again, but do it properly.'

Learning from the failure of the Superior Staff Recruitment process, JRD contemplated relaunching his initial idea as a more structured 'Tata Cadre'. The Committee also looked around for inspiration and sought information on the Management Trainee programmes that companies such as Hindustan Lever Ltd had established, as well as the recruitment schemes and training processes relied upon by multinational oil companies. The Committee members realized that since the Tata Group was a diversified conglomerate, a simple Management Trainee programme would not achieve the many objectives that JRD had in mind.

6
The Origins of the TAS

JRD HAD BEEN DEEPLY INFLUENCED BY JOHN PETERSON WHO HAD WORKED for the ICS before joining the Tatas. His own experience as an Executive Assistant to the Britisher planted the idea in JRD's mind that the Tatas needed something that would be akin to an 'ICS for the Tatas'.

A cadre-based system like the ICS, or the IAS as the service was renamed after Independence, appealed to JRD. He had spent his early years in France and had also served in the French Army. In French society, cadres had come to represent a kind of social reference point. Some cadres also had military antecedents, but their collective identity had jumped the divide from being purely professional, to commanding social position and status.

In French society, cadres had become aspirational social groups and part of the French elite. Moreover, the social esteem enjoyed by cadres was not shallow, merely based on titles. Instead, it was linked to a rigorous education system; premier educational institutions (the 'Grandes Écoles' were able to attract the best students) and the most reputed companies, which chose to come to these institutions to look for bright managers. Over time, a virtuous circle developed—the institutions would select the best students, and the best French companies would recruit them, leading to these Grandes Écoles becoming the destinations of choice for more young bright students. The concept of a cadre-based administrative system has also been part of Indian society for thousands of years. Kautilya's famous text, Arthashastra, talks about a large and complex bureaucracy as a remarkable feature of the governance structure within the Mauryan empire. This was a well-organized, hierarchical and cadre-based administrative system, which allowed the government to regulate the economic life of the kingdom. It was hugely aspirational for the common people to be part of this elite cadre. Kautilya laid down guidelines and qualifications for people who could be part of this cadre. The cadre envisioned by JRD had features of both the French and the Indian systems. JRD and the Superior Staff Recruitment Committee proposed the recruitment of young people from the best universities around the world, including Oxbridge. The importance of choosing officers for the cadre from 'good families', with an appropriate work ethic and values, was emphasized.

The Committee's desire to recruit from well-known universities was also linked to the fact that there were no management institutes in India in the 1950s. Most people started to work straight after their graduation and worked their way up the corporate ladder. But JRD was clear in his direction to the Committee. He was looking for future leaders—people who would not only grow in the Group to take on leadership positions, but also individuals who would perpetuate the Tata values across the Group companies. JRD envisaged that the members of the Tata cadre would be encouraged to move between different Tata companies and functional areas before settling down in one company. JRD was also mindful of the fact that the IAS was the most aspirational civil services cadre in India. It drew the best and the brightest from across the country. IAS officers, immediately after their induction, were given positions of considerable responsibility and power, and regularly moved between various departments/ministries of the Government of India. Those selected were looked upon as men and women of calibre and integrity by others. The administrative framework was described by

India's first Home Minister, Sardar Vallabhai Patel, as the 'Steel Frame' for governance in India.

By 1956, JRD had the recommendations of the Superior Staff Recruitment Committee before him, as well as the myriad inputs he had gleaned from a variety of sources in India, Britain and France. He recognized the value of the equivalent of the 'Steel Frame'—the Indian Administrative Service—represented for the Tata Group. The Tatas were not as complex or disparate as India, but JRD was convinced that the time had come for such a cadre to be put into place.

It was JRD's vision that the members of the cadre would become the mobile superglue that would harmonize the working of the growing Tata Group. They would serve as a cohesive force that would unobtrusively compel the Group's companies to be fully aligned with the values and the larger goals of the Group. The cadre members would work with Tata companies in different sectors, but would not be confined to remain in single companies for their entire careers. Their mobility was to be an asset for the Group; wherever their intervention and expertise would be needed within the Tata Group, they would be sent in to work with senior leaders and make a wholesome impact.

JRD named the cadre the Tata Administrative Service (TAS).

7

The TAS Selection Process

THE MANNER OF THE SELECTION OF PROSPECTIVE YOUNG LEADERS INTO the TAS was deliberated by a core group of Directors close to JRD Tata. They agreed that they were looking for people who were business leaders in the making, and not just those who might have the technical qualifications and expertise required for a specific industry. They would look for a certain 'type' of person, who would demonstrate the essential qualities that the Tatas needed.

It was also agreed that the selection process would be different and more scientific than what was followed by many 'Box Wallah' companies, successful subsidiaries of multinational companies operating out of India in the 1950s and 1960s. As advocated in Kautilya's *Arthashastra,* there was some emphasis on selecting officers from 'good families', with the right work ethic and values that would gel with those of the Tatas.

The Committee found a rich catchment, in the early years, in the pool of scholars funded by the Tata Trusts to pursue their studies abroad. The J.N. Tata Endowment was focused on awarding scholarships to deserving students wishing to study further in universities overseas. The Endowment exercised basic due diligence by vetting the scholars, their family background and academic credentials; all that the selectors had to do was get some of these students to apply. The selection process would then further sift out the candidates, so only a few would make the cut. Dr Freddie A. Mehta (TAS 1956), the first recruit, was in his early twenties and a doctorate in Economics from the London School of Economics when he joined the Tatas. Like almost all subsequent TAS officers, he was academically brilliant and came with impressive credentials that caught the attention of the selection committee immediately.

The selection process—all the way till the mid-nineties—was fairly elaborate. In the early decades of the cadre, the TAS Secretariat would announce the start of the recruitment process in select magazines and newspapers.

At the same time, reputed colleges across the country and a few overseas were sent intimations. These colleges would then reach out to the TAS Secretariat to try and schedule preliminary interviews on their campuses—usually right at the start of the placement season since the TAS was aspirational among the graduating students. The on-campus selection process was rigorous, and there was a high cut-off for eligibility. Candidates who were above this academic threshold but from colleges not visited by TAS were invited to one of the chosen campuses close to them for the preliminaries.

The response to the on-campus advertisements and the announcements was usually overwhelming. Thanks to the values of the Group and the performance of many of the growing number of companies, the draw of the Tatas as an employer and the appeal of the TAS as a leadership development opportunity were powerful. Moreover, Tata companies were playing an active role in contributing to the developmental requirements of the nation—be it iron and steel, hospitality, energy or commercial vehicles. Therefore, it wasn't surprising that the Group was considered to be as important a contributor to national well-being as the government! Furthermore, this orientation of the Tatas gave those committed to a more 'purposeful' contribution to national development an alternative to the Civil Services—albeit with less authority, but definitely more money.

Harpal Singh (TAS 1974) vividly recalls JRD's conversation with the candidates during the selection process. 'JRD first asked us why we were interested in the TAS. Obviously, there were a variety of enthusiastic responses from candidates, with each of them indicating interest in the steel business, the hotel industry or the automotive sector. After JRD had heard us all, he said, in his inimitable style: "We are in none of these businesses. We are in the business of nation-building. And each one of you has a job there." This was the comment that excited me; I informed my family, rather emphatically, that I wanted to be a part of TAS—not Citibank, where I already had a job at the time, or the government services that I had cleared the exam for.'

The Tatas were also known for leaders who were not just committed to doing business ethically, but even had the courage to forego opportunities acquired through 'tainted' means. Furthermore, JRD's chairmanship of Tata Sons without break, from 1938 all the way through till 1991, and that, too, without getting into any kind of public spat for power with his capable and effective colleagues, showed the world that the Tatas were driven by a commitment to values and fair play that were beyond the ordinary. Besides, his long tenure conveyed the idea that the Tatas were steadfast in their businesses and would keep the long term in mind, ignoring short-term ups and downs. Prospective TAS officers knew they would never be forced to do things that would go against their own conscience and expose them to needless risk.

The fear of being 'thrown under the bus' by unscrupulous business owners wasn't entirely unfounded. Even though India's mercantile class was largely patriotic and committed to doing business honestly, the 'licence raj', which became the Indian government's means to regulate business growth and implement a socialist approach to the economy, crimped the entrepreneurial drive of most Indian businesses. A regulatory nightmare forced many businesses to either remain small players, mired in a web of absurd regulations and stymied in terms of growth, if they did not want to strive to discover convenient ways to bypass the regulations or influence the policy-makers so as to relax a set of specific rules to their advantage. When business owners wanted changes in regulations to be made by the government, it would inevitably be one of their professional managers who would be given the job to 'convince' the bureaucrats. This was obviously not up everyone's alley, and often talented people would find themselves without a job because they had refused to do what they were told to. The security of employment was a big positive factor in the Tata Group. The general view was that Tata companies rarely fired anyone for poor performance. Instead, the companies had a system of providing guidance and development opportunities to those who were somehow achieving their full potential. TAS officers were therefore in line for long and steady careers with the House of Tata. Unless they botched things up really badly, they could expect to serve for many years.

The on-campus application process was fairly elaborate. It required prospective candidates to write essays on a variety of questions and themes that would provide a glimpse into the mindset of the young aspirants, and the ideas and values that they were passionate about. This helped assess the clarity of their thinking and the fluency with which they expressed themselves in writing. In a sense, the application process for the TAS was similar to the application process most top global business schools adopt today.

The essays and other details shared by the candidates were used by the selectors to screen the aspirants. Typically, about half the applicants would be dropped at this stage, creating a shortlist. These candidates would then be brought together for group discussions. The discussions provided further insights into the ways the contenders thought things through, and how they interacted with other members of the group. A key assessment also revolved around how quickly the applicants could put their thoughts together, and how clearly they were able to express themselves thereafter.

Inputs from the group discussions were used by the selectors to create a micro-list of usually not more than a candidate or two, from each campus. When the names of those on the micro-list were announced on campus, there would be jubilation across the entire batch! Sometimes colleges would be collectively disappointed if none of their eligible candidates had been selected. Candidates on the list would be flown to Bombay (now Mumbai) for the final round, which would typically be conducted through a weekend, with the last round of interviews and a business lunch with Tata Directors scheduled for the following Monday. The candidates would go through a battery of psychological tests, as well as a host of analysis rounds related to decision-making, value-orientation and thinking capabilities.

'The initial TAS batches were modest in size, and typically had several Oxbridge graduates—officers like Nawshir Khurody, Xerxes Desai and Camellia Panjabi, to name a few,' recalls Francis DaCunha (TAS 1971). This was because, in the first few years, the selection undoubtedly focused on reputed overseas colleges as the candidate catchment areas.

However, universities and colleges in India started to get attention in the mid-sixties. Arun Maira (TAS 1965) mentions that during his selection interview with the TAS Committee, he initially felt at a disadvantage on being compared with Oxonians and the Cantabrigian candidates among the lot, but not for long. 'Despite my feeling a little inferior to the foreign educated candidates initially, I quickly got over it; because the selectors were courteous and caring, and made no attempt to intimidate me. Instead, I was pleasantly surprised when instead of bombarding me with questions, they cared to ask me about my interests and passions. Besides, they listened to me with rapt attention. That really touched me,' Arun says with a sparkle in his eyes.

Francis does mention that the Indianization of the TAS was a shift that was well thought out and planned. He says, 'The 'Indianization' of the TAS Selections commenced with reputed Indian colleges such as St. Stephens getting a look-in. (Arun Maira (TAS 1965) being one such alumnus.) Then around 1967–68, there arrived this new animal on the horizon called the "MBA". Describing the first 'jumbo' TAS batch that followed in 1970, Francis tells us that nine individuals were selected, and all were MBAs or engineers with MBAs, including officers like T.K. Balaji, Richard Masilamani and Gulam Vahanvaty, among others. Francis was part of the very next 'jumbo' batch. There were again nine people selected, but only six joined, including officers like Aubrey Rebello, Raj Kadan and Rajan Jhanjee. 'There was a bright chap called Mundra who committed the sacrilegious act of not joining, and going over instead to Hindustan Unilever (where he rose to become the CFO)!' laughs Francis, mimicking a look of horror.

The Selection Committee, with senior Directors, including the group chairman as members, was supported by the TAS Secretariat, which was steered by a capable Member-Secretary. The Member-Secretary would ensure that the pre-selection formalities—including outreach to campuses and students—were handled efficiently. The Member-Secretary was assisted by a small staff. In the formative years of the TAS, Prof. Rustom Choksi (1902–86) played the role of Member-Secretary. Prof. Choksi was also a trustee of several of the Tata Trusts. His successor was D.K. Malegamwala.

During Malegamwala's tenure as the Member-Secretary of the TAS, there were some initial concerns about the rising influx of MBAs in the organization. Malegamwala was sceptical about the creation of a 'monoculture' in the TAS with mainly MBAs being hired. He had his doubts about how much MBAs would add value to the Group. Wanting to have more diversity in the intake, he therefore commenced a September induction of Oxbridge graduates who could not physically appear for the regular schedule of interviews in India earlier in the year. This practice of mid-year selections continued for some years in the mid-seventies, but was then discontinued. 'The practice was revived briefly in September 1994,' recollects Dr Mukund Rajan (TAS 1995), 'the year I was interviewed for the TAS, only to be rolled back again from the following year.'

Two TAS batches in a year complicated the induction programme. A single intake made it easier to address all the logistics of inducting the growing batch sizes of TAS officers. Perhaps more importantly, and to Malegamwala's utter horror, Tata companies started preferring the new crop of engineers/MBAs. Companies like TISCO and TELCO, the heavyweights in the Group, actively sought out candidates with these qualifications.

'Some of the Oxbridge graduates who had joined the TAS—including one who had a tripos from Oxford in Ancient Egyptian History—felt like misfits, and therefore quit. The historian eventually became an antiques dealer!' remembers Francis.

Meanwhile, uniquely within the Tata Group, one company decided it did not really need generalist MBAs. This was Tata Consultancy Services (TCS), under the leadership of F.C. Kohli, who preferred to identify more Information Technology (IT) and computer science-oriented graduates for the business. 'The TAS never really found much traction within TCS,' says Francis.

8
Those Three Days!

'THE WHOLE EXPERIENCE OF THE SELECTION PROCESS WAS A VERY pleasant one. Not at all like anything I had expected!' says Khorshed Jhaveri (TAS 1958), the first woman in the TAS. (Sadly, she passed away as we were writing this book.) Khorshed seems to have a remarkably clear memory of the interview process she went through in 1958. 'I was the only lady in the whole group of candidates, and I got special treatment, especially from JRD Tata,' she says with a twinkle in her eyes as she recalls the envy of her fellow candidates. Khorshed came from a well-known Parsi family of Bombay and her father was an eminent lawyer.

Arun Maira (TAS 1965), on the other hand, came from a refugee family. He was studying physics at St. Stephen's College in Delhi and had interviewed with some companies in Calcutta and Madras as well. 'I had not heard of the TAS but I applied because it gave me an opportunity to go to Bombay—a city I had always wanted to visit but had never had a chance to, till then,' says Arun.

He went in expecting an interview process similar to the ones he had been subjected to in other companies. 'I was used to encountering interviewers who were very eager to show off their own knowledge,' he says, shrugging his shoulders. 'I remember once [in another company] an interviewer asked me a convoluted question and I answered it. His colleague immediately asked me another complex question and when I hesitated while answering, the questioner looked triumphantly at his colleague, as if to say "See, he could not answer my question!"' laughs Arun. But the TAS process, Arun found, was completely different, and designed to get to know a candidate really well.

The selection process was spread over a few days. Till the mid-seventies, it happened partly in Bombay and partly in Pune at the Tata Management Training Centre (TMTC), before it shifted entirely to Bombay.

The TAS Committee consisted of senior Tata Directors who took their time in getting to know the candidates better. The selection process consisted of a written test, group discussions, a meeting with a psychiatrist (which was later discontinued), a lunch at the Taj Mahal Hotel, and finally, a personal interview with the TAS Committee. The Directors gave their time to the process with full commitment. 'When I was there, I wondered how the Directors found so much time to spend with us. It seemed unique to TAS!' quips Surya Sethi (TAS 1975).

There was a reason for the Committee to spread the selection process over days. The Committee was looking for qualities in the candidates that could not be discovered by a mere question–answer session. The TAS was to be the elite cadre within the Tata Group and its members had to have what the French so articulately describe as '*Je ne sais quoi*' qualities. This French idiomatic expression is used so often by the English that the phrase is today a part of the Webster dictionary. *Je ne sais quoi* is something that cannot be adequately described or expressed but whose existence is understood intuitively.

Debjani Biswas (TAS 1983) agrees. 'During the multiple rounds of the TAS interview process, it felt like Committee members were looking for that indefinable quality we now call 'Executive Presence'', says Debjani in her calibrated voice. The Army, too, has its own equivalent of this—they call it Officer-Like Qualities (OLQ). These intangible qualities took time to discover and the TAS Committee was prepared to invest their time in the process.

Arun Wakhlu (TAS 1980) holds the view that the Committee had to spend time with the candidates because gauging two of the key leadership competencies that the TAS sought definitely required time to assess. 'The TAS seemed to place immense emphasis on the leadership traits of personal integrity and the degree of passion one brought to the pursuit of new learning. I remember the Committee probing deeply my general interest in spiritual matters. It almost seemed as if they were trying to answer the question: Is this young man just a dilettante or does he truly have a deep and abiding interest in what he's pursuing?'

Sanjaya Sharma (TAS 1980) reaffirms this. 'The TAS Committee would ask candidates to indicate their areas of interest. They would then go deep into any area of interest the candidate had mentioned. Even if the area of interest was not related to business or management, it didn't matter,' he says. 'I had mentioned that I enjoyed nonsense poetry and was asked to recite Lewis Carroll's *Jabberwocky'*, he laughs.

The written test and the group discussions were designed to meet a few objectives. One, for the candidates to interact with each other and get comfortable. Two, for the Committee members to watch the candidates interacting in different environments. Three, the Committee was also keen to ascertain if the candidates were authoritarian or followed a consensus approach while resolving issues in a group. The third objective was an especially important quality for the Tatas, where the ability of candidates to work both as a team member as well as a leader, were prized.

While candidates expected to jump various hoops, the one part of the selection process that unnerved even the most hardened candidates was the lunch at the Taj Mahal Hotel. 'We were all told that the lunch was not part of the selection process, but we knew differently,' says Ashok Mehta (TAS 1966). 'Of course, in my time the lunch used to be held at the fourth floor of Bombay House,' he adds.

Since almost the entire top brass of the Tata Group would be present at these lunches, the Taj would pull out all stops to offer a truly spectacular spread. 'But we could not give full rein to our appetites,' says Ashok in his booming voice. The lunch was a formal sit-down affair with an array of forks, knives, spoons, plates and glasses set at each place on the table. Furthermore, there were pristine, crisp white napkins. No candidate wanted to hurt his or her chances by picking the wrong fork or using the wrong glass! And certainly no one wanted to stain the whiter-than-white napkins either.

The smarter ones turned vegetarian for the Taj lunch! Others had more innovative ideas. 'I told Mr Jamshed Bhabha, who was sitting next to me at the lunch table, that I had an upset stomach, and therefore would be able to eat only simple dal and chawal (rice),' remembers Rajeev Dubey (TAS 1975), with a hearty laugh. No one wanted to take the risk of butchering a perfectly cooked piece of chicken with a fork and knife; none wanted to be caught speaking with their mouths full; and nobody, absolutely nobody, wanted to be one to spit out bones, however delicately, onto the plate!

Some of the smarter ones prepared for that lunch even before the final interviews. Ajoy Misra (TAS 1980) remembers his preparation well. 'In preparation for the test lunch, I tried my hand at home carving roast chicken and using all the layers of cutlery laid out in precise order alongside the plates.' He thought he was well prepared. 'However, I was faced with a last-minute decision when the server asked me 'veg or non-veg' on the day of the lunch itself. I hesitated, as a starving meat-eater, but said vegetarian because I was not sure that I could keep the chicken from flying out of my plate!' he exclaims. Ajoy, too, turned vegetarian for the day. He went on to spend many illustrious years at the Taj Hotels as part of the senior leadership and must have eaten hundreds of non-vegetarian meals thereafter.

Sonu Bhasin (co-author of the book and a TAS officer of batch 1987) remembers her lunch table. She was the only candidate at the table and had three Committee members for company. 'I was a vegetarian in any case and had no problem eating my simple dal and chawal,' she says as she mimics taking a spoon delicately to her mouth. 'Though the crisp tandoori rotis looked mouth-watering, I did not order them for fear of dropping the crumbs on the table,' she recollects. 'But the Committee members on my table had no such qualms! I remember the waiter coming with a small brush and a tiny little dust scoop after our main course, to remove the crumbs of the rotis that had been eaten. Clearly, they were not on test!' she says with regret in her voice as she remembers the appetizing food she could not partake of.

'Once we were selected and went to the Taj again as part of our team lunch, you should have seen all of us eat! No one was vegetarian, and no one had an upset stomach. I had two tandoori rotis and the waiter did come after the main course to pick up the crumbs but I did not care—I was not on test anymore!' Sonu laughs delightedly.

The Taj lunch gave the TAS Committee members the perfect opportunity to chat informally with the candidates. Arun remembers the lunch vividly as he was sure that he had blown his chances at it. 'I had always been interested in art and had written about it in my CV.' Jamshed Bhabha, one the Directors, was an art lover, and he decided to bring up the subject after looking at his resume. 'The lunch at the Taj was in the newly opened Apollo Room. There were murals on the wall with nymphs and other such Greek/Western mythological creatures frolicking in a Western-style garden. Hence the name "Apollo Room", I think. The tables were laid out to seat three each. I remember there was Jamshed Bhabha and Dr Parukh, the psychiatrist, at my table,' says Arun.

The lunch was a pleasant experience and Arun remembers that he, too, ate very lightly. The conversation veered to art and Jamshed and Arun talked of various painters and their styles. 'Then Mr Bhabha looked around and pointed to the large paintings on the walls of the Gateway Room,' says Arun. Jamshed asked Arun what he thought of them. Arun looked at the large paintings and expressed his frank view that they did no justice to the otherwise tastefully done-up room. 'I thought I detected a fleeting look of surprise on Mr Bhabha's face, but I was young and had the arrogance of youth,' continues Arun.

Jamshed asked Arun to elaborate, which he did with much enthusiasm. 'I remember we discussed the paintings in great detail. I told him what did not work for me. He was very attentive and discussed each aspect of the paintings minutely,' says Arun.

While they were deep into the discussion, the steward brought them their dessert, which the table of three polished off even as they spoke. As Jamshed pushed his now-empty dessert plate aside, the attentive steward came forward quickly and asked if they wanted a second helping. 'Now, I did love that dessert, but I thought it would be extremely rude if I asked for a second helping. I did not want to blow my chances by not knowing the dining etiquette,' says Arun, waving his hands as if waving away the dessert. Jamshed had no such qualms and requested for another serving, which he then ate with much relish.

When it was time to go back to Bombay House for the rest of the selection process and the announcement of the results, just as they were waiting for the cars to arrive at the porch of the hotel, Dr Parukh invited Arun to accompany him in his car. During the short ride to Bombay House, the doctor mentioned the paintings in the Gateway Room. 'Do you know that Mr Bhabha personally commissioned those paintings and was in touch with the painter throughout to get the output he wanted?' he asked quietly while looking at Arun intently.

Arun's heart sank, but then he responded, 'Mr Bhabha did ask me about my honest opinion, did he not?' While he was wondering if he had shot himself in the foot, Arun almost missed the next question. 'I saw that you had only one helping of the dessert. Did you not know that the Directors all love their dessert and always have a second helping? It is dining etiquette that they do not eat alone at the table,' continued Dr Parukh, still looking at him intently.

'Gosh, I have really blown it,' thought Arun as he agonized over the mistakes made at lunch. He imagined that all the other candidates knew about the second serving and that they must all have ordered accordingly. 'The first thing I did when I reached the candidates' room was to ask if everyone else had a single or a double helping of the dessert,' says Arun. To his immense relief, not a single person had requested for seconds. 'I was back in the game as the playing field was level—dessert wise,' laughs Arun.

The Taj lunch aside, the personal interviews were a key part of the selection process. The interviews, too, were different from the usual fare in other companies, again, because the Committee took time to understand the individual interests of the candidates and talked to them about these.

'I got selected because of dogs and jazz,' says Vijay Rai (TAS 1971). During his interview, he was asked about the most tedious experience he had had in recent months. 'Pat came my reply—registering a pedigree dog,' says Vijay. His aunt had been gifted a purebred Lhasa Apso. 'I needed to get it registered as the dog would not be considered a pure breed till I had the registration papers.' Jamshed Bhabha was also interested in dogs. He talked to Vijay at length about purebreds, the process of registration and the care needed for such dogs.

Francis Menezes, another Selection Committee member, then asked Vijay about the love he had for music. 'I had grown to love jazz (mainly by listening to the Voice of America programmes on radio), and Francis and I talked about jazz and the various singers,' says Vijay. He was later told that the Committee was looking for people who, if they had an interest, would have deep knowledge about it. They were not looking for superficial knowledge. Thus, dogs and jazz came in handy for Vijay, who was a mechanical engineer.

At the interviews, the Committee members made every effort to put the candidates at ease. They were not looking for a stress interview. Surya remembers his interview very well. 'We had to walk into the Board Room at Bombay House, and just at the entrance there was a big bowl with some folded pieces of paper,' remembers Surya. These folded papers each had a topic written in it and the candidate was to speak extempore on whatever topic they happened to pick.

'I had gone to the wash-room and it was while I was there that my name was called out as the next person to be interviewed,' says Surya. 'I rushed out after washing my hands, of course!' says Surya, 'and almost ran to the Board Room.' He was understandably a little flustered as he walked into the Board Room and picked up a folded piece of paper. The bowl was at the entrance and the candidate's seat was at the other end of the room. 'I unfolded my piece of paper and saw only one word: Fate.'

Surya's mind went blank as he could not think of anything that he could talk about. 'The walk to my chair was the slowest of my life,' laughs Surya. He was thinking about what to say as he was walking. 'As I sat down, the only thing I could think of was the song, *Que Sera Sera*!' says Surya. So he launched forth and replaced the lyrics of the song to share fateful events of his own life, ending each stanza with his mother, father or an older sibling reassuring him with '*que sera sera*' ('what will be will be'). 'I ended by saying that now Fate has brought me here and I ask the TAS Committee will I be, will I be—*que sera sera*!' says Surya.

He had been speaking for 10 minutes, and the Committee had been listening mesmerized by all the intriguing stories of his life. As he finished, Jamshed stood up clapping and said, 'Young man, *que sera sera,* you will be, you will be! But before you go zip up that fly of yours!'

Surya knew then that he had cracked the interview and the selection process. It is another matter that Sanjay Johri (TAS 1975) who went after Surya for his interview picked a piece of paper that asked him to talk about his pet. 'Sanjay came out and said that the Committee members seemed a little disappointed with my story about my dog. It was not as interesting as yours,' laughs Surya. Sanjay was also selected, however.

There was one more reason that the Committee took their time to understand the candidates in great detail—they did not have to fill in any slots. The TAS did not have to recruit any prescribed number of officers each year. It depended entirely on the calibre of the individuals. Some years, over half a dozen officers were selected, while in others just one. There was even a time when no one came up to scratch and thus, there was zero intake into the TAS that year. One of the Committee members, Professor Rustom Choksi, told the candidates that they were looking for people who were passionate about what they do and were good learners. Furthermore, there was little purpose served in finding out how good the candidates were at what they had done in the past, because what they would be doing thereafter was going to be completely different. Professor Choksi reiterated that they were not hiring managers but future leaders—especially those eager to embrace continuous learning.

Visty Banaji (TAS 1973) is of the view that while the Committee may have wanted the candidates to be good, and preferably 'lifelong' learners, they could have been misled. 'The difficulty is that super-qualified people may be poor learners,' Visty says, adding that it is never easy to judge, in a brief interview, if a candidate has the right kind of interpersonal skills.

For many of the TAS batches that joined the Tata Group after the early sixties, one of the key persons in the Secretariat was a gentleman named Bhupen Chakravarti—a mild-mannered man who would sport a goatee and who was devoted both to the cadre and to the Tatas. Bhupen was the repository of all the anecdotes and stories of the TAS, and it was customary for him to be the first person to interact with the prospective candidates on the day of their face-to-face interviews with the Committee and their interactions with the Tata Directors. Such was the warmth and spirit of generosity and solidarity Bhupen exuded that a mere mention of his name even today brings a smile on the faces of those TAS officers who interacted with him.

Bhupen was a graduate from the London School of Economics, and then joined the newly established Indian Institute of Management (IIM) at Calcutta on his return to India around the early part of 1963. The TAS had already started to recruit sizeable numbers of candidates, and Tata executives were assigned the tasks of screening and shortlisting suitable candidates on different campuses. Tata companies in the Eastern part of India were requested to send senior leaders to attend the placement seasons at IIM Calcutta, along with the Member-Secretary of the TAS. Bhupen must have come into contact with some of these executives and been of considerable assistance to them. Soon after, he received an offer letter from the Tatas, and happily accepted.

One story that often gets repeated over the years is a particular favourite of TAS officers, and reflects the deep love Bhupen had for the cadre. For every new TAS batch, a series of interactions would be arranged with executives across multiple Tata companies. Bhupen accompanied the batch to all meetings. It could become quite tedious for the TAS officers to have to introduce themselves to a different executive at every meeting. Occasionally, to have a bit of fun, the TAS officers would swap profiles and take each other's names. On one occasion that Sonu vividly remembers, when the customary round of introductions was getting completed, her batchmate Raghuram Rajan (TAS 1987) introduced himself as Bhupen Chakravarti! When Bhupen's turn to introduce himself came, determined not to let the side down, he gamely played along. Haltingly, and with a shy smile, he said in his spidery voice, 'Sir, my name, also, is Bhupen Chakravarti.'

Note: Bhupen is no longer alive and the newer generations of the TAS have remained poorer for missing out on his acquaintance. What has also changed is the recruitment process of the TAS. The times of the three-days-at-Bombay-House with a lunch thrown in are over. Since the early 2000s, a team of senior Tata executives goes to various campuses for recruitment on site. The IIMs at Ahmedabad, Bengaluru, Kolkata, Kozikhode and Lucknow are the ones typically visited by the TAS recruitment team, as are a handful of other institutions like Faculty of Management Studies (FMS), Xavier Labour Relations Institute, now known as the Xavier School of Management (XLRI), S.P. Jain Institute of Management and Research (SPJIMR) and Tata Institute of Social Sciences (TISS). Offers are made on the spot after a group discussion and personal interviews. Currently, employees of the Tata Group can also apply to the TAS, and the winners of the Tata Imagination Challenge get a pre-invite.

TAS officers are expected to complete three business projects and one Corporate Social Responsibility (CSR) stint in their first year. The first-year salaries for TAS officers remain within the 50 to 75 percentile range of the salary spread in the market. The number of probationers recruited each year has increased steadily over the years. Till the year 1999, the number of TAS probationers recruited each year did not exceed ten. Then, between the years 2000 and 2010, the batch size each year increased to twenty and higher. Thereafter, batch sizes have grown even more. Yet, the number of TAS officers recruited since 1956 till now does not exceed one thousand.

Therefore, any young professional desirous of being part of the TAS needs to be aware that, if successful, they would still be part of a very select group!

9

Good Beginnings and Some Challenges

The TAS Committee was successful in attracting applications from and then selecting some of the best young minds in India in the first few decades. One of JRD's objectives—to make the TAS an aspirational cadre in India—was met from the very beginning. However, the Committee was not successful in managing the careers of the officers once they joined the Tata Group. The TAS Secretariat in the initial years was headed by Professor Rustom Choksi followed by D.K. Malegamwala. By the mid-eighties, Dr Francis Menezes, an HR professional working in Voltas, was made the head of the Tata Management Training Centre at Pune, and simultaneously appointed member-secretary of the TAS.

Most of the TAS officers from the early years agree that while they did find the entire induction process useful, the Secretariat could have done a much better job in shaping their subsequent careers. 'Not many companies are successful in having a top-rate induction programme,' says Sonu Bhasin (TAS 1987). 'The problem usually is that new recruits are youngsters full of enthusiasm and energy and the organization is unable to channelize these right from the get-go. Furthermore, the senior management, already under stress from their normal workload, finds it more of a chore to "train" the new trainees,' she continues. The TAS was different in this aspect. Senior Tata Sons Directors and Managing Directors of Tata companies spent quality time with the TAS officers during their induction.

In the early years, the TAS officers of a particular batch all reported at Bombay House on the same date. Once the formalities of a mandatory medical test and some paperwork were completed, the officers—initially called TAS Probationers, and later TAS Officers on Induction, for a year (as in the IAS)—were sent to the Tata Management Training Centre (TMTC) in Pune (once it came into existence in 1966) to go through a thorough induction and 'immersion' into the values and the lore of the Tatas.

Till the inauguration of TMTC in early 1966, the TAS probationers did not have a long induction process. Till the mid-sixties, the batches were small—a couple of people or at most four or five, and occasionally even none. The training, if it could be called that, was customized for each individual in the batch. There was no collective induction or training. The first collective training was when TMTC became fully functional.

Newly recruited TAS batches were, thereafter, inducted into the 'Tata Way' through a well-designed set of lectures conducted at TMTC's sylvan campus. Senior managers from Tata companies were part of the faculty. In the dining room, only formal attire was allowed, and it became the venue of many informal and animated discussions between probationers and the senior management of Tata companies. The dining room was the centrepiece of TMTC, and meals in it were the high point of each day. The chefs there, some say, outdid those at the Taj Hotels. The setting was very British, and the staff were considered a terror as they were not afraid of frowning and pointing out loudly if a probationer picked up the wrong fork. 'And heaven forbid if someone bent down to pick up a spoon that had fallen to the ground!' exclaims Sonu. But this informal training prepared the probationers for the many formal meals that would follow in their careers.

After the stint at TMTC, the batch was brought back to Bombay House for interactions with senior leaders of the Group, as well as for familiarization with the various departments and companies in Bombay. A large part of the induction programme at Bombay was a let-down for the new recruits. 'No one had any idea what to do with us,' complains Khorshed Jhaveri (TAS 1958). 'We were shepherded into a room, told to sit at a table, and then someone would come and plonk a bunch of files on the table,' says Nawshir Khurody (TAS 1960). 'They wanted us to go through the files as they believed that this was the most efficient way for us to get to know a company,' he continues.

The TAS officers of the early years also remember with exasperation their week at Davar's College of Commerce. The new recruits came from diverse backgrounds—some had studied economics, others physics, and yet others had a Master's in law. Most of them had no previous experience of management studies. Davar's College was a five-minute walk from Bombay House, and the TAS Committee worked out an arrangement so that the college would provide the new recruits with a capsule course in management studies. There were modules on subjects like accounting, personnel management, operational effectiveness, marketing and business economics.

'It used to be very boring to sit there and listen to the old teachers go on and on without defining an objective or [offering] practical examples of application,' says Vijay Rai (TAS 1971). 'The only reason we looked forward to going to Davar's was because of the tea breaks,' says Rajeev Dubey (TAS 1975) with a naughty smile. 'The young girls who served the tea and cakes were good-looking and used to wear miniskirts!' he continues.

The classroom training and file readings drained the young minds. On the other hand, the 'Bharat Darshan' energized them. This was a term coined by the probationers, which was quickly adopted by the Committee itself! The Bharat Darshan was a structured tour of the various companies of the Tata Group across the country. The probationers travelled together and spent time, among other places, in Jamshedpur, Kolkata, Mithapur, Cochin, Munnar and Delhi. This facilitated bonhomie within this elite group, gave them exposure to the workings of the flagship companies and allowed them to interact with senior TAS officers across the Group. Even the IAS currently has a system akin to this where every new batch, after being inducted at the Lal Bahadur Shastri National Administrative Academy in Mussoorie, is sent in small groups to different parts of the country.

'My batchmates who had joined multinational FMCG companies were going through sales training in their first couple of months,' says Sonu. 'They were pounding the streets in tier III and tier IV towns, working the market. And there we were—wining and dining with the top brass of the Tatas!' she exclaims. The Bharat Darshan sensitized the TAS probationers to the challenges of managing diverse workforces in Tata companies located in difficult geographies—be it the steel plant in Jamshedpur, the mines of Noamundi and West Bokaro, or the chemical works at Mithapur. They were given a sense of the work culture, the leaders in charge and the people behind the numbers. The Bharat Darshan also helped extend the TAS networks, and thus, strengthened the Tata superglue. Within India and across the world, TAS batchmates, Debjani Biswas (1983) confirms, continue to this day to have annual reunions. This is despite the fact that many of them have left the Group, with their careers (including Debjani's herself) blooming in companies and organizations outside the Tata Group!

There were occasional aberrations in organizing the Bharat Darshan. Bharat Wakhlu (TAS 1985) was one of only two to be selected as TAS officers in his batch. By the time he was asked to join, the other candidate selected with him had quit. Since he was the lone probationer of his batch, the TAS Secretariat decided that his induction—including the stints at TMTC and the Bharat Darshan—could be dispensed with! Instead, Bharat was presented with two books—both written in the early eighties by the affable and urbane Tata chronicler, Russi Lala—titled *The Heartbeat of a Trust* and *The Creation of Wealth: A Tata Story*. When the next batch was due to undergo its induction, the TAS Committee Member-Secretary, Dr Menezes, ensured that Bharat joined them for the TMTC sessions.

Once they had completed the fun-filled Bharat Darshan, it was the real-life assignments that energized the TAS probationers. The probationers had to work on four to five live projects in different Tata companies. In the early years—the fifties through to the mid-seventies—the companies that were in demand for these projects were TELCO (now Tata Motors) and TISCO (now Tata Steel), but later many more Tata companies offered exciting assignments. These assignments often allowed the probationers to engage with the senior leadership teams and observe the manner in which decisions were taken. They also enabled engagement with other senior officers and gave the newbies a taste of the culture of each company and the quality of leadership in the enterprise. All this helped the probationers make up their minds on whether they could see themselves building careers in some of the companies.

'These were hands-on jobs and not the kind that relied on academic learning,' says Ashok Mehta (TAS 1966). 'The one-year induction programme was very thoughtfully structured. Normally, it involved going to the factories of about six major companies that were the biggest in their particular sectors and were spread all over the country, like Tata Steel, Tata Chemicals, Tata Motors, Tata Hydro, Tata Tea, Indian Hotels, etc. In the detailed programme with each company, one was made familiar with the challenges of that industry, the competition, and then sent to each of the major divisions, where it was possible to interact with the senior management. While in the head offices of these companies, usually in Mumbai, one also attended the part-time course specially devised by Davar's College, next to Bombay House, on various functional aspects of business,' he continues. 'Most importantly, I got to know the people in these companies because I worked with them—which proved to be very useful in my subsequent years in the Group. If I had joined, say, Shaw Wallace or Hindustan Unilever, I would have learnt only about one industry, in contrast to the breadth of the extensive coverage of Indian industry of the Tata Group, in which one also got the opportunity of transfer to other companies within the vast Tata Group,' adds Ashok.

The live projects also gave the senior Tata executives in companies the opportunity to gauge the talent of the young probationers better. This helped in the final placement of the probationers once their induction was completed.

The final placement could occasionally throw up some challenges. The TAS had its own pay-scale, which was somewhat higher than that of the Tata companies, with its officers inducted one level higher than other entry-level management cadres. Thus, a TAS officer would join a company with a higher salary than his or her peers, some of whom may have been working for longer years. Not only this, but they also often joined as the bosses of many people who were significantly older than them and had been working much longer. This naturally led to murmurs of resentment within the larger employee base, but since the TAS was identified as JRD's project, even discontented employees had to tolerate the officers.

'Everyone called the TAS officers the blue-eyed boys of the Group,' says Nawshir. Khorshed agrees and says that initially the TAS officers were even called the white elephants of the Group. 'We were described as Tata's Adopted Sons (TAS),' laughs Rajeev.

Notwithstanding the latent misgivings about the cadre, JRD was absolutely clear about where he saw the TAS and its officers in the years ahead. Nawshir remembers the speech JRD gave at the inauguration of TMTC in Pune on 6 January 1966, 'This was the first time I heard JRD talk about the TAS in a large gathering. JRD said, "Young boys and girls, I have not set up this Centre for you to play tennis and croquet at our expense. I have built it because we Parsis don't seem to have any children. Therefore, the Group has to have identified leaders who will be the children of the Tatas and this will happen through the TAS!"' Nawshir continues.

The resentment encountered by young TAS officers was not different from the kind faced by Management Trainees in other organizations. It is a rare organization in which people who have risen through the ranks whole-heartedly welcome professionals who join either as their peers or bosses. Visty Banaji (TAS 1973) mentions that the TAS was seen as somewhat unique over the years. 'TAS officers were brought in laterally at higher levels than similarly aged persons, were often supported by senior leaders, and seemed to be the carriers of the Tata Spirit. All these added [up] to make the TAS something special,' he says smiling, as he remembers his own long stint with the Tatas.

Many organizations develop career plans for the professionals they hire along set paths. The TAS was different, as there were no fixed career plans for the young officers. There was a long-term goal: for the officers to morph into leaders. But the path to that was not defined. 'Maybe it was for the best,' muses Rajeev. 'The selection process ensured that the TAS had talented high achievers. Maybe the Committee did not want to hand-hold them.' He adds that it was up to the officers to sink or swim. They had been thrown into the deep end and each of them had to find their own way to navigate through the waters. Visty disagrees, however. He comments, 'When you bring in talented people into an organization, you have to foresee what will happen to their careers several years down the line.'

'It's not that there was a lack of planning or structure per se,' says Camellia Panjabi (TAS 1963) who was one of the early women in the TAS. 'The persons on the TAS Committee with JRD Tata were Rustom Choksi, J.J. Bhabha and Col Sawhney. These three were not directly running companies; and in fact, the latter two were in staff roles on the Board of Tata Industries. Col Sawhney had not grown up in the Tatas but had come from the British India Army post-Independence. There was huge resistance from the Directors in charge of Tata Companies, and more so from their senior managers, to having TAS officers among them. They feared that these TAS officers would be reporting the goings-on in their companies to these three Directors. So, initially, the only posts available for the TAS were in non-operational functions, such as the Economics Department or as Executive Assistants to the Directors-in-Charge—remember, the Managing Agency system was in operation in the 1950s till early sixties. So they were not called Managing Directors, but Directors-in-Charge,' explains Camellia.

'I remember that Tata Chemicals welcomed me during my induction. The fact that they already had three TAS officers may have helped. Bhagwant Singh, Sabherwal and Vinod Bali were there already,' remembers Camellia.

'But when I was sent to the Indian Hotels Company for induction, the General Manager of the Taj Mahal Hotel of Bombay sent me back to Bombay House on the first day, saying that I was their spy and that they did not have a spare desk for me,' exclaims Camellia. 'Xerxes Desai (TAS 1961) was the Executive Assistant to the Director-in-Charge of Indian Hotels, Col Leslie Sawhney, and he asked me to go and sit in the Taj Kitchen where a young man called Ajit Kerkar had just joined as the Assistant Manager, Catering. I sat on a stool in the kitchen for four months as part of my induction,' Camellia says as she looks back at those months which were mind-boggling. She later rose to be the senior-most woman Director in the same company.

Camellia remembers that Leslie Sawhney had extended her induction at Taj Hotels by six months, asking her to review the Purchase function in the hotel. 'At the end of my review, the General Manager was sacked!' says Camellia. 'So, in a way, Mr Kotwal was right—TAS officers were indeed asked to report on the goings-on!' she adds, smiling widely. After the induction process was over, Camellia was asked to join the Tata Oil Mills Company (TOMCO). 'Now it was they who refused me a posting,' says Camellia who, by this time, had realized what the overall attitude towards TAS officers was. Never one to mince her words, she took up the matter with Leslie Sawhney. 'I told Col Sawhney that as an army man he should be issuing orders and not taking rejection of his requests from subordinates,' she remembers. 'It worked. He issued an office order appointing me as Product Executive in TOMCO's Marketing Department.'

The induction period after the Bharat Darshan may have been frustrating for some TAS officers; for others, it was a time to bond—and for life, too! Abanti and Govind Sankaranarayanan were part of the TAS batch in 1992. They are one of the few TAS couples—officers who had married each other.

'Abanti and I met each other during the interviews and then [our plans] overlapped in the same city, Bangalore, for one of our projects,' remembers Govind. It was at that time that Abanti went over to Govind's and met his parents. 'I remember my mother describing her as a lovely, well-brought-up girl. I, of course, took it as an indication that my other friends were not like that!' laughs Govind.

They decided to get married when they had finished their first year in TAS. 'We did not really hide our relationship from anyone, except KK (Krishna Kumar), who was our common boss in Tata Tea,' says Govind. 'In fact, [even] when I broke the news to him, he was astounded. But his wife just said, "I have known this for the last one year, but KK did not believe me and told me that it was just my imagination,"' Govind adds. 'And of course, dear Bhupen remained very supportive of us, so long as nothing came in the way of his unstinting loyalty to the Tata Group,' Govind concludes.

Govind says that the Group and the TAS, per se, had no issues with their couplehood, but there were some other strange issues that cropped up. 'These situations would seem very odd today—for instance, Tata Tea, for some time, insisted on withdrawing some of the allowances we were both entitled to, saying that one household did not need the same allowance twice!' says Govind. 'But then it was also kind enough to club some entitlements—like a rental deposit—which enabled us to stay in a bigger house than we might otherwise have been entitled to,' he finishes.

Typically, for the first three to four years in the companies they were assigned to, TAS officers would work with the Director-in-Charge or the Managing Director in roles such as the Executive Assistant or its equivalent. This was a persuasive way of familiarizing the newly recruited TAS officers with the manner in which the senior management of the companies worked, while offering them a broad overview of the management processes, quality standards and norms of these enterprises. The TAS officers served their bosses diligently, providing advice when requested, or when essential, while also maintaining confidentiality.

Situations where the boss would be annoyed with the Executive Assistant's ideas were few and far between. The leaders of Tata companies, in the decades from the fifties through the nineties, were typically mature and seasoned veterans, comfortable in their skins, who could take feedback—even critical feedback—without getting ruffled. Most TAS officers developed fairly synergetic relationships with the top brass of the companies, and could have easy conversations with the leaders—including when giving them perspective on matters that ran contrary to the views of many other senior managers in the same organizations.

There are some who believe that assigning a TAS officer the role of an Executive Assistant early in their career could prove to be a double-edged sword. On the one hand, there was indeed a lot for the officer in question to learn. However, some bosses would use the young officer to verbally 'beat up' their subordinates, and pull them up for a variety of operational lapses! Smart TAS officers would learn to do this with the utmost suaveness and ensure that nobody's feathers were unduly ruffled as a result. Experiences of these kinds also helped TAS officers stay humble, because many of the people who had to be given the 'bad news' were experienced and powerful leaders in their own right.

Dr Mukund Rajan (TAS 1995), who served for twelve years as Ratan Tata's Executive Assistant and then as his Chief of Staff, observes that a lot depended on the emotional quotient and maturity of the TAS officer. In the former role, he says, 'I had to often deliver bad news or issue instructions on Mr. Tata's behalf to the senior-most people in the Group. Sometimes, they would want to shoot the messenger!' laughs Mukund. 'In the process, I became a good judge of character, and learnt how to communicate in a way that ensured the right outcomes.'

A few TAS officers seemed to enter into what may be called Faustian pacts with their bosses and would develop a kind of unconscionable loyalty to them that was astonishing and worrisome. As inconceivable as it was for a TAS officer to ignore the values of the House of Tata and become a 'yes man', it did happen, occasionally. It was worrisome because the 'inner gyroscope' of a TAS officer was supposed to be sufficiently robust and capable of withstanding pressure from all kinds of people in authority. Many EAs, as a result of getting too comfortable with their superiors, did develop swollen heads, causing resentment among the capable line executives of the company with whom they would interact.

The ethos of the TAS stayed true for over three decades, after which the selection process began to undergo and effect subtle but meaningful changes. The TAS Committee continued to spend quality time by getting to know the candidates as individuals and focusing on their interests for the most part of the first three decades, but as the number of recruits went up significantly from the mid-nineties onwards, the level of leadership engagement from the upper echelons reduced. The TAS Committee has continued the practice of probationers undertaking hands-on real-life projects with Tata companies in their first year, with projects in CSR at Tata companies and the Tata Trusts also becoming mandatory over the past two decades. Undertaking live projects within companies enable the probationers to experience the breadth and depth of the Tata Group first hand. What has also not changed, unfortunately, is the lack of career planning for the young officers after their probation is over. Later chapters will dwell on this aspect in greater detail.

10
Loyalty on Trial!

THE TAS HAD STARTED WITH A GRAND VISION. ITS COMMITTEE TALKED about this vision at all interactions with potential and selected TAS officers. The vision of an in-house elite cadre of officers who would be rotated across Group companies, and thereby groomed to be future leaders of the Tata Group, caught the fancy of the talented young Indians who applied to be part of it. The entire selection process, along with the fact that the candidates got to interact with the Senior Directors of the Tatas—many of whom were well-known public figures—and the Group Chairman, added to the allure of the TAS. The fact that only a handful of individuals were selected each year made it even more aspirational in the minds of the young candidates.

The early years of the TAS saw mixed success. In the first three decades of its existence, it did see some of its officers rise very fast; some others left mid-way; others followed a moderate career path and a handful languished. One of the main reasons for this mixed success was the fact that unlike other management programmes, for example in Unilever, there was no template career path for the TAS officers. To some extent, the largeness and the diversity of the Group came in the way.

The Tata Group was expanding, with diverse businesses of varying sizes. Each company had its own management ethos, with varying corporate hierarchies and different salary levels. The aspirations of the TAS officers had to be matched with the ability of the corporates to fulfil them. This came in the way of a defined career trajectory. Moreover, several Tata companies, especially the larger ones, had also perfected their own unique approach to attracting, developing and retaining talent.

Jaspreet Bindra (TAS 1994) recalls, 'During the induction, many of the assignments that were given to us were those that were important to the Group but not yet within the ambit of any one Tata company. We were given a responsibility and it was understood that we would deliver. However, the fact that the TAS Secretariat was not very assertive prevented any active involvement in the career development of TAS officers. As a result, talent within the TAS sometimes did not find a fit without some struggle.'

TISCO may have started off by catching young men off the trains but it very soon moved to establishing a Technical Training Institute in 1921 and a Graduate Trainee programme in 1932. The latter entailed two years of rigorous training, after which the GTs were placed in various departments of the company. By the mid-1980s, new cadres of Systems Trainees, Administrative Trainees and Management Trainees had been created in TISCO. In a similar manner, TELCO (now Tata Motors) and Tata Chemicals, too, evolved their own recruitment and training programmes.

The larger companies that were the first choice of many probationers thus evolved their own Management Trainee programmes. And the smaller companies that perhaps needed and may have wanted TAS officers to join them were not usually the first choice of the probationers.

Considering the detailed and meticulous selection process, relatively few stars emerged in the seventies and eighties from the ranks of the cadre. Most of them were handpicked by emerging powerful company chiefs, the so-called 'satraps', and it is important to place in context the influence these individuals wielded—people such as Ajit Kerkar at Indian Hotels, Darbari Seth at Tata Chemicals, A.H. Tobaccowala at Voltas, Russi Mody at Tata Steel and Sumant Moolgaokar at Tata Motors.

JRD Tata had taken over as the Tata Group Chairman in 1938 at the young age of thirty-four. He made up for his lack of formal education in management with his enthusiasm and personal charisma. He was also prudent enough to realize that operating Tata companies would benefit from having talented people at the helm, so he did not name himself as the Chairman of all the Tata companies. He looked for people with greater experience than himself and delegated powers to them. Meanwhile, he focused on exploring opportunities for new businesses, while identifying and grooming talent to lead these new companies. Unlike many other Indian corporate leaders, JRD did not yield to the temptation of placing only family members at senior levels in the various Group companies—albeit there is a view that had the family had more members they probably would have been part of the senior management of the Group.

The one family member that JRD did depend upon was his brother-in-law—Colonel Leslie Sawhney. Douggie, as he was popularly called, had an English mother and had served as an Officer in the Indian army, with the 16th Light Cavalry, also known as the 'Brown Pandits'. He had been a contemporary of Army Chief General Cariappa and was one of the officers on the fast track. However, he left the army when he married JRD's sister, Rodabeh, and joined his brother-in-law in the business. The army's loss was Tata's gain.

JRD came to depend on Leslie Sawhney on all matters, especially when it came to identifying and managing talent. Many are also of the view that it was Col Sawhney who fleshed out the idea of the TAS with JRD Tata. For the two larger companies in the Group, TELCO and TISCO, JRD had already identified Sumant Moolgaokar and Russi Mody, respectively, as the ones who would lead these businesses. It was Leslie who identified a young Darbari Seth and Ajit Kerkar as the individuals who would eventually go on to lead Tata Chemicals and Taj Hotels.

Leslie Sawhney had a powerful and commanding personality. Good-looking and affable, he strode confidently across the corridors of Bombay House with as much ease as he did while zipping down Mumbai's Marine

Drive in his yellow convertible with the roof folded down. His army background had given him a focus on discipline and his insights about people gave him the ability to groom talent.

'He could identify talent instinctively,' says Nawshir Khurody (TAS 1960). 'I've sat in interviews with him, and Colonel Sawhney would tell us within five minutes of talking to a candidate if it would work out or not. We were surprised many times, because the candidate, on the face of it, had the best academic qualifications. But Colonel Sawhney would just shake his head and say "No".'

Since he was part of JRD's office, and was senior in the hierarchy, Leslie Sawhney was able to identify and groom talent without any HR processes coming in the way. If they did, he quickly overruled them, as was the case with Nawshir.

'It was early 1963 and I had just got married,' remembers Nawshir with a fond smile. He got a call from Leslie Sawhney's office asking him to come for a meeting. Leslie asked Nawshir to go to Munnar in the southwestern Indian state of Kerala to head the Instant Tea project. 'He told me that it was not doing as well as the Tatas wanted, and he expected me to turn it around. It was a Friday, and he told me that I needed to be there on Monday!' exclaims Nawshir.

'Sir, I will do this, but you do know that I recently got married,' said Nawshir hesitatingly.

'Oh, yes, I am aware of this, Nawshir,' said Leslie Sawhney in his crisp voice. 'And I forgot to tell you that it is a non-family posting,' he continued, looking Nawshir straight in the eye.

Nawshir did reach Munnar and took over the Instant Tea project. It was the first project of its kind, and the young TAS officer had been directed to oversee it. 'I went out of my way to prove myself,' says Nawshir. Working hard, he did make the project a success.

When he returned to Bombay on completion of the project, Leslie Sawhney asked the TAS Secretariat to move him into the senior grade of pay. 'I was in the junior grade in the TAS. Prof. Rustom Choksi, who managed the TAS at that time, was flabbergasted,' remembers Nawshir with a laugh. 'Prof. Choksi practically told Col Sawhney that he was mad to think that someone could move into the senior grade of the TAS without going through the medium grade,' he adds, as he continues to recount the interaction and chuckle.

"This young man has done the work of a Senior Officer, and it is my decision to move him into the senior grade." And I was moved into the senior grade,' Nawshir continued, 'When Leslie Sawhney took a decision, it had to be implemented.'

Leslie Sawhney was a charmer. Khorshed Javeri (TAS 1958) remembers him with a fond smile. 'Every time I met him, he said, "What's wrong with these Parsi men? I expect to see a line of them behind you!"' says Khorshed, blushing prettily.

A cavalry man by background, Leslie Sawhney had a striking personality. He also had a sharp temper. Sanjaya Sharma (TAS 1980) remembers a story told to him by his friend Sivaraman.

'A.V. Sivaraman had joined Bombay House after his stint in Kerala as Secretary to Col Sawhney,' recounts Sanjaya. 'It was well known that Col Sawhney had a short fuse. It so happened that one morning, as he reached Bombay House, he saw that there was a small car parked in his parking space. The short fuse blew! "Slam it," he told his chauffeur! And the loyal driver did just that,' laughs Sanjaya. 'It was a different world,' he reflects.

Arun Maira (TAS 1965) has another story about Leslie Sawhney. 'This is about how Col Sawhney fixed Russi Mody,' chuckles Arun. 'Sawhney was the Chairman of CIEL, later converted to Tata Exports, through which all Tata companies had to export,' says Arun as he starts narrating the story. Russi Mody was in charge of marketing and exports of TISCO at that time and Sujit Gupta worked for Mr Mody. 'TISCO was not happy with Tata Exports' service levels, and Mody was unhappy at the commission being charged. So he asked Sujit Gupta and me to prepare a case against Tata Exports and how it should do its job better,' remembers Arun. They prepared the report and, along with Russi Mody, went to meet Leslie Sawhney at Bombay House.

'In the meeting, we did a good job of demolishing Tata Exports,' says Arun. Once the presentation was over, Leslie Sawhney asked everyone to leave the room but asked Russi Mody to stay behind. 'Sujit and I returned to our fourth floor office delighted with our performance,' says Arun. Then they waited for their boss, Russi Mody, to return.

After about half an hour, Russi Mody came back to the office. 'He looked very excited,' says Arun. 'Sujit was also excited and he jumped up at the sight of Mody and said, "We did it, huh?"

"Did what?" said Mody. "Douggie Sawhney has fixed me! He said that since I know how Tata Exports should be run, he has made me the Chairman! Now, both of you—stop criticizing Tata Exports and start singing the praises of the company immediately!"'

Besides identifying talent for businesses, Leslie Sawhney also helped JRD identify new businesses. In fact, it was he who was responsible for the creation of TCS, a company that would become wildly successful some decades later. It was in the mid-1960s that Leslie Sawhney suggested JRD pool the Group's need for data processing support within a single business unit, which grew into TCS.

Many believe that Leslie Sawhney and his contributions have been overlooked whenever the history of the Tata Group is talked about. Rajvir Kadan (TAS 1971) is one such person. 'Col Sawhney does not appear to get the recognition or recall for his immense service to the Group,' says Rajvir. 'The three companies for which he was the Managing Agent had been in poor shape when he took charge; he was able to turn things around in a short time. Furthermore, he is the one who selected the new heads for these large companies—Darbari Seth for Tata Chemicals, A.B. Kerkar for Taj Hotels and Wadud Khan for TOMCO,' points out Rajvir.

Rajvir and some of his contemporaries, like Vinod Bali, Xerxes Desai, Nawshir Khurody and Krishna Kumar, started their careers in the TAS when Leslie Sawhney was part of the senior leadership at Bombay House. 'He was one of the biggest supporters of the TAS, and he had the courage to put young people like us in positions of responsibility at a young age,' asserts Rajvir. He further said, 'For example, look at Vinod Bali who was appointed as a General Manager in TOMCO at the age of twenty-eight after he finished a short stint as Col Sawhney's Executive Assistant. Vinod, like many others handpicked by Sawhney, lived up to his expectations and did him proud.'

Camellia Panjabi (TAS 1963) remembers Leslie Sawhney as the person who had her induction at Taj Hotels extended by four months. 'I spent those four months sitting on a stool in the Taj Kitchen,' exclaims Camellia in frustration. After the induction process was over, Camellia was asked to join TOMCO.

'TOMCO refused me a posting,' says Camellia who by this time had had enough. 'I went straight to Col Sawhney and told him that as an army man he should be issuing orders and not taking insolence from subordinates,' she remembers. 'It worked. He issued an office order appointing me at TOMCO.'

JRD confided in many that he saw Leslie Sawhney as his successor. 'Oh, I have no doubt that Col Sawhney would have led the Group,' asserts Nawshir. 'Even though he had no formal education about management, he knew a lot of about people and could identify business problems as well,' he says. 'Sawhney was tipped to be successor to JRD,' agrees Camellia.

Leslie Sawhney may have had an eye towards this future as he identified and then delegated power to several young leaders who he imagined might be his lieutenants in the later years. Fate intervened, however, and he died suddenly after suffering a massive heart attack on a golf course. This loss would lead to a concentration of power in the hands of the satraps. Some people in the Tatas say that had Leslie Sawhney lived longer, the satraps may not have been allowed to wield almost unchecked power. 'Had he not died unexpectedly, I believe that the TAS and the Tata Group may have taken a very different path than they did,' says Rajvir a bit wistfully.

The other reason that led to unbridled power in the hands of the satraps was the abolition of the Managing Agency system in April 1970 and the introduction of the Monopolies and Restrictive Trade Practices (MRTP) Act around the same time. Each Tata company was nudged to become a more independent entity with its own corporate governance structure. Tatas were rarely the majority shareholders in any of their companies, but their writ had run large on the companies—thanks to the Managing Agency contracts. As the Tata companies now became more independent, Bombay House's influence was wielded more through advice and persuasion.

The satraps revelled in their increased autonomy. With Tata Sons not even being the largest single shareholder in companies like Tata Steel (where the Birla Group held a larger stake for much of this period), there would even be murmurs at the top of these companies about why they needed to follow diktats from Tata Sons.

Arun recalls, 'Tatas became more decentralized than they wanted to be during JRD Tata's time because they were required to, by the MRTP Act. Tata Industries, the erstwhile Managing Agency, was forbidden to manage the listed Tata companies. The Managing Directors of the companies were even forbidden to meet together every Wednesday to exchange ideas as they used to. Centrally directed processes across the Group became legally fraught. The TAS became harder to implement across the Group, with big companies like TISCO and TELCO having their own Graduate Trainee and Management Trainee Development programmes.'

In a Group increasingly functioning like a loose federation of companies bound together by some common values, TAS officers had to wade their own way through this amorphous structure. In the absence of a structured career path and consistent career support, it was each officer for himself. The TAS Secretariat worked essentially as a coordination service, helping the probationers in their first year find the right projects across various Tata companies. The new probationers were encouraged to explore opportunities in these companies for their final placements.

What followed was based more on personal rapport with senior managers built during the probation rather than a structured plan for the officers. 'Bombay House was very involved during the probationary period,' explains Rajeev Dubey (TAS 1975). 'Once the probation was over, however, there was almost no involvement of Bombay House in the career trajectories of TAS officers,' he says.

Francis da Cunha (TAS 1971) recalls that the TAS 'was reduced to recruitment and placement. You only went crying to the TAS Committee if you were desperately unhappy. I doubt if the Committee even kept tabs on individual progress.' Nawshir admits, 'In my time, TAS was a concept. Without a supporting architecture. The HR heads of the large Tata companies had no formal relationship with the TAS Secretariat.'

Rajvir also confirms, 'When I joined, the total size of the TAS was only about forty, and few formal practices for the development, training and evaluation of TAS officers existed. It was all still a work in progress. In reality, once you were assigned to a Tata company, there was little or no involvement of the TAS Secretariat. Their role effectively ended after the recruitment and induction cycle. However, they did assist when an officer wanted a change and needed to be reassigned to another Group company. Even this was largely done informally, by speaking to the CEOs of companies that might provide a suitable opening.'

The absence of a structured career planning approach and the limited influence of the Secretariat with the satraps contributed to the fact that after three decades in existence, the TAS still had only a handful of rising stars. Less than 10 per cent of its officers had reached the level of Chairman, Managing Director or Vice President in Tata companies. A study in the mid-1990s showed that out of 176 TAS officers selected between 1956 and 1986 in a Group that straddled more than 100 operating companies, only one was a Director at Tata Sons or Chairman of a large Tata company; six were Managing Directors of some of the larger Tata companies or chairmen of smaller Tata companies; and twelve were Managing Directors of smaller Tata companies or Vice Presidents of larger Tata companies.

Among the satraps, some, like Darbari Seth and Ajit Kerkar, proactively brought TAS officers into their companies. Sumant Moolgaokar at TELCO did induct several TAS officers and also simultaneously built a Management Trainee programme for the company, but the intake slowed down as the number of Management Trainees increased.

At the Group flagship, Tata Steel, chairman and Managing Director Russi Mody's disdain for TAS officers was well known. Some did trickle in, but it was due to the fact that they impressed Russi during one of their interactions with him. Russi Mody would boast of having his own management cadre, informally described as the Mody Administrative Service (MAS).

Most of the early rising stars in the TAS were officers identified by the satraps and then groomed for leadership. These included individuals like

Freddie Mehta, Arun Maira, Camellia Panjabi, V.S. Mahesh, Xerxes Desai, V.S. Krishnan and Krishna Kumar. Arun was merely fifteen years into the TAS when he was sent on an important and visible assignment to Kuala Lumpur, where he headed the Tata joint venture company promoted by Tungku Arif Bendahara, a powerful member of the Malaysian royal family. On his return to India, Arun Maira was put in charge of the Pune Plant of Tata Motors (TELCO at that time) and inducted to the Board of the Tata automotive company; he was an influential figure whose presence at the helm of TELCO reinforced the importance placed by the Tata Group on young and effective TAS officers.

The Indian Hotels Company, too, had its share of TAS officers who were visible and delivering value. Camellia worked closely with Ajit Kerkar, the Managing Director of the Indian Hotels Corporation, and was seen as the creative marketing force within the company. V.S. Mahesh (TAS 1971), who had worked with Arun Maira in TELCO, moved to Indian Hotels where he brought about changes in the approach to Human Resources Management with the same enthusiasm that he'd shown in TELCO. Several TAS officers were fairly visible by virtue of being assigned to the offices of the Managing Directors of their respective Tata companies. With these young persons attached to powerful Tata leaders, especially the satraps, the perception was that they commanded considerable clout and influence within their companies.

The satraps, however, demanded total personal loyalty from their proteges. For example, a young officer joining TISCO was told unequivocally that he should no longer think of himself as a TAS-person but as a Mody-person. Another TAS officer was told that he was henceforth a Finlay-Man and not a Tata-man!

Many TAS officers quickly understood that if they wanted successful careers within the Tata Group, they needed to hitch their respective wagons to either a satrap or a Senior Director in the Group. They also understood that their loyalty needed to be transferred from the TAS, which was a nebulous structure, to their mentor in the Group. In the absence of a formal retirement policy, there was practically zero attrition among the Directors of the Tata Group, including the satraps, and many

TAS officers presumed that their loyalty to a person, rather than to the institution, would pay off in the long run. For the most part, such loyalty did pay off, except when, in later years, the Mentor-Director himself got into trouble!

In picking up young TAS officers to work with them, the satraps typically went by their instincts based on their interactions with the officers. 'I got picked up by Darbari Seth because I told him the truth when no one else wanted to,' remembers Vijay Rai (TAS 1971), who later went on to head Rallis India Ltd. Vijay was at Mithapur working on a project for Tata Chemicals during his probation, when Darbari made an unscheduled and sudden visit to the workshop at the factory. 'It just so happened that there was no senior engineer or manager present at the workshop or even in the factory when Darbari Seth walked in,' says Vijay. Darbari had left to go to Bombay that morning and the employees were relaxed as the boss was away. 'His plane, however, developed some snag, so Darbari Seth decided to come back. And he came straight to the workshop because there some equipment critical for capacity expansion was being fabricated. He wanted to check on its progress,' continues Vijay. Since he was the only one present on the shop floor and prepared to answer, Darbari initiated a conversation with Vijay to get an update.

'This was my first one-on-one interaction with Darbari Seth. I wasn't too keen to stay on in Mithapur, so I did not worry about being politically correct with him,' Vijay laughs wickedly as he remembers that afternoon. Darbari wanted to know when that critical machine would be ready for operations.

'I looked at him and told him, "Oh, not for another couple of years." Just like that!' chuckles Vijay as he remembers the look of shock on Darbari's face. 'What are you saying? How is this possible? I can't wait for that long for this machine to be operationalized,' shouted Darbari. 'Well, I don't know what you have been told, Sir, but here are the reasons why it will take two years to ready the machine if you go about it the way you are going about it now,' said Vijay calmly. And he went on to explain why the current method of assembling the machine would take time. He also explained how it could be done faster. 'Of course, it will take more money to do so,' Vijay cautioned Darbari.

Darbari told Vijay to go ahead and explain to the Chief Engineer what needed to be done. 'My solution worked and after my probation I was picked up by Darbari to be his Executive Assistant,' says Vijay. Thereafter, Darbari would lean on Vijay to solve any problems around engineering and then later in marketing. 'He groomed me completely. He gave me opportunities that people my age would never have got,' says Vijay. 'Darbari Seth gave me the opportunity to learn. I also saw the way his mind worked and learnt from that as well.'

Darbari groomed Vijay and the young officer rose quickly in the hierarchy. Under his tutelage, Vijay got to be a part of many business ventures across India and around the world. At the age of thirty-one, he got to handle TOMCO exports; at thirty-four, the fertilizer project; and soon after, he became a Director of a major company, Tata Fertilizer. He was given the reins—as an independent business head—for Rallis India at thirty-nine, and was made the Managing Director of that company in 1987, at the age of forty-one. However, when Darbari died, it was over for Vijay as well. 'My career ended a few months after my boss, Darbari Seth, died,' accepts Vijay, acknowledging the reality of corporate life.

It was sheer coincidence that Vijay Rai was identified and then groomed by Darbari. In Rajeev's case, it was his own initiative that got him to work with Russi Mody. 'I was absolutely clear that I would stay on in the TAS only if I got to work with Russi Mody as his Executive Assistant, posted in Jamshedpur,' remembers Rajeev. Having watched his father's successful career as a senior bureaucrat in the government, he had plans of taking the IAS exam himself, in case he could not get to work with Russi.

'Don't ask me why—it was a mix of a vision of Russi as a leader to work with (despite my never even having seen him!), a romantic notion of steel as an industry and its role in nation-building, an image of the hills, forests and rivers in the Jamshedpur region, of getting away from the concrete jungle in Bombay,' reminisces Rajeev. 'But I was certain that the only job I wanted after my probation was that of Executive Assistant to Russi Mody and to work in Jamshedpur,' he continues. Rajeev was vocal about his preference and shared it with the TAS Secretariat as well. 'I was told that I was stark raving mad!' chuckles Rajeev. "You must be out of your mind! Don't you know that Russi Mody hates the TAS and has his own cadre, the MAS?" This was what one senior Committee member told me,' says Rajeev.

His mind made up, and Rajeev looked around to find a way to get an appointment with Russi. A good option was to take up a project in Jamshedpur during the probationary period. Rajeev went to TISCO, Jamshedpur and managed to secure an appointment with Russi after a few days.

'I remember walking into that large room of his,' says Rajeev as he speaks about their first meeting. 'He was sitting there wearing a colourful shirt, smoking a cigar. I could see a gold medallion resting on his heavy chest. The first question he asked me was, "Young man, why do you have a beard?" I replied that I had it because I liked it. But he said "No, I think it is because you want to hide your weak chin,"' continues Rajeev. He then says, 'I told him categorically that I did not have a weak chin!' The banter, small talk and discussions on myriad issues went on for almost 45 minutes, after which Russi suddenly turned serious and asked Rajeev if he wanted to work for TISCO.

'I said yes, but only as your Executive Assistant,' recollects Rajeev. Russi was surprised at Rajeev's assertiveness and told him that he already had an Executive Assistant—Aditya Kashyap. 'I replied that I knew that but still wanted to work as his Executive Assistant,' says Rajeev.

Russi looked at Rajeev intently for about thirty seconds; and Rajeev, sitting right across the table from him, looked right back at him. 'Then he nodded and said "Okay",' remembers Rajeev. 'But he told me there and then that I had to get off my fancy TAS grade. I would have to trust him, surrender to him and he would look after me,' continues Rajeev.

Rajeev agreed to Russi's condition and joined TISCO after his probationary period. 'He protected my pay and fitted me at an appropriate level. But I was off the TAS grid. Bombay House played no role in my career thereafter. I would sink or swim based only on what Russi Mody and other Tata Steel executives thought of me,' clarifies Rajeev.

He went on to serve as Russi's Executive Assistant for two years and then he was moved to a line-job in sales and marketing. 'For all practical purposes I became a TISCO man, a Russi Mody man. But the stamp of the TAS remained,' says Rajeev. 'It may just be a *chhaap* (stamp) but, boy, it was a great *chhaap!* For me that is what the TAS remained—a powerful stamp that served me well throughout my working career, even after I left the Tatas. There was almost no interaction with the TAS Secretariat after I joined TISCO, except for receiving the annual list of TAS officers with their current postings, but this list, too, was discontinued after a few years.'

After five years of service, Rajeev took a two-year sabbatical to go to Yale for his MBA. When he came back, he again worked in TISCO and other Group companies for a number of years. 'All my Tata achievements were because of Russi Mody and, after him, Dr Jamshed Irani,' says Rajeev categorically. He went on to head Tata Metaliks and then Rallis India. He left the TAS in January 2004 to join Anand Mahindra as a member of the Group Management Board of Mahindra and Mahindra.

Interestingly, despite the fact that Russi had his own unique way of identifying talent for the MAS, he remained fairly open to TAS talent flowing into TISCO. Steve Godinho (TAS 1986), who also served as Russi's Executive Assistant from 1987 through 1989, says, 'Russi always enjoyed having people around him, especially young people with whom he could engage and converse. It was this form of interaction that enabled him to discover hidden talent and identify individuals whom he would then develop for bigger roles.' Steve adds that one of the reasons Russi agreed to his serving as Executive Assistant was that he shared Steve's eclectic interest in a broad range of topics—sometimes as distant from everyday life as the Napoleonic Wars.

As one of the largest companies of the Tata Group, with plants flourishing in Jamshedpur and Pune, it was natural for young TAS officers to make a beeline to TELCO. The company did not have a structured Management Trainee programme till the mid-seventies, but Sumant Moolgaokar who led the company always welcomed young TAS officers. Several became rising stars in the company.

Arun Maira was working at TISCO in Jamshedpur when he was picked as Sumant Moolgaokar's Executive Assistant. Moolgaokar was looking after TISCO as well as overseeing TELCO. 'I was at Jamshedpur when I was asked to meet JRD,' remembers Arun. 'JRD was visiting Jamshedpur. He called me and interviewed me. I did not know where the conversation was heading,' continues Arun. At the end of the interview, JRD asked Arun to come and work as his Executive Assistant. 'I was over the moon as I would get a chance to work with the great man himself,' smiles Arun.

'But it was not to be,' he continues ruefully.

'Sumant Moolgaokar got the news that JRD had met me and had offered me an Executive Assistant's position. He promptly went to JRD and told him that the young man needed to do some serious work and therefore he wanted me as his own Executive Assistant! It seemed that the Executive Assistant to Moolgaokar would do more meaningful work than what he would do with JRD,' he laughs out loud.

Arun thereafter spent almost twenty years at TELCO, rising to become an Executive Director and a member of the Board. He would eventually leave the Group in the late 1980s to go to the US to work with Arthur D. Little before coming back to India as the head of the firm of international strategy consultants, Boston Consulting Group (BCG). He would later also serve as a member of the Indian government's Planning Commission.

For V.S. Krishnan (TAS 1972), an engineer-MBA, 'joining TELCO was a no brainer'. 'I was a mechanical engineer and TELCO was a rising star among companies. Perfect match!' he explains. Engineer-MBAs were a rare breed in the early seventies, and Krishan had specialized in Finance and Strategy as part of his MBA. 'Suddenly I was in demand as people in TELCO saw me as a man who could speak to the engineers as well as the finance people. I understood both languages,' laughs Krishnan.

He worked with Sharad Jakatdar, one of the main architects of the Pune factory. 'Moolgaokar was of course the big name in the company but Jakatdar was the one who implemented the plans on the ground. I was fortunate to work with him for several years,' says Krishnan.

Within a short time, Moolgaokar pulled Krishnan out of Pune and brought him to Bombay to set up and head the Corporate Planning Group for TELCO. 'It was a first for the Tata Group as well. Corporate Planning was a new concept back then,' continues Krishnan. The Corporate Planning team was responsible for putting together the strategic direction for the company, backed by financial plans, and also for presenting the capital budget to the Board, and monitoring it thereafter. 'As the Head of Corporate Planning, I received fantastic exposure to business and strategy. I had a fantastic time. The best of the TAS officers would come to work for our group,' says Krishnan. As the Corporate Planning Head, Krishnan sat on the Management Committee, the highest policy formulating forum under Moolgaokar, along with the Executive Directors of TELCO.

He was soon made the Head of Corporate Planning and Finance. 'It was one of the most integrated roles in the company, which itself was the largest automotive company in India at that time. It was also the largest TATA Group company at that time,' Krishan says. 'Responsibility for Product Pricing and presenting of the profit and loss account to the Board came with this new role,' he adds.

However, after Moolgaokar passed away in 1989, TELCO went through a management overhaul. 'I felt that I would be better somewhere else. So, I left,' asserts Krishnan. He went to work for the Harsh Goenka-led RPG Group and was the management board member in charge of strategy for the forty odd businesses of the Group. 'That kind of a role could never exist in the Tatas, as the Tatas were not a consolidated group in any case,' explains Krishnan.

Visty Banaji (TAS 1973) credits luck for his career at TELCO. He was doing a project at TELCO, Pune during his probationary period when Dinshaw Malegamwala, Member-Secretary of the TAS Committee, asked him to go to TISCO for a project. 'I wasn't too keen on it. It was known to all that TISCO did not welcome TAS officers. Just then, I came down with jaundice and that put a stop to all talk of travelling to Jamshedpur,' continues Visty in his gravelly voice. While still in his probation, he joined TELCO as Executive Assistant to Sharad Jakatdar, head of the Pune plant.

At the time, TELCO was looking to reinvent its approach to dealing with non-unionized employees. A new department was created, called Manpower Development. V.S. Mahesh headed it. 'I got to report to Mahesh, and after five to six years worked directly under Arun Maira as his Executive Assistant,' says Visty. 'Arun recommended my name as the Head of the Manpower Planning Cell in Mumbai and I moved there in 1980. I was a bit young to be in the reckoning, but full credit to Arun and to the TELCO of those days for taking that call,' continues Visty.

For the next seventeen years, Visty continued to head that department which he helped build into a full-fledged corporate HR function. 'The role grew as the scope of Corporate HR expanded. I enjoyed my role and would like to believe that I made a difference. We did some pioneering work—pioneering for India and pioneering for the Tatas,' ruminates Visty. He left the Group in 1997, first to work with ALSTOM and then with Godrej Industries and Associated Companies as an Executive Director.

If TISCO and TELCO were the largest companies of the Tata Group, Ajit Kerkar had a vision to bring the Indian Hotels Company—owner of the Taj Hotels—into the same league. In the early seventies, he spotted a talented young TAS officer, Camellia, then working in TOMCO in the marketing department. Camellia was amongst, the first few women in the TAS. She was recruited at a time when not many women were being taken into the service. Camellia, during her interview, apparently told the Selection Committee that she could fire a gun; this would appear to have been an important factor in her recruitment!

Ajit was on a mission to modernize the Taj Hotels and institute a merit-based recruitment programme in all departments. Sales and Marketing was Camellia's department, and taking her cue from Ajit, she travelled the country interviewing every applicant herself. Over a short period of time, she was able to build a handpicked team of dedicated sales and marketing professionals. Camellia rose in the corporate hierarchy to become the senior-most female TAS officer in the Group and was one of the very few women on the board of a large Tata company—she served on the board of the Indian Hotels Company for over two decades. It was shortly after Ajit left the Tatas that she, too, left to be an entrepreneur.

This is a common thread that runs through the career paths of TAS officers picked up and groomed by the satraps. Many of these fast-tracked officers left the Tatas soon after the superiors departed.

Ratan Tata took over as the Chairman of the Tata Group in 1991. Some news reports of that time termed him the wrong choice and accused JRD of nepotism. Ratan Tata himself has been quoted as saying, 'There were other aspirants for that position, so there was quite a vocal set accusing him (JRD) of having made the wrong decision.'

Among the first tasks Ratan Tata focused on, as we will discuss in more detail later in the book, was to bring greater cohesiveness within the Group. To achieve this, the wings of the recalcitrant satraps had to be clipped. Moolgaokar had passed away a few years before Ratan Tata became the Chairman of Tata Sons, but others such as Russi Mody, Darbari Seth and Ajit Kerkar were all there, larger than life. Within a few years, all were gone. Several of the senior management staff who had spent years with these satraps became collateral damage.

The TAS officers who had risen swiftly under the satraps were part of the 'casualties'. When Ratan Tata took a broom through the fiefdoms of the satraps, a number of TAS officers who were seen to be close to the erstwhile bosses were side-lined. Rather than serve in reduced roles or under new bosses, they preferred to leave the Group.

It is ironic that a Group cadre like the TAS was not able to incentivize and appropriately reward institutional loyalty in the first few decades of its existence. Visible rewards often came from personal loyalty to a satrap: because that's how the system was functioning. For TAS officers not picked up by one of the senior leaders in the Group, institutional loyalty did not generate great payback. This had further strengthened the belief among the fraternity that officers needed to find a senior mentor and a benefactor within the Group.

The question about loyalty to a boss versus loyalty to the institution has been debated across a variety of organizations over the years. Every boss demands loyalty in any case. When the boss and the organization are seen to be one, as is the case in family-owned businesses, loyalty to the former easily translates into loyalty to the latter. The satraps of the Tata Group, unfortunately, saw their businesses as their fiefdom, and saw the people working in their businesses as their own people. They ran their businesses like patriarchs of a family-owned business. The employees, including the TAS officers, also saw the satraps as patriarchs and were happy to pledge their loyalty to them. No one believed that the satraps were 'going anywhere' or could be ousted! Several of the satraps had also identified the 'inheritors' of various businesses. These were truly managed like family businesses!

Then came Ratan Tata, and this personal loyalty suddenly became a liability. Simultaneously, TAS officers who had been working with Ratan Tata now saw their fortunes turning for the better!

Having noted the risks of concentrating power in the hands of a few individuals, Ratan Tata would ensure that no Chief Executive of any Tata company became too powerful during his watch. He introduced fixed terms for the Managing Directors, and he was comfortable bringing in many CEOs from outside the Tata Group. Even the central team at Bombay House saw new faces from outside the Group. TAS officers who had risen to senior roles in the Group did not see significant new opportunities to demonstrate their leadership capabilities, and the debate about the relevance of institutional loyalty continued, inconclusively!

11

A Stepping Stone to Success

ATTRITION IN THE TAS STARTED ALMOST FROM THE INITIAL YEARS. IN the sixties and seventies, very few left it to join other Indian corporate houses as there were few organizations as large as the Tatas, with the potential to offer a wide range of career-growth opportunities. The TAS officers who left during this period typically did so to pursue higher studies overseas or to join the government or to join multinational banks that paid considerably higher salaries than Tata companies.

The TAS lost officers to multinational banks with surprising regularity. The latter offered salaries that the TAS could not match. About 10 to 15 per cent of TAS officers left within the first two years to join these banks. They were attracted by the salaries, perks and structured career plans on offer. The multinational banks were of course delighted to use the TAS as a recruitment pool. They were aware of the meticulous selection process that had been put in place.

The early entrants to the TAS were graduates of economics, history, physics, mathematics and even geology. After they joined the corporate world, a number of them came to recognize the benefits a formal MBA degree could offer. Of those TAS officers who left to pursue the degree, almost none returned. The exposure they received to other organizations during their course highlighted the lack of structured career planning within the TAS. They saw this as a major shortcoming, and thus, preferred to build their careers elsewhere thereafter. A further problem emerged when the TAS started competing with individual Tata companies for talent at the IIMs. The TAS, Arun Maira (TAS 1965) argues, had ridden into the IIMs on the back of Tata Motors's success in recruiting from these institutes. It offered higher salaries to the candidates selected from the IIMs, and in the process, upset the senior managers at Tata Motors. For some years, Tata Motors even chose to avoid inducting TAS officers into its managerial cadre. One outcome of this bickering was the induction of Dr Francis Menezes from Voltas as Director of the TMTC, and his appointment on the TAS Committee, with a mandate to 'professionalize' the TAS Secretariat.

Dr Menezes succeeded Dinshaw Malegamwala. He was known to be critical of the 'amateurish' ways in which the TAS was being managed. Also, some Tata companies, Voltas included, were unhappy with not being provided 'professional' managers. 'The smaller companies like Voltas and Indian Hotels made the case that they wanted more professional managers hired for them, leveraging the Tata brand,' explains Arun.

But little changed even after Dr Menezes was brought in. The TAS Secretariat had no real powers of placement, and the Group itself did not really have a central HR policy at the time. Each company decided for itself under the generously broad framework suggested by Bombay House. Frustrated by the absence of clear career paths, TAS officers kept leaving at regular intervals.

The divergence in starting salaries between the TAS and the multinational banks also persisted. By the 1980s, it seemed to have become a pattern—within a couple of months after their selection, bright TAS probationers would be lured away from the Tatas. Bharat Wakhlu (TAS 1985) recalls that Dr Menezes was livid when he discovered that in one batch a good number of probationers had all landed jobs in the same multinational bank! Though Dr Menezes did write to the Directors on the TAS Selection Committee, salaries remained unchanged for a while longer.

Bharat, who was one of only two TAS officers in the 1985 batch, soon became the lone TAS officer because the other candidate joined a multinational bank, within a month of her joining the TAS! Since poor salaries were an important factor in the flight of TAS talent, Bharat broached this topic with Bhupen Chakravarti at the TAS Secretariat, a few months into his probation. His suggestion was reasonable: he wanted to meet, and make a pitch on the matter, to Jamshed Bhabha, at that time a Director of Tata Sons, who was responsible for overseeing the functioning of the TAS, and to Dr Menezes. Bhupen, however, was appalled that a member of the prestigious TAS was even concerned about money!

When Bharat persisted with his request, after considerable internal discussion, it was agreed that he would be allowed to write a letter to Jamshed on the matter. Bhupen agreed that he would 'put up' the letter to Jamshed, 'duly'. Bharat's salary as a probationer didn't change, but the subsequent batches did secure higher starting salaries!

A few candidates selected for the TAS, after some introspection and due reflection, chose not to join. Rahul Singh, the well-known journalist, was almost coerced by his father, author Khushwant Singh, to join the Tatas. 'Dad told me again and again that I was an idiot for giving up an opportunity like the TAS, but somehow I did not see myself there,' says Rahul as he sits on his sun-dappled balcony in South Bombay. He had spoken to some of his friends who were already part of the TAS and had heard about the lack of a structured career plan. 'I decided I wanted to follow my heart and went into journalism,' he adds.

Nitin Paranjpe was selected in 1987 but chose to join Hindustan Levers instead. He says that it was a difficult decision but he had made an informed choice after speaking to some people who were in the TAS and others who were in Hindustan Levers. The fact that Levers did not have two levels of Management Trainees coming into the company stood out for him. Some of the TAS officers also pointed out that the TAS programme was not a structured one. Nitin chose to join a company that had a structured Management Trainee programme and went on to head Hindustan Unilever in India.

The Tatas were not happy with the attrition. The Senior Directors were invested in the TAS and their commitment was visible from the time they spent on the interview process. Even thereafter, the Directors were available to the TAS probationers and officers for advice, discussions or guidance. The Directors were aware of the reasons for attrition but in the prevalent structure they could not do much to change the set up. Nor did they want to address the below-market salaries, as it was believed that the high brand equity of the TAS offered sufficient compensation. The flow of exits consequently remained steady. The only bright spot was that the TAS officers who left ended up becoming Brand Ambassadors for the TAS as well as the Group.

'I remember my time with the TAS with great fondness,' says Arun Kumar (TAS 1973). After his probation, he had spent five years at NELCO working with a young Ratan Tata. During that time, thoughts about an MBA took root when he interacted with some alumni of the Sloan School of Management in MIT. Arun left for the USA six years after joining the TAS. After the MBA from MIT, he ended up staying on in the country. He built an illustrious career first with Elxsi as a Silicon Valley entrepreneur, and then with KPMG. He served the Obama Administration as the Assistant Secretary of Commerce and Director General of the US and Foreign Commercial Service. At the end of that tenure, he returned to India as the Chairman and CEO of KPMG India. 'But the Tatas and the TAS remain firmly a part of my happy memories. In fact, when I was in the Obama Administration, and even before that on many occasions, I would meet people in many places who also had been part of the TAS fraternity. We always connected with them immediately and talked warmly of our days at the Tatas!' says Arun with a fond smile on his face.

Vinay Pande joined the TAS in 1979, worked at the Taj Hotels and left within four years to do an MBA at Wharton. He then joined the World Bank as part of their Young Professionals' Programme. Vinay was rotated through various departments before settling down in the Treasury department of the World Bank.

The trend of young officers leaving within the first few years to pursue higher education overseas has continued through the years. Once the TAS started recruiting MBAs into the service, the young TAS officers who left for higher education usually went on to do either a second MBA or a PhD. These included Dr Ashish Nanda, who became Dean at the Harvard Business School and later served as the Director of the IIM at Ahmedabad; Dr Sunil Vacchani, who became the Director of the IIM at Bangalore; and Prof. Raghuram Rajan (TAS 1987), who became a Professor at the Chicago Booth School of Business, was appointed the youngest Chief Economist at the International Monetary Fund, and later served a term as the Governor of the Reserve Bank of India.

Some TAS officers left to join the government. The civil services have traditionally attracted some of the brightest students from Indian universities. Navtej Sarna (TAS 1980) had written the UPSC exams in November 1979 but was not sure if he would make the service he really wanted to join—the highly coveted Indian Foreign Service (IFS).

Navtej made it past the regional round of TAS interviews and then spent a week in Bombay for its final selection process. 'I remember feeling very special during that week,' says Navtej. 'The interviewers were all very dignified and talented people. The fact that they spent almost five days with us, the candidates, and made us aware of ourselves in terms of our own strengths and weaknesses was an unforgettable experience,' he continues. As one of seven selected that year for the TAS, Navtej joined the Group in the summer of 1980. 'The results of the UPSC exams came out soon after and I found that I was number thirty in the All-India list,' says Navtej. In a couple of months, he received news that he had indeed been offered the IFS cadre. He knew he had to resign. 'I went to Malegamwala, who was not angry but, shall I say, a bit disappointed. But when I told him that I was leaving to join the IFS, he told me "We don't have any quarrels with the IFS, young man! I wouldn't have let you go for the IAS,"' laughs Navtej. 'But Malegamwala had a condition.' 'He told me that I should go quietly and not make a noise about my resignation. He said that my leaving may have a bad effect on the morale of my batchmates at the TAS,' says Navtej. He did leave quietly. He says, 'So quietly that in fact that day, after my meeting with Mr. Malegamwala, I left by the side exit of Bombay House!'

Even though he spent only a few months with the TAS, Navtej remembers them with great fondness. 'After our initial induction, I spent time at the Taj Hotel working on some project in the HR department. It was a lovely experience,' says Navtej. His association with the Taj continued, even after he joined the government. When he became the spokesman for the Foreign Ministry, most of his interactions and meetings took place in Taj hotels. 'The difference was that as a probationer I could sign the Kitchen Order Tickets (KOTs) at the Taj. Now my office had to sign the bills!' he quips. He went on to become India's High Commissioner in the UK before being posted to Washington DC as the Indian Ambassador to the US. 'My connection with the Tatas continued and I kept meeting people from the Group. There was a great sense of warmth and friendship in our interactions,' says Navtej.

Some TAS officers quit to turn entrepreneurs. Siddharth Kak (TAS 1971) was one such individual. He had joined the TAS after graduating from St. Stephen's College. 'To tell you the truth, I had absolutely no idea what the TAS was all about,' says Siddharth. 'All I knew is that the TAS was an elite service. It was not advertised at all and the aura was built by word-of-mouth publicity,' he continues. It was only during his interview that Siddharth got to know what TAS officers were expected to do!

After his probation, Siddharth landed up at the Taj Mahal Hotel in Bombay and worked as the Front Office Manager. 'This was before the Oberoi, Nariman Point was built,' remembers Siddharth. 'My biggest problem used to be how to say "No" politely to people who could not get a room at the Taj,' he laughs wryly.

'ABK (as Ajit Kerkar was known) was a very hands-on person. His entire life revolved around the hotel,' continues Siddharth. Ajit knew that the Oberoi Hotel was coming up at Nariman Point, and he wanted to protect his clientele. 'He told me that I needed to spend time with our existing clients. Starting with breakfast, I had to have every meal in the hotel with a client. Besides the meals, I also had to have tea, coffee and drinks with them,' says Siddharth, his voice irritated even after fifty years. 'I could not do this and must have made it apparent to ABK. Thereafter, our relations were, shall we say, not the very best,' he continues with a laugh.

With the satrap's hand no longer on his head, Siddharth moved out of the Taj. He first went to Tata Exports and worked there for a couple of years before being asked by Jamshed Bhabha to be his Executive Assistant. 'I had always been interested in the creative arts. Even as I worked with the Tatas, I spent a lot of my free time in creative pursuits. Maybe Jamshed Bhabha saw me as a like-minded person,' says Siddharth by way of explanation.

Jamshed gave Siddharth several different assignments. 'I think he recognized my core strengths and interests and gave me jobs accordingly,' says Siddharth. These included a role in the Public Relations Department of the Tatas. The assignment that he enjoyed the most, however, was as the Business Manager for MARG Publications. MARG was a quarterly art magazine and a publisher of books on the arts. It was started by the noted author Mulk Raj Anand and was supported financially by the Tata Group. Siddharth already had a mentor in Jamshed; at MARG he got another one—Mulk Raj Anand himself.

Working with both Jamshed Bhabha, who was then setting up the National Centre for the Performing Arts (NCPA) in Bombay, and with Mulk Raj Anand, who was expanding the MARG portfolio, Siddharth's creative juices had occasion to flow freely. When the urge to do something in the creative field became stronger, he went to Jamshed, who encouraged him to take the step. 'He told me that I could go on leave for a year—a kind of sabbatical. If I found that I was better off outside the Group, I could then formally resign; if, on the other hand, I found the going hard, the doors of the TAS were open. I cannot tell you how much of a security that was,' says Siddharth.

Siddharth left, went through a couple of turbulent years, and then went on to set up Cinema Vision. He became the Producer and Presenter of *Surabhi*, a very popular television programme which he co-hosted with Renuka Shahane. The show went on to become the longest-running cultural series on Indian television, and Siddharth became a household name. 'But I will always remember my days at the Tatas with great fondness and will always go that extra mile for them,' says Siddharth with a wide smile. 'I owe Tatas, they don't owe me!'

Vir Chopra (TAS 1971) plotted during his initial years with the TAS on how he might earn enough money to fund the management programme at the Harvard Business School. 'I really wanted to do an MBA from Harvard,' says Vir. (Vir Chopra, sadly, passed away during the writing of this book).

Vir recalls returning to Delhi after his TAS interview in Bombay, and calling his parents in Srinagar. 'My father picked up the phone,' remembers Vir. 'Before I could tell him about my interview, he got emotional and said "Mubarak, Mubarak" with his voice breaking. The telegram from the TAS Committee had reached Srinagar that morning! It was a hugely emotional moment for me and for my whole family. Getting selected in the TAS was a big thing.'

After his probation, Vir joined TISCO. 'Those were the pre-Russi Mody days. R.S. Pandey used to be the MD, and Russi Mody was the joint MD of Operations. Pandey had asked the Committee for a few TAS officers and I was one of those sent,' remembers Vir. He spent just over three years with TISCO but felt constrained in the bureaucratic environment of the large company. He had caught Ajit Kerkar's eye during his probation days, and when Pandey left TISCO, Ajit saw his chance and asked for Vir. 'I spent three wonderful years with the Taj. I was the Group

Marketing Manager working with Camellia who was the Vice President of Marketing,' remembers Vir. One day, one of his senior TAS colleagues, Kishore, who was posted by the Taj in Muscat, called him. 'He started speaking to me in French. I knew a bit of the language, of course, but was puzzled nevertheless. Kishore told me that he was speaking in French because he did not want the telephone operators at the Taj to understand what was being said!' Vir laughs. Kishore told Vir that there was a local businessman, Mr Mustafa, who ran a large guest house in Muscat and was looking for a General Manager. The money would be good. 'I thought to myself that this was my chance to earn some serious money so that I could go to Harvard for my cherished MBA,' exclaims Vir. But it was a big decision and he told Kishore that he would call him back. After two days, he called Kishore back, and said, '*je suis d'accord*!' Kishore told him that Mr Mustafa was coming to Bombay a week later and would like to meet him.

'Ironically, he had booked a room at the Taj and I went for my interview to his room!' Vir recounts. After they chatted for over an hour, Vir had the job. 'The Taj and the TAS were loath to let me go but my mind was on the money I would earn, which would enable me to do my MBA,' says Vir. His plan was to work for a couple of years, earn enough money for an MBA and then leave. 'But I worked there for over thirteen years!' Mr Mustafa was so happy with him that he kept increasing the scope and range of his work.

'Very soon I found that I was running sixteen companies. Their strategy, their foreign collaborations, their business plans all had to be run past me,' says Vir. 'I got so much exposure to doing business that I realized that an MBA would not teach me anything new.'

The bug of higher studies never left Vir. Eventually, he enrolled at the London School of Economics and earned a doctorate, before returning to India. 'When you spend so much time outside the country, you start feeling more deeply about the country,' he explains. 'And I wanted to do something by way of giving back in whatever small way I could.' Vir worked with the government on a paper on electoral reforms, which gave him much satisfaction.

By this time, his brother Vidhu Vinod Chopra had established himself in Bollywood and was working on *1942: A Love Story*, a movie that went on to become a box office hit in 1994. Vir joined his brother and worked with him on this movie and several more that followed—*Mission Kashmir*, *Munna Bhai MBBS* and *3 Idiots*, to name a few.

However, the pull of hospitality continued to tug at him. 'Once a hotelier, always a hotelier!' says Vir. He went on to set up a luxury resort in the Maldives, and now spends much of his time there. 'But I look back at my days with the Tatas with great reverence. I learnt so much there and if I had to re-do my career, I would not change it a bit. Even the TISCO stint taught me so much,' Vir reminisces.

While the call of higher education, entrepreneurship, working for the government or even the need to earn more money each played a role in the exit of many TAS officers, some were forced to leave simply because they could not see any further career opportunities in the Group, despite being members of an elite cadre.

Vibha Paul Rishi (TAS 1982) had been working with Titan in Bombay. When her husband was transferred to Delhi, Vibha too looked for opportunities within the Tata Group there. The TAS Secretariat, however, was unable to identify any opportunities for her. She therefore decided to quit.

'I went to Bombay House to go to the TAS Secretariat and submit my letter of resignation,' remembers Vibha. As she got into the slow-moving lift, she found that she was sharing the small space with Ratan Tata. 'He used to call me Watch Lady. I am sure he did not remember my name but he did know that I had been part of the Titan team from the early days,' she continues as she laughs fondly at the memory.

As the lift slowly groaned its way to the second floor, Ratan said, 'So, Watch Lady, where are you going?' ' I told him that I was quitting because I was moving to Delhi and you guys have nothing there for me,' Vibha recounts briskly. 'He looked at me oddly and said, "No, no, no—why don't you check with Zahid? There may be something for you in Delhi."' Zahid Baig was the head of the Corporate Office of the Tata Group in Delhi.

Baig asked Vibha to meet with Ramesh Vangal who was setting up a new Pepsi project in India. PepsiCo had entered India through a tie-up with the state-owned Punjab Agro Industries Corporation and Voltas. 'I met Ramesh and he said immediately, "Come, come let's build this,"' remembers Vibha. Thus, Vibha became part of the Pepsi project.

'I continued to be part of the TAS but I honestly don't know when I left,' she says, shaking her head. She would get some communications from Bhupen Chakravarti at the TAS Secretariat in her initial years at Pepsi. 'But those communications, never regular to begin with, slowly just petered out. I guess at some stage, I stopped being part of the TAS, though there was never a formal communication from them to me to that effect,' she continues. She went on to make a name for herself as a marketing expert at Pepsi.

The attrition levels of TAS officers in the first three decades of its existence were not trivial. Of the 169 TAS officers selected between 1956 and 1984, only fifty-seven remained with the Group after thirty years. About 67 per cent of this cadre of top-flight talent and future Tata leaders had instead chosen to move on. The fact that many of those who left made a name for themselves outside the Group is testimony to the outstanding talent selection process of the TAS.

Even in the current times, the attrition has not slowed down and TAS officers continue to leave at regular intervals. The silver lining for the Tata Group, however, is that almost all of them still retain a warmth for their erstwhile employer. The TAS Committee was not wrong when it said that TAS officers, including those who left, would be the Brand Ambassadors for the Group.

12
A Few Good Women

'So, tell me Sonu, why did you leave the TAS?' asked Percy. Percy Siganporia (TAS 1974) and Sonu Bhasin (TAS 1987) were having lunch in Delhi at a fine-dining Chinese restaurant. Sonu had recently quit the TAS after working with the Tata Group for over thirteen years. Percy, Executive Director of Tata Tea, was visiting Delhi and had invited Sonu out for lunch. As Percy waited for Sonu to answer his question, he focused on his food. He used his fork to twirl up some noodles that were on his plate.

Sonu answered Percy's question with a question of her own. 'Percy,' she said looking at him with a glint in her eye, 'can you name five senior women in the Tata Group?'

Percy had finished gathering up the noodles with his fork by now. As Sonu asked her question, Percy looked up at her and said 'Yeeaaah' in a tone that said, '*What-a-stupid-question-is-this, why-five? I-will-name-ten-women.*' And then, as he took the fork to his mouth he stopped; realization dawned on him. Sonu looked at him steadily with a knowing smile. It was the moment when Percy realized that he could not name even five senior women in the entire Tata Group. 'There! You have the answer to why I left the Tatas, Percy,' said Sonu with a rueful smile. 'Seems to me that the glass ceiling for women in the Group is made at Tata Steel!' she muttered under her breath.

This was in the early 2000s. After more than twenty years, if he were asked the same question again, chances are that he would still not be able to name five senior women with executive powers in the Tata Group!

The Tata Group is known for a lot of things; one thing it is not known for is its women leaders. Because there are so few. The Tata Group now spans scores of countries and has over 700,000 employees spread worldwide, with more than 100 companies. But the Group hardly has a woman Managing Director or CEO anywhere, in any Tata company, in any country.

The TAS, too, has been unable to provide its women officers sufficient opportunities to lead businesses. Khorshed Jhaveri, the first woman TAS officer, joined in 1958. Silloo Surti (TAS 1962) joined a couple of years later, followed by Camellia Panjabi. While Khorshed left after a decade and a half, having run into the unbreakable glass ceiling, Silloo continued in a support role, hidden away in the backrooms of TELCO, Jamshedpur. Camellia stayed with the Group for many years and rose to become the senior-most woman TAS officer in the Group.

The early years of the TAS were considered to be progressive as women were selected during the time to be groomed as future leaders. In the 1950s and early 1960s, there were not many corporations making this 'bold' statement of intent. The women selected were told categorically that the Group hoped that they would lead Tata companies in the future. 'This was something that excited me. It was thrilling to be thought of as a future CEO,' remembers Khorshed. 'We were told at our induction that we would become role models for others.'

But it was not to be. Inexplicably, for twenty years, between the 1960s and the early 1980s, the TAS simply stopped taking applications from women. 'There may be an explanation of sorts,' says Camellia Punjabi (TAS 1963). 'The first two women hires were sent to Jamshedpur for their induction. Now, they got married there and refused to move out of that town. So the Tatas simply decided that they would not hire any more women in the TAS!'

The notices sent out to educational institutions, including the IIMs, had specific instructions that women were not to apply to the TAS. Unfortunately, there is no one else who knows, or is willing to speak, about the reason for this bizarre decision by the Committee. It seems odd, considering that JRD Tata himself was supportive of women leaders.

There is some speculation that the Factories Act of 1948, which governed the manner in which factories had to be regulated and managed, and restricted the working hours for women, may have incentivized the preference to only hire men. Another view that prevails is that women in management positions in the US were few, and the Tatas—who would eagerly look to that country for inspiration in matters related to technology and management—might actually have believed that this was 'normal'. Harvard Business School was lukewarm towards women taking up key leadership roles in management, and their influence and support in the setting up of IIM Ahmedabad (IIM-A) allowed the same overseas biases and mindsets to get transposed to corporate India.

Many suggest that Dr Kamla Chowdhry, a formidable researcher, academic and a brilliant teacher at IIM-A, who had obtained her doctorate in social psychology from the University of Michigan in 1949 and was the de facto Director of IIM-A, was stalled from becoming the Director of the prestigious management institute precisely because of the discriminatory mindsets that prevailed at that time.

Interestingly, when a graduating woman candidate from IIM-A brought the TAS campus selection announcement in 1981 to Dr Chowdhry's notice (which clearly indicated that 'women need not apply'), she promptly called JRD Tata. JRD must have been suitably impacted by the illustrious Dr Chowdhry, because he went on to ensure that this glaring discriminatory aspect of the TAS was done away with the next year onwards.

'We were the first batch after more than twenty years to have women,' says Vibha Paul Rishi (TAS 1982), adding with a wry laugh, 'Though it seemed that we were an afterthought.' The notice inviting applications to the TAS had come to FMS—the Faculty of Management Studies—where she was a student, just as it had gone to other educational institutes. As was the norm then, it did say that applications from women would not be accepted. 'And then one day, the placement cell got a cable which said that women could apply! Can you imagine a communication like that in these days?!' she asks rhetorically, her eyebrows raised. 'So, of course I applied.'

Vibha made it to the shortlist at the Regional Round in Delhi and went to Bombay for the final process of selection. 'One thing that struck me was the fact that the TAS Selection Committee had absolutely no idea what to do with us women candidates!' says Vibha shaking her head. 'They were deferential, almost putting us on a pedestal, being like ultra-nice and stuff like that.'

That year, the TAS Committee selected the largest group of women since the cadre's inception—three. Interestingly, Vibha recalls, 'When we went to various Tata companies to do our projects in the first year, we found that each company had its fair share of women.' The women were not at senior levels, but nevertheless, the Tata companies had not stopped recruiting women. It seemed that the Tata companies had been more progressive than the TAS! 'No one can quite say why the TAS stopped taking women for twenty years,' says Vibha.

Since there had been no women in the cadre for two decades, the pipeline of women leaders was empty. Thus, by the time green shoots around gender diversity started appearing in the late eighties, and then became stronger in the nineties and after, the TAS had no women who could be showcased as leaders, with the exception of Camellia. Gender diversity, or the lack of it, was definitely a problem.

Debjani Biswas (TAS 1983) recalls, 'During the recruitment process, I was asked a question about gender diversity by the TAS Committee. Specifically, as to why there was such a skewed male to female ratio in the senior Tata leadership.

'I gave a "controversial" answer to this question,' she says, smiling. 'If memory serves, I chose a risky way to respond, with specific examples of systemic gender bias. Since I was eventually selected, we can conclude that the Committee was open to, and perhaps even appreciated, candid feedback.'

In Debjani's opinion, the strong principles and business practices that served the Tatas well in the past should be adapted to current times. 'The world has changed, and all of us have to adjust accordingly. This advice applies to other organizations, all over the world, as well.'

'I routinely conduct diversity, inclusion and equity assessments for large organizations,' she says. 'It can be disheartening to see how many still have dated rules around female attire, for instance. Perhaps these are merely errors of omission; but outdated codes of conduct can negatively impact workplace morale.'

To be fair to the Tatas, however, it was not a problem only within the Tata Group. Gender diversity, especially in senior roles, was, and continues to be, a systemic problem within the corporate world across countries.

In a larger context, India has seen the participation of women in the workforce decline over the years. Everyone agrees that there should be more women working outside the home. These days when there is a heightened understanding of political correctness, even people who may disagree have to be careful not say it out loud! There are statistics from the Centre for Monitoring Indian Economy (CMIE), the World Economic Forum (WEF), the World Bank and the UN Development Programme (UNDP) that point out that India is actually losing women in the workplace. Currently, as per IndiaSpend, 27 per cent of Indian women are part of the labour market. Contrast that with China, which has 64 per cent of women working. A McKinsey report of 2015 highlights that if women were at par with men at the workplace, India could increase her GDP by a whopping 60 per cent.

The problem is compounded by the fact that even though the number of women graduating is increasing, the number of women joining the corporate sector and then rising to the top remains low. Only three out of 100 Managing Directors and CEOs of companies listed on the

National Stock Exchange are women. Fortune, a business publication, brings out its list of top 100 and 500 companies for different countries and the world. For the year 2020, the Fortune India 500 list has only twenty-nine women leaders with executive powers. Of these twenty-nine women, twenty-two are on the list because they are a part of the promoter/owner family. The statistics are no different when it comes to more developed countries. The Fortune 500 in the US had thirty-three women CEOs while in the Fortune Global 500 listing, which ranks the world's largest companies, the number of women CEOs was even smaller—only fourteen.

Thus, it would be right were the Tatas to say in their defence that they are no different than the rest of the corporate world. 'But this is a lazy argument,' says Sonu, a trifle irritated, her hands waving the excuse away. 'The Tatas have always prided themselves as being different and being progressive. Look at their track record in employee welfare programmes,' she asserts. 'How can they now hide behind a we-are-like-the-others-only argument?'

It is true that the Tatas are known for many progressive welfare programmes in the workplace. The eight-hour working day was introduced in the Tata Group in 1912 and free medical aid for staff in 1915. This was much before it was set down as law by the government. The Tatas also pioneered maternity leave, leave with pay, provident fund schemes, accident compensation and other such welfare schemes. The noteworthy point is that many of these were set up well before they were introduced either in India or even, in some cases, the so-called developed world. The Tatas were also among the first ones to involve employees in management through departmental councils which included representatives of the workers.

Considering all this, it is surprising that the one area in which they have fallen behind is having women leaders in senior roles. Experts say that the problem in the corporate world is less at the junior or middle management levels; the number of women steadily diminishes at the higher management levels. What is essential, according to experts, is the presence of a conducive environment at the workplace with supportive policies, including maternity benefits, and flexible career options with options for short-term sabbaticals.

Women TAS officers did encounter some misguided efforts within their organizations to be supportive. Debjani says, 'When I was with the Tatas, I found the environment quite supportive.' She had joined Voltas after her probation and was assigned to the sales department. 'When I went on sales calls, I was always accompanied by a colleague. This was the norm then, particularly for females—though it might feel old-fashioned today.'

'The Tatas have always been patriarchal in their approach,' says Kalpana Kohli Kar (TAS 1984). 'The overall environment is that of patriarchy, and while it is there in dealings with men as well, when it comes to women it is even more pronounced.'

'It did seem to me that the Tatas could have used their patriarchal approach as something that was enabling; instead, they used it as shackles,' says Sonu.

'At junior levels, it is great to be part of an organization that is so caring and at the same time gives you major responsibilities,' says Abanti Sankaranarayanan (TAS 1992). 'We got so much responsibility and when I looked at my peers from my MBA institute, I was happy that I was doing so much more than them. But at some stage, the caring culture turned into the restrictive atmosphere around a Victorian father—almost stifling.'

The 'Victorian' culture was felt by other women officers as well. 'When I was there, the overarching culture was very much that of patriarchal fiefdoms,' says Indira Pant (TAS 1984). After her year of probation, Indira was appointed as Executive Assistant to Ratan Tata. 'There was a lot of veneration of authority, with distance between levels. All of this played out to a male-dominated, authoritarian culture. I don't think that there was a conscious plan to keep out women, but the environment was not conducive to women climbing up the corporate ladder,' she continues in her measured voice.

'The fact that you have so few women at the top means that there is no contra-leadership style in the Group,' explains Abanti.

'The typical leadership styles that are over-indexed for women, like collaboration, empathy, sensitivity and orientation towards consensus and inclusivity, were lacking, as a result. Therefore, we always felt that there was only one style that was needed to succeed—an alpha male kind of leadership, hierarchy-driven, command and control. That was the leadership style that was visibly rewarded. If we did not have that kind of leadership style, one was left feeling that there might not be place for us at the top.'

This culture was prevalent in other companies as well but maybe we were a little more patriarchal, who knows? I saw a lot of kindness—it felt like a bunch of men high up on the organization ladder being protective towards much younger, somewhat wide-eyed, lost souls. Being a lost young soul myself, I found it deeply comforting initially. But I imagine a more experienced, capable, ready-to-lead kind of a woman would likely have found the same kindliness oppressive, even offensive', continues Indira. 'I didn't stay long enough in the Group to find out. However, I can say almost with certainty that while there was no intent to limit the rise of women in the Group, there was no active enablement either,' she concludes.

Women, especially in the workplace, do need that bit of enabling. The TAS seemed just the right platform to provide this. It actively encouraged all its officers to work across Tata companies. For the women officers, this could have been a great benefit as one of the main charges thrown at women in the corporate world is that they will get married and then will choose to follow their husbands instead of prioritizing their careers and commitments. Since the Tata companies are present all across India, and even overseas, women TAS officers could have transferred from one Tata company to another, should the need have arisen. Furthermore, women officers could avail of longer leave for maternity without losing out on their seniority. The leave enabled them continuity of service.

'I was fortunate that the TAS protected the seniority of women even when they were on leave,' says Sonu. 'I went on maternity leave as a manager in one Tata company and joined back a year and a half later as a Deputy General Manager in another Tata company. Protection of my seniority with no break in service proved to be a valuable stepping stone for my future success,' she asserts. Data shows that most women who step off the corporate ladder do so at mid-management levels. This is the time when they have children and need to take a break from work. Gender diversity initiatives take time to show results, and CEO and Managing Director appointments in any company are the outcome of human resource decisions taken years earlier. If the supply of women middle managers and CXOs reduces, there will never be enough women in the pipeline to reach the top in any company.

The TAS could have fed that supply line, as it identified and trained women leaders from an early age. The women officers should have risen to leadership positions. However, their attrition continued to be high with most of them leaving within five years of joining. Furthermore, even the ones who stayed in the Group for more than ten years left when it became evident that the leadership opportunities for them were restricted.

'I left once I realized that the path to the next level was not visible,' says Abanti. She had spent more than seventeen years with the Tatas across various companies and geographies. Her last role was as the deputy CEO of Mount Everest Mineral Water, a Tata Global Beverages subsidiary. 'But it just wasn't clear to me when and how I could get the next break,' she says.

'And then there was the fact that there was no one we could look up to and say, "That's where we can reach." There were simply no senior women in the Group,' says Abanti. 'There was nothing really negative against women; rather, it was simply that there was no affirmative action to get more women into senior roles or even build a pipeline of women to reach senior levels. I felt the next level of roles may well be out of my reach.'

Abanti left the Tatas to join Diageo, where she quickly rose to become the Managing Director of its 100% subsidiary Diageo India Pvt Ltd and subsequently, the Chief Strategy and Corporate Affairs Officer, in addition to being a member of the Executive Committee of United Spirits Ltd, Diageo's biggest acquisition in the world.

The alpha male environment along with strong patriarchy could result in yet another obstacle for women to cross—that of the gender pay gap. This is essentially the average of the difference between the total remuneration paid out to working men and women. In the US, the salary of an average female worker is 78 per cent of the average male worker. In India, too, the gender pay gap is stark and spans industries. Studies show that in IT services, there is a pay gap of 26 per cent in favour of men, while in the manufacturing sector, men earn 24 per cent more than women.

The pay gap increases as leaders climb the corporate ladder. Experts blame this on the fact that while men do not take breaks in their careers to have children, women do. However, even without breaks in their careers, women are 'expected' to be happy with the salary they get, while men are 'expected' to negotiate for more.

Kalpana was extremely happy working at Titan in the early years of her career with the Tatas. 'It was a new company in the 1980s, it had young people and it was fun to be there,' she remembers with a fond smile. 'The idea of a contemporary design company representing lifestyle retail was a breakthrough and the team had several bright talented women. The opportunities to contribute and make a difference were equal and large, but when it came to salary and compensation, the story of gender pay inequality persisted!' she exclaims throwing up her hands.

Her husband had started his own venture, which was a success and had become a recognized name in the Information Technology industry. 'They said Pradeep (my husband) is doing so well, so why do you need so much money? And my first thought was, "*Who are you to decide how much money I need? And what does my husband's success have to do with my salary? I should get what I deserve.*" I just felt so undervalued,' she says, first frowning and then sombrely. Kalpana left the Group and helped her husband to grow Microland.

'Actually, there is little difference between a senior Tata executive sitting in his plush office and a diamond merchant sitting in a cramped office in Zaveri Bazaar,' quips Indira. She had left the TAS and joined the non-profit, Child Rights and You (CRY). 'One day, CRY's founder, Rippan Kapur, and I had gone to meet a diamond merchant to ask for donations as CRY was perpetually short of funds,' recalls Indira. 'While describing CRY's work, this diamond merchant interrupts me to ask, "Do you get a salary from CRY? How much is it?" What infuriated me was that he did not ask Rippan, a man, the same question. Ignoring my incredulous look, he pronounced that I should not be paid at all. He felt that paying a salary to me—a woman—was a waste of money, particularly in the non-profit sector. It reflected a widely prevalent view at that time that it was okay for a woman to be paid less than her male counterparts—after all, there was always a father, a husband or a son around to support her,' Indira fumes.

And then there is the stereotyping of women in certain kinds of roles. There is the well-known case of Sudha Murthy being forced to write to JRD Tata so that she, as a woman engineer, could be considered for a job at TELCO. Sudha Murthy was able to work in TELCO and be taken seriously as an engineer in the 1970s, but the stereotyping tended to continue.

'I had gone to meet a senior Tata executive in a large Tata company in the mid-1990s,' remembers Sonu. She was looking for a larger role, having spent a few years in a small Tata company. 'The TAS tag got me a meeting with the senior executive. I went for the meeting in my normal work attire—a vibrant silk saree, and I remember I had a string of pearls round my neck,' she says as she recalls the scene. 'We had a good meeting and then the guy turns to me and says, "We have a role in the PR department." He saw me, well dressed and articulate, and the first role that came to his mind was in PR!' she splutters with indignation.

'Here I was, managing all aspects of business in two big regions and looking for a larger business role. Maybe it was the string of pearls that worked against me—maybe women leaders are supposed to be dowdy and not dressed in vibrant colours,' she goes on, the indignation still strong. The millennium has brought with it a renewed focus on gender diversity and inclusion. No longer can employers hide their diversity figures. All research data points out that the gender gap has increased at the higher corporate levels. With more women being educated and joining the workforce, at the entry and junior levels there tends to be gender parity; but the number of women steadily decreases in middle management and then almost falls off a cliff at senior executive roles.

Regulators around the world are doing their bit by mandating a certain percentage of women in the Board of Directors. Furthermore, search firms are increasingly instructed to shortlist at least one 'diversity candidate' for CXO and CEO roles. The Tata Group, too, had to take visible action. In March 2014, the Group launched an initiative called 'Tata Lead' and announced that the programme was a reflection of the Group's commitment to diversity and inclusion. The Group maintained that increased representation of women provided a broader talent pool and also drove a more collaborative culture. The programme promised to double the number of women in the Tata Group by 2020, and triple the number of women at the CXO/CEO levels. The sad truth is that both these targets have been missed by large margins.

In 2008, the Group also launched a much-publicized programme called the Second Career Internship Programme (SCIP). This was a programme designed to facilitate the onboarding process of women returning to work after a break. This has offered opportunities for several hundred women to get back into the workforce.

The jury is still out on whether these programmes will eventually throw up some women leaders with executive leadership powers or not. What will certainly be of interest is to see when a large Tata company gets its first woman CEO.

Part II

The Post-JRD Era

13

The Ratan Tata Years: The Beginning

By 1991, JRD Tata had presided over the fortunes of the Tata Group for 53 years. During this time, he had led the Group through India's freedom struggle and independence from colonial rule. Along with other Tata leaders, he had witnessed the new-born republic's developmental challenges and the struggle to overcome widespread poverty; he had probably been disappointed by India's post-Independence tilt towards socialism.

Meanwhile, decades of poor growth under the licence raj and profligate government spending in the late 1980s significantly weakened the Indian economy. The last nail in the coffin was driven in by a massive and unanticipated fuel price hike caused by Iraq's invasion of Kuwait and the Gulf War. The IMF and the World Bank extended their conditional aid linked to economic reforms to an Indian economy that was teetering on the edge of default on its international debt obligations.

What followed was what JRD Tata might have wished for—only that it may have been what he wanted to happen in the prime of his life, rather than at the fag end of it. Led by an astute Prime Minister, P.V. Narasimha Rao, and a brilliant Economist-turned-Finance Minister, Dr Manmohan Singh, the Indian government undertook a series of far-reaching reform initiatives at the start of the nineties. This set India on a path to greater openness to foreign investment and greater engagement with the global economy via increased trade, and dramatically improved the choices available to customers.

From an economy committed through a 1976 Constitutional Amendment to 'socialism', the 1991 economic reforms pushed India on the path of free enterprise, lifting many of the shackles of the by then infamous licence raj. Indian businesses were no longer obliged to rush to the government every time they saw the opportunity to increase production to address market demand. Quality standards that were often suspect in the era when India was a closed and protected economy started rising. And with the entry of world-class foreign competition, Indian businesses were pushed to become more competitive.

An ageing JRD, in a choice that surprised some, decided that the time had arrived for him to hand over the baton to Ratan Tata and bring speculation over his successor to an end. Many were of the view that the succession planning for an empire that was as diverse and large as the Tata Group had become should have been done much earlier when JRD was younger. This would have provided ample opportunities for the outgoing Chairman to provide guidance and mentorship to the new incumbent. Over five decades with the same individual in the leadership role meant that a certain degree of stasis had crept into the Tata Group. Many Tata watchers also surmised that JRD's legendary laissez-faire style, and his gentlemanly approach to management, gave the powerful satraps too much leeway. The satraps started to function in ways that suited them—and which were not always in alignment with the best interests of the Tata Group.

Bharat Wakhlu (TAS 1985) worked at TISCO (Tata Steel) in Jamshedpur when JRD visited the Steel City in March 1991. 'As it turned out, it was the last trip JRD made to Jamshedpur as the Group Chairman,' recalls Bharat. 'He came to be part of the Founder's Day celebrations, which used to be celebrated on a grand scale. Russi Mody was heading TISCO at that time.'

At an Officers' Dialogue that was organized by TISCO, JRD started his speech by thanking Russi for inviting him to Jamshedpur. 'I am very glad to be here with you all,' he said from the lectern, 'and I am grateful to you, Russi, for inviting me to Jamshedpur,' he continued, looking towards Russi who was also on stage. 'You, Russi, are the Maharaja of Jamshedpur, and I couldn't have come here unless you deigned to invite me,' JRD said impishly, with a big smile on his face. While most of those in the auditorium laughed, the message was not lost on the more discerning members of the audience. In the same month that year, Ratan Tata succeeded JRD.

The fifty-three-year-old Ratan was a spring chicken in comparison with several other potential contenders for the role of Chairman of Tata Sons, including veteran leaders like Russi Mody, Darbari Seth and Nani Palkhivala—all in their seventies by then. Ratan's selection by JRD suggested his suitability across several important dimensions.

Ratan was younger than his principal contenders on the Board of Tata Sons, with many years of active leadership still ahead of him. He had already acquired considerable experience, having served on the Tata Sons Board since the 1970s and having been involved in the leadership of various businesses in the Group, including electronics, textile and automotive. He also had a personal interest in areas of emerging new technologies, and had helped to seed some Tata Group investments in the rapidly emerging and exciting information technology sector, notably in Tata Elxsi, a company originally formed to deliver high performance computing solutions.

Perhaps most importantly, the research Ratan had undertaken in 1983 while preparing a Strategic Plan for Tata Industries, the erstwhile Managing Agency of the Group which he had been appointed to Chair, had equipped him with many ideas for the Tata Group's future growth. Rajiv Dube (TAS 1990), Ratan's Executive Assistant in the early and mid-1990s, recollects the significance of the 1983 Strategic Plan. Even though much of the Plan was not implemented at the time, Rajiv says, 'It possibly gave JRD visibility into the mind of his potential successor and the manner in which he thought. JRD would also have been impressed with Ratan's views on technology, internationalization, and how the Group ought to prepare for the future.'

Exciting new sunrise opportunities were identified in the 1983 Strategic Plan. Tata Industries became the vehicle to launch a series of new projects, including joint ventures with the likes of IBM, Honeywell and AT&T, and new forays into sectors like telecommunications. Senior executives like S. Ramakrishnan (TAS 1972) were brought in from other parts of the Tata Group to help Tata Industries launch several of these projects. A number of young TAS officers, like N. Srinath (TAS 1986), Hasnen Varawala (TAS 1988), Shayesth Desai (TAS 1990), Suneel Bandhu (TAS 1989) and Eric Vas (TAS 1991) would cut their teeth in strategic planning and project management roles at Tata Industries under the watchful eye of Ratan Tata.

Eric recalls the enormous learning he acquired in project management while at Tata Industries. 'I was a young and inexperienced TAS officer in the mid-1990s,' he says candidly. 'But I was, at one time, the principal project manager handling three substantial capital-intensive projects at Tata Industries, namely the Utkal Alumina project, the proposed new Bangalore Airport, and the proposed Tata–Singapore Airlines joint venture. My interactions within the company were directly with the senior executive overseeing projects at Tata Industries, S. Ramakrishnan (SR; TAS 1972), and the Chairman, Ratan Tata,' he says excitedly.

Eric notes the enormous responsibility placed on the shoulders of young TAS officers like him in Tata Industries. He gratefully acknowledges the support managers like him received from SR. 'SR gave you a huge amount of space, but he would step in when it was necessary. If he saw you doing something stupid, he would help you refocus on what really mattered,' he says. The exciting new opportunities being pursued by Tata Industries made it an attractive destination for many young TAS officers through the 1990s.

As it happened, in Eric's case, none of the three projects he was assigned at Tata Industries could materialize. He says, 'I felt terrible at a personal level. But those years taught me a lot about project and risk management that I could carry through in my subsequent career. After my stint at Tata Industries, I felt I needed P&L and operating experience. I therefore moved to the new car business being set up at Tata Motors, where I worked closely with Rajiv, and oversaw the network development and commercial activity.'

Rajiv observes, 'Almost all the substantial elements of the 1983 Strategic Plan were delivered over the time Ratan Tata was Group Chairman. The internationalization agenda commenced in the 1990s, but was firmly embraced in the second decade of Ratan Tata's chairmanship. Perhaps what did not get fully executed was the integration of the Group's older international assets in the form of Tata International, Tata Inc., Tata Zug and Tata Ltd. The 1983 Plan, as I understood, called for a unified international face for the Tata Group, and that is something that is yet to be achieved.'

Ratan was as prepared as anybody could be to lead the Tatas into a brave new world, as India opened its hitherto protected markets to foreign investment. A new era was set to commence at the Tata Group.

But the changes that would follow would not be to the liking of everyone in the Tata Group, particularly the satraps, and those TAS officers who had developed specially close relationships with those satraps.

14
Getting Rid of the Satraps

THE HASTENED PACE OF CHANGE IN THE INDIAN ECONOMY SOUNDED THE death knell for many Indian businesses as foreign companies moved into the Indian market with better-designed products and services, superior technology, efficient supply chains and proven business models. The 'Bombay Club', which consisted of some of India's most prominent industrialists, including Rahul Bajaj, Lala Bharat Ram, Lalit Mohan Thapar, Hari Shankar Singhania, M.V. Arunachalam, B.K. Modi, C.K. Birla and Jamshyd Godrej, agitatedly demanded a 'level playing field' for Indian corporates.

As a result, the government imposed some constraints on foreign companies, including caps on the equity that foreign players could hold in Indian companies. And some sectors of the Indian economy were entirely shut to foreign investors. Still, by the end of the decade, many of India's leading business groups from the beginning of the 1990s were no longer in positions of leadership.

In this rapidly transforming economic landscape, Ratan Tata chose to stay away from the Bombay Club. He felt that though there would be pain involved in adjusting to an increasingly open and transparent economy, hitherto cosseted Indian companies needed to learn to be more competitive. By continuing to seek the protection of the government, they were only kicking the can further down the road and postponing the day of final reckoning.

Ratan knew that he had to move with urgency to prepare the Tata Group for the unprecedented challenges the new environment presented. The old ways of doing business had to change. The first of many critical internal challenges he had to address was to limit the influence of the satraps, whose style of doing business he did not endorse.

In a key departure from JRD Tata's latter years, Ratan resolved to centralize decision-making at Tata Sons and unify the Group under its umbrella. He believed that the satraps had moved too far from the centre and had shown limited interest in leveraging the Group's institutional strengths. In the companies they ran, there was excessive reliance on their personal charisma and management capabilities.

Ratan's belief was that the whole could be far stronger than the sum of the parts. The prospects of success for individual Tata companies would be far greater if they were to be guided by a powerful Tata Sons, rather than each trying to compete on its own in a very competitive market.

The satraps were typically a couple of decades older than Ratan and had cut their teeth building businesses in a tough, socialistic environment when Ratan was still a rookie. They owed their positions and true loyalties to JRD, not Ratan. The first to throw down the gauntlet and challenge the younger Tata's authority was Russi Mody, the 'Maharaja of Jamshedpur'.

Already in his seventies when Ratan was appointed as JRD's successor, Russi was the Chairman and Managing Director of TISCO. He was widely respected for his people management skills and the way he ran the very successful enterprise in Bihar, one of the most underdeveloped and poor regions of the country. He had hoped that he would have a shot at the top job after JRD laid down office. When this did not happen, he smarted at the perceived insult and was determined to show the much younger man his place.

Russi did this by appointing a number of his favoured executives to key positions in the company, without adequately consulting Ratan or the TISCO Board. Matters came to a head when Russi sought to anoint one of his closest associates, Aditya Kashyap, as the Managing Director of the company. In doing this, he overlooked the claims of another long-serving and well-respected TISCO executive preferred by Ratan, Dr Jamshed J. Irani. Many of the senior leaders in TISCO were asked to demonstrate their allegiance to Aditya Kashyap by writing letters in support of Russi's action to the Board of Directors, and a number of executives who were beholden to Russi and Aditya, did so with alacrity.

The company, at the top, was thereby split from within. Jehangir Ardeshir (TAS 1983) was a young TAS officer working in TISCO at that time. He vividly recalls the tense situation. 'Dr Irani came in for a weekly production meeting, one morning. Our meeting was just a few days ahead of a critical Board meeting,' he says. 'Dr Irani told all of us at the meeting that this might well be his last meeting as he "may not have a job by next week"'. As it turned out, Dr Irani was retained by the Board and would, in fact, soon become the Managing Director of the company.

Following a bitter exchange of words and missives between Russi and Ratan, the Board of TISCO, with JRD as Chairman Emeritus lending his weight, decided to drop Russi from the Board, ending his over fifty-year association with the Tatas. The decision to terminate the association with one of the most powerful managers in the Group sent a clear signal that JRD would stand firmly behind his chosen successor, Ratan. It dampened the enthusiasm of the other satraps to take on Ratan and bought him time to implement his own plans for the Group.

Three years later, Ratan was compelled to quell dissent within the Indian Hotels Company Ltd, where another satrap, Ajit Kerkar, ruled the roost as Chairman. Ajit was perceived to be running Indian Hotels like his fiefdom, and fell out with Ratan when former employees of the company made allegations accusing the former of financial mismanagement and violation of various laws, including the draconian Foreign Exchange Regulation Act (FERA). Ajit initially enjoyed the support of a majority of the Directors on the company's Board. However, in the course of clever boardroom management tactics following the induction of two TAS officers loyal to the Group as additional Directors, R.K. Krishna Kumar

(TAS 1963) and S. Ramakrishnan (TAS 1972), Ajit was ousted from Indian Hotels in September 1997.

Peeved with the periodic challenges to his authority from the satraps, Ratan Tata hit upon a stratagem to secure the exit of the remaining holdovers from JRD's era. Recognizing that several of the Group's ageing leaders had fears about how their lifestyle and healthcare options might be impaired were they to surrender their grip on their jobs, he proceeded to create a generous retirement scheme to secure their graceful exit. The 'special retirement benefits' at Tata Sons included a pension for the retiring individual's lifetime, as well as a smaller amount to the surviving spouse for the spouse's lifetime; maintenance of an office for the use of the individual; provision of a car and driver; and medical benefits for the individual's and the spouse's lifetimes.

For the remaining satraps and the older group of Tata leaders, the new retirement scheme offered welcome insurance against any decline in their quality of life. Renowned Tata leaders like Nani Palkhivala, Shahrokh Sabavala, Jamshed Bhabha, F.C. Kohli, A.H. Tobaccowala, Homi Sethna and Dr Freddie Mehta (TAS 1956) stepped down from the Board of Tata Sons from 1999 onwards in quick succession, immediately yielding a generational change in the Board's composition.

The departure of the satraps through the 1990s had a major implication for the TAS. Many of the officers who had hitched their wagons too tightly with those of the satraps—and who may have broken the compact of standing up for the best interests of the Tata Group even as they were working in different Tata companies—found the going getting tough under the Ratan Tata dispensation. In the wake of the departure of their bosses, they also chose to exit the Tata Group.

A steady stream of TAS officers who had been close to satraps like Ajit Kerkar, Darbari Seth and Sumant Moolgaokar left Tata companies like Indian Hotels, Tata Chemicals, Rallis and Tata Motors through the 1990s. The departure of these TAS officers in the 1990s and the depletion in the ranks of senior TAS officers had obvious implications for the fewer number of CEOs of the Tata Group who would emerge from the TAS in subsequent decades.

15
Ratan Asserting His Authority

For many TAS officers, the starting assumption when they joined the Tata Group was that careers in Tatas were for a lifetime. That changed after Ratan Tata took over. It became strikingly evident following the exit of a number of TAS officers alongside the satraps.

Meanwhile, the creation of a retirement policy was, on the whole, welcomed by the TAS community. It meant that the leadership profile of the Group would begin to look younger. It also meant that leadership roles across the Tata Group began to open up, offering the first generation of TAS hires a stab at top jobs across a number of large Tata companies; this resulted in their elevation as Managing Directors at large listed companies. Those who benefited included Nawshir Khurody (TAS 1960) at Voltas and R.K. Krishna Kumar (TAS 1963) at Indian Hotels.

Ironically, the retirement policy instituted at Tata Sons, insofar as it might apply to its author, Ratan Tata, was tweaked on multiple occasions. This gave Ratan a much longer run in the job than appeared likely initially. Dr Mukund Rajan (TAS 1995) was Ratan's Executive Assistant at the time. 'I remember that Ratan Tata was very keen that the retirement age at Tata Sons be fixed at sixty-five. In informal chats we would have in the office, he would sometimes mull over the hobbies he was planning to take up after retirement. He was particularly concerned about putting the right governance system in place at Tata Sons before he turned sixty-five in 2002,' Mukund says as he remembers those conversations.

Ratan had intensive discussions on the subject of succession through 1999 with several people close to him, including Prof. Kumar Bhattacharyya, the head of the Warwick Management Group at Warwick University, who had become a mentor to him. Indeed, after he hired R. Gopalakrishnan in 1998 as an Executive Director at Tata Sons, the media was agog with speculation that the new recruit might be anointed as Ratan's successor, since he had previously served as Vice Chairman at the large and respected multinational enterprise, Hindustan Lever.

When Gopalakrishnan's former boss at Hindustan Lever, Keki Dadiseth, was appointed as a Trustee of the Sir Ratan Tata Trust, media speculation changed course. The spotlight shifted to Keki, whom they suspected could become the successor instead. Of course, neither did. Instead, Ratan was persuaded by some colleagues to differentiate between executive and non-executive roles, and fix the retirement age for the former at sixty-five and for the latter at seventy. Then, as he approached seventy, he allowed himself to be persuaded by colleagues to extend the retirement age to seventy-five.

Ratan finally retired only in 2012, by which time he had spent over two decades in the top job. There is perhaps a cautionary tale here for other ageing leaders; had Ratan stepped down, as he had originally planned, at the age of sixty-five, he would have been spared the many stresses that took their toll on him in later years—the global financial crisis, the terror attack on the Taj, the financial setbacks at the Tata Group after the overseas buyout (the largest one in Indian corporate history) of Corus Steel, the reputational smears as a result of the so-called 2G scam and, eventually, the existential crisis for the Tata Group sparked by the ouster of his successor, Cyrus Mistry.

With the exit of older colleagues under the new retirement policy at Tata Sons, he now had a completely free hand in appointing individuals of his choice on the board of Tata Sons, as well as at the helm of various

Tata companies. His forceful personality, combined with the elimination of voices of dissent from the boards of the companies he chaired, left just a few individuals who might question his judgement or vision for the Group, or even offer constructive counsel. All of this meant that Ratan's authority over the Tata Group was complete. It would have serious implications for the Group's handling of the series of crises it would face in the new millennium.

It is important for senior leaders to receive (and be accepting of) feedback and constructive criticism, even tolerate occasional dissent. This allows them to get the best possible inputs—which is what they need to make the right strategic calls. In Ratan's case, sadly, and not entirely by design, very few of those around him in his immediate circle would appear capable of standing up to him and offering alternative points of view to those he might have himself considered.

Interestingly, several TAS officers from the time recollect the series of meetings convened by Jamshed Bhabha in 1996 over dinner at the Taj Mahal Hotel in Bombay, between select serving TAS officers and the Chairman. Jamshed had played a key role in the development of the TAS earlier, and was keen that Ratan hear first hand the concerns in the minds of TAS officers, particularly in the wake of the stream of departures of officers from the Group.

Bharat Wakhlu (TAS 1985) recalls being part of one such intimate dinner interaction. The Chairman was attentive, and Jamshed played the role of a facilitator with aplomb. At the end of the two-hour meeting, there were a number of actionable points that had been put forth. However, Bharat was struck by the manner in which the meeting ended. Jamshed said, 'Ratan, it would be good for the Tatas if these excellent suggestions for the strengthening of the TAS are implemented. Will you instruct the right people, please?' Ratan nodded and walked away, without saying a word.

16
Ratan—The Man

THROUGH HIS YEARS IN THE TATA GROUP, RATAN TATA WOULD BE surrounded by a number of TAS officers. None spent as long with him, though, as Dr Mukund Rajan (TAS 1995), his longest-serving Executive Assistant and Chief of Staff, who worked with him from 1996 to 2008.

Mukund recalls that his final interview for induction into the TAS was with a three-member panel comprising Ratan, Shahrokh Sabavala and Jamshed Bhabha, all three Directors of Tata Sons. He describes how he came to work for Ratan, and his experience with the man.

'I came to understand, years later, from Bhupen Chakravarti, the much-loved manager of the TAS Secretariat, that Ratan Tata, after my interview, had left instructions that I was to be earmarked for his office once I completed the obligatory one-year induction programme. As the first year of induction drew to a close, I received a call from the Member-Secretary of the TAS, S. Ramakrishnan (TAS 1972), asking me to meet Ratan Tata. I had an inkling that this might be connected with a job offer and was relieved when I was told that I should first introduce myself to the Chairman's Executive Assistant, a TAS officer named Rajiv Dube, before

I met the Chairman himself. I felt that Rajiv would be able to give me tips on how to conduct myself at the meeting with Ratan Tata.'

'On the appointed day in December 1995, I walked into the Chairman's office on the fourth floor of Bombay House—and ran straight into Ratan Tata, who was emerging from his conference room into the reception area. He immediately ushered me into the small conference room, so there was no preparation for the interview, no opportunity to get inputs from Rajiv on how I should conduct myself, and no guidance on whether I should ask any questions to the Chairman or just listen to him. But the meeting turned out to be quite interactive and very cordial and pleasant.'

'Ratan Tata asked me how I had spent the year of induction and then mentioned the role he wanted to offer me, that of his Executive Assistant. I would help Rajiv, as a precursor to taking over all the responsibilities that Rajiv was then discharging.'

Mukund adds, 'on hearing that I was to be the Chairman's Executive Assistant, I felt it fair to point out to Ratan Tata that I had not done an MBA and had very little business-related experience. His answer will remain etched in my mind—all I needed to succeed in the corporate world, he said, was "good common sense".'

'Ratan Tata emphasized the responsibility one would carry as part of the Group Chairman's office—this office he told me, would be the court of final appeal for many Tata stakeholders with grievances, and one would be tasked to live up to their expectations, right from acknowledging receipt of their communications to finding solutions for them. He underlined the importance of humility and the need to show empathy in dealing with these stakeholders. Ratan Tata went out of his way to make me comfortable and I left the meeting relieved but also inspired to work with this man.'

'I never asked why Ratan Tata picked me for the role. I always assumed that it was a function of being at the right place at the right time. I was a TAS officer available for deployment at just the time Rajiv Dube was looking to move out of the office. But I do know that Ratan Tata and I got on very well, and until the time I started getting very involved in matters relating to telecom, around a decade after I joined his office, I was pretty much the principal staff support he had.'

'The Ratan Tata I saw for most of the next twelve years that I spent in his office was a delightful personality. At well over six feet in height, with wide shoulders and a broad frame, he had a formidable presence. In office, he would always be immaculately dressed in sharply cut fine suits (the only exceptions being weekends, when he would occasionally pop in wearing shirts and khaki trousers) and carried himself with grace.'

'He was extremely grounded and well spoken, and in all my years with him I probably heard him raise his voice only on a couple of occasions. He gave his staff a great deal of autonomy, and to have that at a young age was hugely empowering for me. He was extremely friendly for the most part, but you could sense when he was displeased from the coolness, or even coldness, he could convey.'

'Among Ratan Tata's excellent qualities was his ability to laugh loudly, sometimes at himself, and his incredible mimicry of his colleagues. These were thc times when he was most lovable, and even senior colleagues otherwise known for their reserve and aloofness would warm up to him despite themselves. He would doodle during long meetings, and once he drew the bald heads of three senior Tata Sons' Directors, Shahrokh Sabavala, Jim Setna and Noshir Soonawala, viewed from the back. They all had a hearty laugh when he showed them his work, and Ratan Tata was so pleased that he gifted each of them prints of the drawing, titled "The Three Ss".'

'On another occasion, Ratan Tata and Farokh Kavarana, having quietly kicked fellow Tata Sons Director Jamshed Bhabha's shoes to the far corner of the august Tata Board Room, were sharing a chuckle. Bhabha, who was getting along a bit, used to slip his shoes off his tired feet and place them under the table. He was singularly distressed after the meeting when his colleagues started filing out of the Board Room and he was unable to find his shoes! I once even had to restrain Ratan Tata from planting a very life-like green plastic snake in the recess of the chair Jamshed Bhabha used during the Board meetings of Tata Sons—I was worried lest the senior Director be frightened into a heart attack!'

'In the years to come, and certainly after I left his office in 2008, the Ratan Tata I first came to know and whose many warm qualities I learnt to appreciate became increasingly invisible. He was replaced by a senior statesman with a larger-than-life figure. Most of his colleagues came to be intimidated by his personality and stature. And the woes that were visited upon the Tata Group, particularly the 2008 terror attack on the Taj, the financial struggle in the aftermath of the global financial crisis and the so-called 2G scam and its fallout, took their toll on this essentially decent, fair and fun-loving human being.'

Like Mukund, Bharat Wakhlu (TAS 1985) was also interviewed by Ratan before he was selected to join the TAS in 1985. JRD Tata was travelling at the time and Ratan was therefore chairing the TAS Selection Committee. From the over-dozen finalists interviewed, when the names of the selected candidates were announced after the sumptuous luncheon with the Committee members, only two were selected—Bharat and a woman who was an MBA from IIM Ahmedabad. It was what Ratan did after the selections were announced that struck a very positive note with even those who were not selected.

He spoke to the candidates with empathy, and indicated that if any of them would be interested in joining a Tata company, his office would gladly process their requests. Bharat was struck by Ratan's compassionate nature and his appreciation of the talent that had allowed these candidates to make it to the final selection round of the TAS. Indeed, one of the TAS finalists who had (like Bharat) also served as a Graduate Engineer in TELCO was able to secure a role in Tata Industries Ltd. He went on to serve the Tatas as the CEO of a company that Tata Industries incubated.

Years later, Ratan was the Chairman of the Board of Tata Inc. in the US when Bharat took over as the President of the company in 2003—a position he held till his return to India as the Resident Director of the Group in New Delhi in 2008. The years when Bharat was in the US were heady days for the internationalization of the Tata Group, as we will see later in the book. In 2005, when Tata Inc. completed sixty years in the US, Ratan blessed the idea of having a gala to commemorate the event. The only caveat he added, in conversation with Bharat, was that it had to be an event that was befitting the stature and the cache of the Tata Group. The gala was a grand success and gave Ratan Tata and the Tata Group companies visibility in a subtle manner, helping to blunt some of the negative commentary and media attacks in the US against the Tatas and TCS for being at the forefront of 'outsourcing' and therefore taking away American jobs!

At a subsequent Board meeting of Tata Inc., when Bharat proposed that given the growing footprint of the Tata Group in the US, some efforts at advocacy in Washington DC would be helpful, Ratan was emphatic that while the pursuit of business and advocacy were both important, they were to be done by different organizations. Accordingly, Tata Sons created a separate 'Representative Office' based out of Washington DC for advocacy, while Tata Inc. continued to pursue its business goals.

Ratan was ever supportive of new business ideas and possibilities for the Group. During his years in New York, Bharat forged a very good relationship with the senior leadership of Sikorsky Aircraft Corporation, based in Stratford CT, with the help and guidance of his friend, Robert Kaplan. When Bharat broached the possibilities of collaborating with Sikorsky, Ratan was enthusiastic. In a series of moves, the Tatas and Sikorsky Aircraft Corporation (now a part of Lockheed Martin) forged a joint venture that paved the way for the Tata's entry into aerostructures manufacturing and design.

Sonu Bhasin (TAS 1987) has her own memories of Ratan. 'The first time I interacted with him was, of course, at the final interview process at Bombay House,' she remembers. 'I walked into the Bombay House Board Room and was immediately intimidated by the number of senior Tata Directors sitting around the long table. I walked to the strategically placed lone chair on one side of the table and was about to sit down when Jamshed Bhabha asked me to close the door. In my awestruck mode, I had forgotten to close the door of the Board Room as I walked in. "*There goes my chance of getting in*", I thought to myself,' she says, hitting her hand on her forehead to express the momentary dismay she experienced back then. 'As soon as I sat down, the first question I was asked was by Ratan Tata. I was surprised at how mild he sounded as he asked me about my stint as the Captain of the Women's Judo Team at St. Stephen's College. As I started telling him, he interrupted me midway and asked me "Tell me, how do you manage to do Judo with that long hair of yours?" I had waist-length thick hair at that time and I had left it open that day,' Sonu says with a grimace as if regretting not tying up her hair that day.

'Without blinking and almost spontaneously, I replied, "Oh Sir, I tie my hair up in a bun when I am at the Dojo (judo place)." To my surprise, the entire room erupted in loud laughter. I saw the Directors looking at Ratan Tata, pointing a finger at him as they laughed. One of the senior Directors gesticulated as if to say, "What a stupid question, Ratan!" A couple of people even gave me a thumbs up sign at my answer! I was horrified as I thought that Ratan Tata would be upset at my answer as he had become the butt of everyone's joke. But to my surprise, he had an impish look in his eyes as he, too, joined in the general laughter.

The next time I met Ratan Tata was also in Bombay House. I was doing my project at TOMCO, which had its offices in Bombay House. I was running up the stairs to the TAS Secretariat one day. As I reached the landing of the second floor, I saw Ratan Tata coming down the corridor towards the glass door. I guess he saw me running up the stairs. As he walked to the door, he held it open, waited for me to come in and then walked out. For me, it was a reflection of the man himself,' says Sonu.

17

In the Shadows of the New Group Centre

RATAN TATA'S BIGGEST CHALLENGE WHEN HE TOOK CONTROL OF THE Group from JRD Tata was to prepare the Tata companies to compete better in an Indian market that was rapidly opening up. Foreign companies were entering India with better technologies, sophisticated business processes, efficient supply chains, and better-quality products and services, and were rapidly increasing their market share. If the Tatas were to hold their own against world-class competition in a liberalizing Indian economy, the Group would need to build strength and capability.

Towards this objective, Ratan undertook a series of key initiatives that would play out through the decade. These included investing in talent and capabilities at the Group Centre, to manage and direct the Group's portfolio and investments going forward; promoting a culture of quality consciousness and ensuring Tata Group companies shared their best ideas and good practices with each other; and securing access to key technologies and intellectual property required to help companies improve their competitiveness internationally.

The TAS played a valuable role in the execution of several of these initiatives. However, for a cadre that was meant to play a vital role in uniting the Group and spreading the message of the core Tata values, it enjoyed relatively little visibility within the Group Chairman's core team. With the exception of influential staffers like Rajiv Dube (TAS 1990) and Dr Mukund Rajan (TAS 1995) in Ratan's immediate office, strategic support offered during regular meetings by Rajendra 'Raju' Bhinge (TAS 1975) of the Tata Strategic Management Group, and years later, the elevation of R.K. Krishna Kumar (TAS 1963) to the Board of Tata Sons, few TAS officers enjoyed particularly close proximity to Ratan.

Rajiv says, 'Ratan Tata valued the TAS. He was clear that if you had made it through the successive rounds of the rigorous selection process to gain entry into the TAS, you certainly had the talent and the potential to do well.' But Ratan was clear that the TAS could not be an elite structure, where wearing a TAS hat came with a career-long entitlement; the head start a TAS officer received was sufficient, and once the officers were placed in Tata companies, they needed to earn their spurs and merge with the company's leadership as equals. This would only be fair so far as the other colleagues in the TAS officer's company were concerned, and it was important that TAS officers continued to prove themselves.

Rajiv himself achieved distinction as the first in-house candidate to break the glass ceiling and get into the TAS. As a Graduate Engineer Trainee at TELCO in Jamshedpur, he observed, 'The TAS used to be shrouded in myths, which became more unreal the farther away from Bombay House one was. One such myth was that Tata officers could not apply and hope to get in, and you had to be a fresh postgraduate from an IIM or a prestigious overseas university to be selected.' Rajiv was at the Tata Management Training Centre (TMTC) for a 6–8-week programme for promising young Tata executives, coincidentally around the same time the recently selected TAS batch was undergoing training there. While there, he met and asked Dr Francis Menezes, who ran the TAS admissions process, whether interested Tata managers could apply to the TAS. Dr Menezes told him that anyone who had, in fact, only a graduate degree and was interested could apply for entry into the TAS—'There are no such rules that prevent your entry into the TAS if you do well in the selection process'. Rajiv applied to the TAS, was interviewed at IIM Calcutta along with others from the institution, and then called to Bombay House for the final interview where he was selected for the TAS.

In Rajiv's view, during JRD's time, the TAS was treated quite distinctively in most companies, and the officers were often given an edge over other managers. But under Ratan, certainly in the companies that he directly oversaw, 'the progress of TAS officers was based primarily on merit; they had to perform, and would not be treated differently just because they came from the TAS.' Where earlier the TAS got a certain visibility and push because officers of the cadre were considered 'entitled to lead', in Ratan's era, the entitlement went away and performance and delivery held sway.

Rajiv also points out that after 1991, when Ratan took over, India changed with the liberalization of its economy. He says, 'Before 1991, many Tata companies straddled stable and ready markets with limited competition under government-licensed control, and life was about managing what you already had and growing within defined limits. After 1991, the calls on leadership and the management skills required to succeed were very different. The Managing Agency system had long been abolished and TAS officers, like other managers, had to roll up their sleeves and fight competition hard—and many unfortunately didn't fare as well as in the pre-1991 years.'

Rajiv also concedes that success often requires risk-taking, and this in turn needs the backing of well-disposed seniors; unfortunately for the TAS officers, while within the Tatas there were many believers in the idea of the TAS, there were as many non-believers. And then some TAS officers hurt their own prospects by trying to perpetuate the myth that they had some 'blue-bloodedness' to them.

Visty Banaji (TAS 1973) points out that Ratan was keen to do things differently from the past. He was uncomfortable with the clutch of senior TAS officers who were closely associated with or highly regarded by the satraps. Rather than leverage their experience and elevate them to yet more senior roles in the Group, he chose repeatedly to turn elsewhere to find talent—not just outside of TAS circles, but also often outside the Tata Group, and even outside the country. This was clearly reflected in the composition of the Group Executive Office (GEO) that he created, which did not have a single TAS officer in it.

In establishing the GEO, Ratan looked for talent both within and outside the Tata Group. From Tata Steel, Ratan pulled in the company's Finance Chief, Ishaat Hussain, ten years younger to him, to support the older Noshir Soonawala and to eventually take over from Soonawala as Group Finance Director. From the well-regarded and very successful British and Dutch multinational, Unilever, he inducted the Vice Chairman of its Indian subsidiary, R. Gopalakrishnan. From ICICI, the fast-growing Indian financial services company, he brought in one of their senior-most executives, Kishor Chaukar. And from another much-admired US multinational, General Electric, he inducted as the Group's HR Head, Manab Bose.

Into the early 2000s, Ratan would induct Arun Gandhi from the chartered accountancy firm, N.M. Raiji & Co., to oversee mergers and acquisitions. He also hired the British Alan Rosling, Chairman of Jardine Matheson in India, to oversee the Group's internationalization thrust. Around the same time, he would also construct a new Group Corporate Centre (GCC) to provide strategic guidance to the GEO. Membership into the GCC included GEO as well as additional members drawn from the ranks of senior executives in Tata companies. Thus, leaders like Dr Jamshed Irani (Tata Steel), Syamal Gupta (Tata International) and R.K. Krishna Kumar (Tata Tea and Indian Hotels) made their entry into the GCC.

Ratan's experiment of inducting professionals from outside the Tata Group had mixed results. Some, like Manab Bose, found it difficult to integrate into the Tata culture, and exited rapidly without leaving a perceptible mark. Others, like Gopalakrishnan, Chaukar and Gandhi, continued in the Group till their retirement and made useful contributions. Bharat Wakhlu (TAS 1985) is of the view, however, that many of those brought in laterally from the outside directly into senior positions never fully imbibed the values and ethos of the Tata Group, and they didn't even comprehend the role that the TAS was meant to serve.

As a long-serving Ratan aide, Mukund suggests, 'It became clear over time that the most fundamental contributions to the Tata Group's future would continue to emerge, for the most part, from the ideas of one man—Ratan Tata—rather than as the collective contribution of "Team GEO".'

18
A New Thrust on Quality

To encourage Tata companies in their journey towards operational improvement and process excellence, the JRD Quality Values Award Programme was launched in 1995. Predicated on what would come to be known as the Tata Business Excellence Model (TBEM), the awards, to be given on JRD Tata's birthday (29 July) each year, were meant to recognize the leading companies in the Group that were doing the most to advance the former Chairman's passion for excellence.

The famous JRD quote, 'You aim for perfection, you will attain excellence. If you aim for excellence, you will go lower' was mounted on the walls of many a Tata factory and office. Rather than create a brick-and-mortar memorial to the longest-serving Chairman of the Tata Group, it was felt that the most appropriate way of recognizing his contribution would be to institutionalize a programme that recognized excellence within the Group.

The TBEM evolved over the years and was eventually based on the Malcolm Baldrige National Quality Award instituted by the US Congress in 1987. By benchmarking critical business management criteria for Tata companies, such as leadership, market understanding, customer care, information systems, human resource practices, process excellence and business results against those of competitors, the model showed a mirror to them. Scores derived from detailed assessments by teams of assessors now allowed Tata companies to recognize where they stood in terms of global performance excellence and leadership.

The TBEM framework allowed Tata companies to share their best practices and learn from each other, nurturing the testing and adoption of world-class practices across different Tata companies. Assessment teams were pulled together from different Tata companies, with expert resources drawn from different functional areas. This approach yielded rich dividends, bringing the Tata companies ever closer to each other, highlighting the value of collaboration and sharing, and inculcating in them a sense of being part of one unified group, or 'One Tata'. A number of TAS officers trained to become TBEM assessors, and played their role in seeding and institutionalizing the framework model.

An early convert was Jamshed Daboo (TAS 1986). Jamshed worked closely with S.A. Vaneswaran, the first Head of Tata Quality Management Services (TQMS), when the latter operated from an office within the Titan facilities in Bangalore. He eventually took over from Vaneswaran as the CEO of TQMS, from 1999 to 2000.

'I vividly recall the thrust given at the time to ensure Tata companies went beyond participation in the TBEM process as a route to winning recognition or an award, and instead saw this as a means to achieve continuous improvement, excellence and develop leadership in their businesses,' says Jamshed. The TBEM framework was also continuously refined with the testing of concepts such as the Balanced Scorecard to ensure it evolved beyond financial management to total stakeholder management. This ensured it also upheld the broader community orientation of the House of Tata.

To see to it that the Group companies participated in and demonstrated continuous improvement in their performance under the aegis of the TBEM, and shared best practices drawn from their business operations, Tata Sons inserted a key clause in the Brand Equity and Business

Promotion Agreement it signed with each Tata company. Under this clause, Tata Sons, as the Group investment holding company, reserved the right to withdraw the use of the Tata brand from companies that did not shape up in terms of a commitment to achieving business excellence under the TBEM framework.

Among the companies helped the most by the new focus on quality consciousness was TISCO. By diligent adoption of best practices and benchmarking its processes against the global best in class, the company became the first winner of the JRD Quality Values Award in 2000. It would also go on to win the international Deming Prize, and eventually the Grand Deming Prize for Total Quality Management.

'The process of quality transformation at TISCO commenced in 1987, under the leadership of Dr Jamshed Irani, the President of the company at that time,' Bharat Wakhlu (TAS 1985) points out. 'Till that time, the sales effort of the company had been what the sales people would wryly call "rationing". The demand for steel in India far outstripped supply, so reputed companies with a good track-record, like TISCO, were always in a position to command which customer got how much of their requirements. But it was clear that this happy situation would not persist for much longer, and the company had to become more competitive or perish,' he continues.

Dr Irani formed a Total Quality Management (TQM) Group, directly reporting to him, which was headed by an experienced and dedicated executive from the works. Bharat was made the Deputy Head of the TQM Group and was given a free hand to add other key members to the team. Dr Irani was clear that alongside a massive change in mindsets among the executives and officers in TISCO, what was also needed was change in the manner in which the quality output of the company was measured. When an opportunity was presented to him to understand from the Union of Japanese Scientists and Engineers (JUSE) how TQM is practised by companies in Japan, he promptly took up the offer and flew to Tokyo to attend their fortnight-long programme.

The programme was impressive and Dr Irani returned enthused. He had made copious notes, which were passed on to the TQM Group. He also made sure that a senior executive from the plant, C.D. Kamath, accompanied by Bharat, attended the next programme by JUSE in Japan. In the months that followed, TISCO embarked on a massive training exercise in which every workman and officer had to participate. Simultaneously, TISCO changed the manner in which output was measured, with greater emphasis being placed on the more remunerative grades of steel and the tonnages that customers wanted. TISCO also embarked upon a process of creating a template called the J.N. Tata Total Quality Matrix to assess the relative progress that departments within the steel company were making. Under Dr Irani's personal leadership, the transformation to a more market-driven, quality-oriented company was decisive and sustained.

A few months after the end of the financial year 1989, the annual retreat of the Heads of TISCO companies was held in the Taj Fisherman's Cove Resort on Covelong Beach. Ratan Tata was the Chief Guest. C.D. Kamath and Bharat were asked to make a presentation to the gathering on what it would take to transform their respective companies from a Total Quality perspective.

'Ratan Tata listened to the presentation with rapt attention and asked a number of questions on what TISCO was doing, how the process outcomes were being measured, and how customer feedback was brought to bear on the improvement cycle,' recalls Bharat. It was evident to Bharat that Ratan Tata was making mental notes of the initiatives that the Tata Group companies as a whole would need to take to become more competitive and customer-centric.

For his achievements in steering TISCO to great heights in overall performance and TQM, the company's Managing Director, Dr Jamshed Irani, would be rewarded by Ratan with a place on the Tata Sons' Board. Dr Irani would also take over the reins of the TBEM Executive Council from the Tata Sons Director, Jim Setna, who helped launch the programme. Jehangir Ardeshir (TAS 1983), who had served as Dr Irani's Principal Executive Officer and stewarded major quality improvements at TISCO in the plant operations, simultaneously took over the reins as the CEO of TQMS.

Jehangir oversaw the wide deployment of the TBEM process across the Tata Group during the critical years between 2002 and 2005. The number of Tata companies participating in the TBEM process grew from thirteen when he joined to thirty-nine when he left.

Many CEOs of the Tata companies that participated in the TBEM process acknowledged how much it helped them in becoming more customer-centric, process-driven and effective, while relying on benchmarking with global best practices to consistently improve competitiveness. Over time, the average TBEM company score at the Tata Group increased substantially, more than doubling to enter the 450–550 score band, regarded as 'good', and just below the band of 'emerging industry leadership'.

19

Championing Technology

THE NEED TO COMPETE WITH FOREIGN COMPANIES ENTERING THE INDIAN market with world-class products after the 1991 economic reforms meant that Tata companies required quick access to new technology. In the make versus buy debate that followed, the fastest route to building technological capability often seemed to be through joint ventures with global majors.

A good example of this strategy is offered by Tata Auto Components Ltd (TACO), the new vehicle created within Tata Industries to support the plans of Tata Motors to build its first small car, the 'Tata Indica'. The new company's mandate was to introduce world-class technologies in the Indian auto-components sector, hitherto largely the preserve of small and medium enterprises that operated with dated technologies. To access these technologies and build key components in the Indian market, TACO resolved to enter into a series of joint ventures with global Tier 1 component manufacturers.

TACO was set up under the leadership of Devender Gupta, the former Marketing Chief of Maruti Udyog, India's largest car manufacturer. A number of TAS officers, including Dr Mukund Rajan (TAS 1995), R. Mukundan (TAS 1990) and Prashanth Nayak (TAS 1995), were assigned to work closely with Devender Gupta and TACO. Under Gupta's direction, Tata Industries entered into joint venture partnerships with companies like Toyo Radiators of Japan to manufacture radiators, Johnson Controls of the US, to manufacture seating systems, and Yazaki of Japan to manufacture wiring harnesses.

Similar partnership strategies were entered into by a clutch of Tata companies across a spectrum of industries. Thus, Tata Motors entered into a joint venture with Mercedes Benz to manufacture the luxury end E-Class car. A joint venture deal was struck with Cummins to produce fuel-efficient engines for Tata Motors trucks. Tata Finance, too, undertook a series of partnerships across several financial services verticals with entities like American Express, TD Waterhouse, Abbey National, and others. In emerging areas of information technology and telecommunication, Tata Industries undertook joint ventures with leading multinationals—IBM to manufacture personal computers in India, Honeywell in the space of process control systems and automation, AT&T for telecom switches, and Bell Canada to launch mobile and fixed line telecom services.

Attractive career options were offered for TAS officers by the many new joint ventures the Tata Group created in the 1990s. A number of the officers moved into these ventures, drawn by the exposure they would receive to foreign cultures, work processes and new technologies. Some, like Ratan Tata's Executive Assistant, N. Srinath (TAS 1986), who joined the Tata IBM joint venture, and Harsh Chitale (TAS 1993), who joined the Tata Honeywell joint venture, would quickly become part of the leadership teams of these new enterprises.

A number of TAS officers who joined in the 1990s, like Jaspreet Bindra (TAS 1994), admit to being attracted to the Group because of its apparent focus on technology. Jaspreet was drawn to the telecom vertical, which had only recently been opened to private sector participation in India. 'There was a palpable sense of excitement about launching a new business in this sector. It soon became the sector that attracted the single-largest investment in the Tata Group's history. The joint venture with Bell Canada offered individuals like me the opportunity to learn about a new sector, and to embrace some of the best international practices and cultural influence of the Canadian partners,' says Jaspreet, as he remembers those exciting days.

Indeed, one of the draws of the TAS has been the opportunity provided to TAS officers to chart a new course for the Group and for individual Tata companies, including in areas of emerging technologies. Vipul Jain (TAS 1980) recounts how the Indian Hotels Company led by Ajit Kerkar entrusted him with the task of automating the front office, points of sale and the back office for the Taj hotels. 'I was given a free hand to decide the best course of action for the hotels,' he says, 'and because I was young, and given the autonomy to arrive at the best solution, it felt good. People knew that, by and large, TAS officers, despite their relative youth and inexperience, could rise to any occasion and deliver the goods.'

Vipul's experience also had an interesting twist. 'When the time came to make a decision on the hardware and software that we would use to run our system, my team and I evaluated a number of options, including offers from Burroughs Systems, DEC, NELCO and WANG Computers,' he continues. 'Burroughs had a collaboration at the time with the Tatas, and there was an offer from another Tata company, NELCO. However, on the basis of our evaluation, we settled for WANG, primarily because we were getting the software source code with rights to modify and replicate at our will.'

The decision not to buy Tata-supported machines didn't go down well with Burroughs and NELCO and the matter was escalated to the level of the Group Chairman, JRD Tata. Vipul was a little nervous when a few weeks after his decision he was summoned to Bombay House. 'Prasun Sengupta (a TAS senior and Executive Assistant to Ajit Kerkar at that time) and I were ushered into JRD's room on the fourth floor of Bombay House, on the appointed day,' he recalls in a soft voice as he relives the nervousness. 'However, when JRD heard my logic that having the source code would make us independent of the vendor, he was convinced that the best interests of the Indian Hotels Company had been upheld, and he blessed our decision to acquire the WANG solution. I was elated with

JRD's support of a young twenty-three-year-old and my appreciation of the Tata values went up several notches that day.' In hindsight, the decision proved to be a good one and Taj Palace Hotel became the first hotel in the country to have a fully functional Property Management System, and Vipul and his team went on to enrich and deploy the solution at many other hotels in India and overseas.

Another TAS officer, Sanjaya Sharma (TAS 1980), recollects the promising idea he had for a new line of business in computer-based learning solutions, while working in Tata Unisys. He took the idea to Ratan Tata. Ratan saw the opportunity in the idea, and backed it fully, enabling the creation of Tata Interactive Systems (TIS), a pioneer in e-learning, simulations and serious games. Sanjaya founded the company in 1990, and served as its CEO for the next twenty-five years.

Well before the Tata Group's recent foray into the arena, Tata Steel, too, was assessing the opportunities and the possibilities around e-commerce. In 1999, an e-commerce group was created within the company, which Bharat Wakhlu (TAS 1985) was asked to lead. Based on information gleaned from visits to leading enterprises in this space, an assessment of the global e-commerce landscape and advice from experts, including professors from Massachusetts Institute of Technology (MIT), this group decided that the supply-chain and procurement functions were the most amenable to using e-commerce—from both a price-discovery as well as disintermediation perspective. This led to the creation of a new company, Metaljunction, a joint venture with the Steel Authority of India Ltd (SAIL), and brought about significant changes in the process of acquisition of non-strategic commodities, and the sale of secondary products such as scrap, slag and a host of other materials. The Kolkata-headquartered company boasts of being India's largest business-to-business e-commerce company today.

20
Sustaining Tata Values

THE 1991 ECONOMIC REFORMS UNLEASHED THE ANIMAL SPIRITS OF Indian entrepreneurs, and with consumers lapping up the new products and services being offered in a newly open market, growth was a given. However, with government intervention still being invoked by Indian corporates used to the old style of doing things across various industries, and with divided electoral mandates ensuring that a succession of weak coalition governments were installed in Delhi from the mid-1990s onwards, the Tata Group had to conduct business in an environment that allowed corruption to flourish.

It was supremely important to Ratan Tata that while stamping his authority on the Tata Group, he also sent the right signals about his genuine commitment to uphold the values the Group was famous for, in particular, its intolerance for corruption. The case that perhaps best showcases this commitment is that of the Tata Group's long struggle to enter the Indian civil aviation market.

The story begins in the early 1990s, when Prime Minister P.V. Narasimha Rao and his Singapore counterpart, Lee Kuan Yew, were fleshing out a new 'Look East' policy for India. They hit upon a great idea for collaboration between the two countries in the form of a joint venture airline to enter the newly opened-up aviation sector in India, something that had hitherto been a public sector monopoly. The joint venture partners selected were the best-known companies in the two countries, the Tatas from India and Singapore Airlines, long regarded as the best brand out of Singapore.

After due consultations with both entities, appropriate public announcements were made by the two governments. Then followed a period of market study and business plan development by a joint team of Tata and Singapore Airlines executives. S. Ramakrishnan (TAS 1972), then a Vice President at Tata Industries and one of the key project executives at the company, was appointed to lead the team from the Tata side, which also included TAS officers like Eric Vas (TAS 1991) and a stream of TAS officers on induction.

Before the airline could be launched, however, Prime Minister Rao's government was unseated in the general elections, and India entered a very unstable period of coalition politics for several years through the mid-1990s. One of these coalition governments announced a new civil aviation policy, which prohibited equity holdings by foreign airlines in any domestic Indian airline. The new policy was clearly targeted at the Tata–Singapore Airlines joint venture.

Many years later, Ratan, while speaking about this to an audience in the US where Bharat Wakhlu (TAS 1985) was present, said, 'The Government of India's new aviation policy was blatantly biased against our proposal, because according to the rules, a foreign biscuit-maker could invest in a domestic Indian airline; but not a foreign airline that could bring in best practices and expertise, apart from the capital.'

Among the more absurd reasons advanced in favour of this policy was the specious argument that it was against national security interests to allow foreign pilots to fly in Indian airspace. Dr Mukund Rajan (TAS 1995), part of Ratan's office at the time, describes with a frown on his face how shocking this argument was: 'It made no sense and fell flat, given the vast number of foreign carriers operating international flights manned by foreign pilots in Indian airspace, charting paths on a daily basis to various parts of the world. Yet, this policy remained in force for the next seventeen years as successive coalition governments sought to avoid criticism for undoing a move that ostensibly protected Indian domestic airlines from global competition.'

To overcome the policy prohibition on receiving equity investment from Singapore Airlines, a smart alternative was devised. Singapore Airlines agreed to become a technical advisor to a domestic airline to be started by the Tatas, but would hold no equity in it. The understanding was that if and when the aviation policy was amended and it so permitted, Singapore Airlines could take an equity stake in the airline. But the Tatas had not reckoned with the strength of opposition they would face from within the central government.

The Tata application for an airline licence just languished in the ministries concerned. In an interview to a media publication, Ratan explicitly pointed to corruption behind the holding back of the licence.

In 1999, the election of a more stable BJP-led coalition government, the National Democratic Alliance (NDA), under Prime Minister Atal Bihari Vajpayee, promised winds of change. The government discreetly approached the Tatas, suggesting that instead of applying for a licence for a new airline, would the Group instead consider bidding to acquire management control of the national carrier, Air India?

Such a step would suit the government's interest in securing credible potential investors for the carrier, in line with its desire to reduce the footprint of the public sector and allow more private players to play a role in the growth of the national economy. A Tata bid for Air India, it was felt, would get broad public approval, given that the Tatas had created the original airline under the leadership of JRD Tata before it was nationalized in 1953. JRD had served as Chairman of Air India till 1977, and for a couple of years in the 1980s, even Ratan had served as the Chairman of the carrier. The historical ties between the Tatas and Air India were undeniable.

Ratan agreed to shift the internal focus to a possible acquisition of Air India. With Singapore Airlines agreeing to stay the course as technical advisors, the due diligence of Air India commenced. After several rounds of dialogue with the government, the Tatas eventually emerged as the sole preferred bidder for Air India. And then ... nothing! Once again, the strong vested interests in the airline industry managed to stall the award of management control of Air India to the Tatas. (Interestingly, as we are giving finishing touches to this manuscript in October 2021, the Narendra Modi-led government at the Centre finally decided to accept the new bid of the Tatas to buy Air India! A full twenty years after the first efforts remained stillborn.)

After having waited for many months, Ratan finally lost his patience and wrote a strong letter to Prime Minister Vajpayee, withdrawing the Tata bid for Air India. 'This demonstrated the high values of the Tata Group. Under Ratan Tata's leadership, the Group had shown that it was willing to withdraw from a business opportunity, sacrificing years of effort and expense, in order to adhere to its Code of Conduct,' says Mukund assertively.

But the story does not end there. In 2012, after more than a decade had elapsed since the decision by the Tatas to withdraw their bid, India decided to amend its policy and allow foreign airlines to invest up to 49 per cent in Indian domestic airlines. Who did Singapore Airlines approach first for a partnership under this new dispensation? The Tata Group.

Singapore Airlines could have had its pick of partners for a tie-up in India. Yet, it chose to come back to its old partner, Tata, to create a joint venture airline that came to be called Vistara. Proof, if any were required, that ethics and good corporate governance together create trust among stakeholders and help nurture strong bonds and relationships that can last decades.

And fulfilling the close association of TAS officers with the Tatas' tryst with aviation, Mukund found himself appointed to the founding three-member Board of Directors of Vistara.

21
Growth at the Tata Flagships

THE TWO FLAGSHIP COMPANIES OF THE TATA GROUP IN THE 1990S WERE Tata Motors and Tata Steel. The rapid growth of the Indian economy after liberalization allowed both companies to modernize, expand capacities and start new lines of products. A number of TAS officers in these companies received excellent exposure to the growth of these behemoths, and made huge strides in their personal growth and careers.

In the mid-1990s, Tata Motors embarked upon a project to design and build India's first indigenous passenger car. This was a long-standing dream for Ratan Tata and Tata Motors. The company was already the market leader in commercial vehicles in India, and had acquired some experience and learnings from its production of sports utility vehicles, like the Tata Sumo and the Tata Safari. But getting into the more refined space of passenger vehicles would present qualitatively different challenges for the company; moreover, it would have to break into a market where several world leaders were already entrenched, including Ford, Suzuki, Daewoo and Hyundai.

Driven by ambition and growing confidence in the capabilities of his team, Ratan defined the key parameters for the proposed new car, benchmarked with the competitive options then available in the Indian market—'the size of the Maruti Zen, the internal dimensions of an Ambassador, the price of a Maruti 800 and the running cost of a diesel vehicle'. The individual tasked to lead the marketing and sales of the new vehicle was his trusted Executive Assistant, Rajiv Dube (TAS 1990).

Rajiv vividly recalls the moment in late 1997 when he was told that he was being considered for the new car project. By then, he had spent six years in Ratan's office. Given his pre-TAS employment with TELCO, and his involvement on Ratan's behalf in many of the interventions relating to the new car, Rajiv already had a ringside view of what was happening with the project. He was privy to the design iterations and drawings, mock-ups, the engine assessments at the Engineering Research Centre (ERC), and even the identification of Italy-based IDEA as the design firm that would work with TELCO on the product.

Rajiv chuckles as he remembers, 'I could have so easily, while segregating Ratan Tata's office mail as his Executive Assistant, overlooked the cold call letter from IDEA seeking a partnership with TELCO. I didn't and, if I remember correctly, I highlighted the approach. This eventually led to a successful relationship with IDEA, which yielded a very well-designed vehicle for the Indian market.' Rajiv was a natural choice to be moved into the new passenger vehicle division being created in TELCO.

The then Executive Director and Head of the Automobile Business Unit at TELCO, Vinod Raval, spoke to Ratan, seeking Rajiv's services for the new passenger car division being created. Ratan then spoke to Rajiv, and said that he thought the move would be good for Rajiv and the project was an exciting one to be involved with. 'Without blinking an eye, I said yes', says Rajiv. While Rajiv's previous experience in the company had been on the manufacturing side, he was now given the opportunity to lead marketing, sales and service for the Indica project.

Rajiv speaks appreciatively about the Tata leadership's willingness to take chances with young people like him and give them significant responsibility. 'I did say to Ratan Tata that I had no working experience in functions like marketing, sales and service, only an academic understanding, but I would do my best. I also hoped that he had thought this through!' Ratan responded that the company and he believed Rajiv had both the inclination and the ability to learn, and supported the move. Rajiv became Employee Number 2 in the new passenger car division. At the age of thirty-six, he became the youngest General Manager of TELCO.

The new car, christened the Tata Indica, was unveiled at the Auto Expo in Delhi in January 1998 to thunderous applause. The Chief Guest, India's Commerce Minister, Murasoli Maran, lauded the Tata Group as the 'Kohinoor' of India. The stylish car, with a distinctive vertical tail-light assembly, had met the key parameters Ratan had promised when the vehicle was being designed. The Tata Indica was a dream car for many Indians and received 110,000 bookings, unprecedented in Indian auto history up to that point.

Unfortunately, design flaws soon emerged in the components, such as the fan belt in the Tata Indica, and customers complained about the car's poor fit and finish. It took some redesigning of the product, an overhaul of manufacturing processes, improved quality control and a clever advertising campaign that rebranded the vehicle as Tata Indica V2 before the sales team was able to retrieve lost ground.

Notwithstanding the temporary setback, Tata Motors went on to acquire significant double digit market share in the Indian passenger car market. The learning associated with being an intimate part of one of the most complex and ambitious initiatives undertaken within the Indian auto industry was immense.

At the same time, the other Tata flagship, TISCO, was on its own transformation journey. As recently as 1992, a firm of management consultants brought in by the company, Arthur D. Little, said the Tata Group might have to consider shutting down TISCO, an inefficient player in a traditional smokestack industry. A couple of years later, another strategy consulting firm, McKinsey and Company, advised TISCO to diversify, and shortlisted several options the company could pursue, including branded retail, telecoms, and establishing gas pipelines. None of the diversification possibilities were eventually pursued.

Bharat Wakhlu (TAS 1985) recollects heated discussions within the TISCO senior leadership team on the invitation to participate in the equity funding of the new telecoms business that the Tata Group was trying to create at the time. Ultimately, the consensus view was that TISCO would not invest significantly in the telecoms business. This did not go down well with the Group Chairman, Ratan Tata.

Bharat recollects that at a huge Tata Steel employee dinner event in the Tube Makers' Club grounds in Jamshedpur, where those who had successfully completed Quality Improvement Projects in the preceding year were being recognized, Ratan Tata made his displeasure known in public. He was distinctly unhappy and felt that Tata Steel was being myopic.

Bharat emphasizes that the senior leadership of TISCO was clear about two things: first, as a developing country, the need for different grades and varieties of steel would only grow in India in the coming years. And, second, TISCO had, at that time, over nine decades of steel-making expertise and competitive access to raw materials (iron ore, some coking coal and fluxes) which needed to be leveraged. The senior team took a call that they would stay with steel and work to improve the performance parameters of the steel plant, including labour productivity, and energy consumption, to compare favourably with the best integrated steel plants in the world.

Under the leadership of Dr Jamshed Irani and with strong support from the Board led by Ratan, Tata Steel reduced its work force on the back of a very generous voluntary retirement scheme, executed plant modernization and bottleneck-removing projects in Jamshedpur, and deployed industry-leading practices in the management of its mines and steel-making assets.

During Phase III of Tata Steel's modernization, Jehangir Ardeshir (TAS 1983) was in charge of a Steel Melting Shop in the Jamshedpur Plant, at the heart of TISCO's operations. He laughingly says that after the vitally important Blast Furnaces, the Steel Melting Shops and Rolling Mills were the 'heavyweight departments in the plant'. Later on, during the expansion programme in Jamshedpur, he was asked to take on the responsibility of managing the Total Operation Improvement (TOP) centre, a key strategic focus for the company to reduce operating costs without additional investment, conceptualized and run with help from McKinsey and Company.

While he was initially reluctant to move away from his shop-floor responsibilities, Jehangir soon came to appreciate the significant value the programme could (and did) add to the company through the work of the TOP centre. Over the years, it delivered a bottom-line impact of several hundred crores and contributed towards making Tata Steel globally competitive. At the heart of TISCO's improvement lay the adoption of new technology, exposure of people at all levels to global best practices, and operational improvements driven by multiple initiatives including TOP. By putting its house in order, TISCO became by 2001, the top-ranked steel manufacturer in the world, according to World Steel Dynamics.

Projects like the Tata Indica launch at TELCO and the modernization activities at TISCO ensured these companies continued to attract TAS officers. Corporate HR Head of TELCO Visty Banaji (TAS 1973) never found this a challenge. From the days of Sumant Moolgaokar, TELCO had underlined the sense of national spirit in the production of commercial vehicles, haulers for the nation, and while trucks were not a glamorous product, this factor did not prevent the company from bringing some very talented and committed people on board.

Visty narrates how TELCO TAS officers in their youthful enthusiasm for their company would wonder how their counterparts could sell soap at TOMCO, when they might instead contribute to building the nation through the design and backward-integrated manufacture of complex products like commercial vehicles in TELCO. With the passage of time, however, and with more opportunities emerging beyond TELCO and TISCO across the Tata Group, fewer TAS officers would opt to join these flagship companies—the ones who did were typically those who, in Prakash Telang's (TAS 1972) words, 'truly had their heart in working for a powerful engineering driven company'; many others took the 'softer options'. Sadly, Prakash Telang, too, left us as this book was in its final stages, succumbing to an illness in December 2021.

22
Portfolio Restructuring

For many TAS officers, the attraction of working for the Tata Group was the diversity of opportunities the over-100 operating companies offered, across myriad industries in both manufacturing and services, including automobiles, steel, power, hospitality, financial services, insurance, software, telecommunications, aerospace, defence, business process outsourcing, and many more. In many of the smaller companies, the learning opportunities and growth that they experienced were particularly large and prepared them for bigger leadership roles elsewhere in the Group or indeed, outside the Group.

On IIM campuses, as Prateek Pashine (TAS 1995) recalls, careers in investment banking, management consulting and general management were the real draws. The TAS, at that time, Prateek says, 'with its offer of diversity within the Tata Group, and multi-industry, multi-function exposure, was able to attract good talent. Wannabe managers appreciated the opportunity through the TAS to spend five years after their typical engineering/MBA degrees finding their feet within a vast organization like Tata that offered immense choice.'

Yet, open and competitive markets are no friend to sprawling, highly diversified conglomerates like Tata. Companies belonging to such conglomerates can find themselves under significant pressure from focused, nimble competitors. Unless they receive adequate attention from the Group Centre, including the timely infusion of financial and human capital, they can suffer from poor performance. It doesn't help even if the conglomerate is large and financially well-endowed—the struggles of smaller companies within the conglomerate can often get ignored, and they can suffer in terms of the priority their issues may receive in comparison with larger and more complex operations within the conglomerate.

With an increasingly strong Group Centre at Tatas, the risk increased during Ratan Tata's chairmanship of sudden decisions that could be taken to divest smaller companies that were not seen to be core to the Group's growth ambitions. Such divestment decisions could disrupt the careers of the TAS officers working in these companies.

Many smaller entities in the Tata Group came under the scanner during Ratan's tenure. Among the first to be churned from the Tata portfolio was the Tata Oil Mills Company Ltd (TOMCO). This company produced one of the early, better-known and regularly advertised brands of soap for the Indian market, 'OK', and even pioneered the launch of India's first-ever detergent powder for use in washing machines. However, Ratan was clear that the company's products did not feature in his strategy or growth plans for the Tata Group, and with a limited product portfolio, he doubted that the company could succeed in the market against competition from global multinationals.

The buyer identified for TOMCO was Hindustan Lever Ltd, the Indian arm of the multinational company, Unilever. Ratan would justify the sale to Unilever as a means of providing a safe new home for the employees while preserving the asset base and growth prospects of the company. A few years after the 1993 sale of TOMCO to Hindustan Lever Ltd, Ratan would undertake the sale of another Tata company, Lakme, to Hindustan Lever. A small but well-respected brand in the area of cosmetics, Lakme did not have the scale or products that would allow it to fit within the technology and engineering-dominated large enterprise into which Ratan was busy reshaping the Tata Group.

Ratan could be ruthless when he needed to make a point about the lack of a company's fit within the Tata Group. This was experienced by Nawshir Khurody (TAS 1960), who chaired the erstwhile Tata Press Ltd, subsequently re-christened Tata Infomedia. This was a relatively small company in the publishing industry, with a well-regarded yellow pages business that would eventually come under pressure from developments online. These would transform the ease of organizing information and searching for it, thus making the yellow pages redundant.

In the late 1990s, Tata Infomedia was looking for diversification opportunities to expand its top line. It hit upon content creation for the entertainment industry as a possible new line of business. Bollywood was just beginning a transformation at the time that would professionalize film production and secure producers' access to transparent banking lines of credit. After a series of scandals linking Indian movie stars and films to the Mumbai underworld, Tata Infomedia felt it could profitably participate in this new trend, and with the Tata reputation of trust, facilitate the clean financing of Bollywood movies. The first such movie it sought to produce, *Aetbaar*, had one of India's biggest names, Amitabh Bachchan, starring as the hero.

The company, however, had not reckoned with Ratan's ire about its flirting with a tainted industry. He was worried that dabbling in the glamorous world of Bollywood would result in compromising several of the Tata values. When he sensed that Tata Infomedia was reluctant to step back and withdraw its plans, he issued firm orders for the company to be divested and for the use of the Tata name to be speedily withdrawn from it. He was determined to send a strong signal within the Group that companies that did not toe the line would face swift repercussions.

Under pressure to arrange an urgent sale of the company, the Group's Finance Director, Ishaat Hussain, managed to locate a private equity firm, ICICI Ventures, that was willing to take the company off Tata Sons' hands. The sale to a private equity player was the first such in the Tata Group's history.

Through the 1990s, a series of divestments took place, of Tata companies that Ratan Tata regarded as non-core to the Group's future. These included companies like Merind in the pharmaceuticals sector (sold to Wockhardt); Goodlass Nerolac, the paint company (sold to Kansai Paints); Lakme in the cosmetics space (sold to Hindustan Lever Ltd); ACC in the cement sector (sold to Gujarat Ambuja); and over a dozen others.

A number of joint ventures were also exited, as it became increasingly clear in several of them that the contribution of the Tata Group was modest in comparison to that of the joint venture partner. Joint ventures which were terminated included the partnerships with Mercedes Benz, IBM, Lucent Technologies and Honeywell; the foreign partners controlled the key drivers of success in these ventures including the technologies and intellectual property rights.

The portfolio restructuring under Ratan left the Tata Group as a major player in essentially seven large sectors, with companies within each that were market leaders and had prospects to grow into successful international players. The sectors and the companies included under their purview were Automobiles (e.g. Tata Motors); Materials (e.g. Tata Steel); Energy (e.g. Tata Power); Consumer Products (e.g. Titan); Chemicals (e.g. Tata Chemicals); IT and Communications (e.g. TCS and Tata Teleservices Ltd); and Financial Services (e.g. Tata Finance and Tata AIG).

The churn in the Group's portfolio did not unsettle most TAS officers. In the case of several of the joint ventures, some exercised their choice to move with the foreign partners. At Tata Lucent Technologies, for instance, the joint venture between Tata Industries and Lucent Technologies, two TAS officers, P. Balaji (TAS 1990) and Prateek Pashine (TAS 1995), oversaw the venture's procurement and commercial activities. When the venture broke apart after four years, Balaji moved out with the joint venture partner, eventually going on to serve in leadership roles across a number of organizations, including Sony Ericsson, Nokia and Vodafone India, while Prateek chose to stay with the Tatas.

Prateek's batchmate in the TAS, Prashanth Nayak (TAS 1995), would have a different experience with the joint venture he would join. Prashanth was initially assigned as an Executive Assistant to Devender Gupta, the Managing Director of Tata Auto-Components Ltd (TACO), in 1996. After two years, he moved to Corporate Planning in the same company, and subsequently became Head of HR, and then from 2003 to 2005, Head of HR as well as Corporate Planning. From 2005 to 2009, he served as the CEO of Tata Yazaki, the TACO joint venture with Yazaki of Japan, to produce wiring harnesses for the Indian auto-market. Prashanth's rapid rise (he became a CEO at the age of thirty-four) and his cross-functional moves made him a poster boy for the TAS, with the Secretariat showcasing his profile in pre-placement talks at business schools.

Prashanth left TACO due to disagreements on corporate governance with the Tata representatives on the Board. He firmly felt that the CEO of a joint venture firm should be insulated from differences between the partners, and instead be directed by the Board to take action based on whatever they discussed and agreed on; the CEO should not be required to take sides and get caught in the crossfire.

However, the Tata representatives were keen that all the TACO 'group companies' should function as an integrated unit and be responsive to directions from the TACO centre, including in relation to things such as having a common SAP platform, using the same security services, and so on. Some of this made sense, but it quickly became more controversial when addressing issues like technology transfer from the joint venture partner, localization to reduce the cost of parts, royalty payments, and the like. Payments due to vendors and supplies to customers were held up while differences between the two joint venture partners were being sorted out.

When Prashanth was summoned to a face-off meeting with the TACO group centre officers at TMTC, a place where he had started his career in the Tata Group, he became emotional during the showdown that took place. Clear that he did not want to hurt his vendors and customers for no fault of theirs, and upset by the 'orders' he was receiving, Prashanth decided to quit the Tata Group. Prashanth's one-line letter of resignation did not go down well with the then TACO management. The Managing Director wanted him, as a TAS officer, to at least explore other roles in the Group. But Prashanth had not maintained any real connection with the TAS Secretariat, and was anyway keen to explore a career as his own master, so he chose to leave.

Several managers had rotated through the TAS Secretariat during Prashanth's years with TACO, and his connections with the Secretariat had significantly weakened. Having served with one company throughout, Prashanth had no sense of being regarded as a 'Group resource', and had experienced no interface or investment by the TAS Secretariat in his growth as a manager. 'Nobody from the TAS Secretariat even called me when I quit!' says Prashanth. Yazaki, on the other hand, maintained regular contact with Prashanth. A few years later, after their joint venture with TACO fell apart, they approached him to take charge of their India operations, a role which he accepted.

In an India that was beginning to experience the highest growth rates in its history, there was really no cause for TAS officers to rue missed opportunities. From the perspective of the Group, with expansion across the board, TAS officers were being requisitioned to staff many new projects. With more opportunities becoming available, larger numbers of TAS officers came to be hired. In the long run, this would, however, prove to be a double-edged sword.

As Prakash Telang (TAS 1972) put it, by the early 2000s the TAS had become only a recruitment and placement agency. Little attention was paid by the Group HR team to the grooming of TAS officers through their careers after they had completed their initial orientation stints. With a considerable increase in TAS recruitment numbers, there was no accompanying increase in senior progression opportunities or brand enhancement, and the median quality the Group could attract was bound to decline. Visty Banaji (TAS 1973) observes, 'There was no way the

Group was going to be able to create 20–30 CEO-level jobs annually in future for the several dozen TAS recruits it began to hire each year. This knowledge could not have aided retention of the better ones.'

This issue would play out in the following two decades. At the time, however, all around there was a palpable sense of optimism about the future. This was significantly stimulated by the agenda of internationalization that Ratan embarked upon in the early 2000s, which saw many Tata companies make overseas forays.

23
Going Global

At the Annual Group Management Meet (AGMM) in 2003, Ratan Tata called for a greater thrust towards internationalization. This spoke to every TAS officer's dream of becoming part of a global landscape where capability and merit would earn them opportunities for personal growth and exposure to international best practices.

Jaspreet Bindra (TAS 1994) underlines how this changed the attractiveness of the TAS from the time in the early 1990s when he joined the cadre. The TAS in the early 1990s had a great deal of prestige attached to it. It was flattering to be interviewed by a committee headed by Tata Group Chairman Ratan Tata. A career with the TAS promised a variety of opportunities, and the Tatas enjoyed a stature in India that made the decision to join the TAS an easy one.

The decision for somebody like Jaspreet to join the TAS, he says, was 'driven significantly by considerations of the past glory of the Tatas. It was only later, in the early 2000s, that a much stronger sense of the future began to take hold among young TAS officers, a perception that the Tata Group was destined for greater glory. This was driven by events such as the acquisition of Tetley, the largest corporate buyout in Indian history up till that point of time; the successful Y2K deployments by TCS and its explosive international growth in the new millennium; and the successful acquisition of management control of Videsh Sanchar Nigam Ltd (VSNL) by pipping Reliance Industries to the goalpost in the final bid. There was now a sense of a Group that had shed its past conservatism, and was willing to take big, audacious decisions that would stimulate growth and expansion.'

The international acquisitions the Group started making from the early 2000s were a 'game changer' for Jaspreet. Where in the past the Group seemed content to source technology and market access through joint venture partnerships, it was now jettisoning many of these ventures, and instead, acquiring direct control of entities overseas.

The emergence of a new liberalized global economic architecture, and the expansion of global trade under the auspices of the World Trade Organization (WTO) were opening up opportunities for Indian companies in foreign markets. Ratan firmly believed that Tata companies, having once consolidated their domestic footprint, inevitably needed to think about expanding overseas. In line with this international mindset, the Tata Code of Conduct even incorporated a clause that required all Tata companies 'to support the development and operation of competitive open markets and the liberalization of trade and investment in each country and market in which we operate.'

Ratan was encouraged in his belief that the time was right to start expanding globally by the success he saw with the first major move towards internationalization made by Tata Tea. It was a TAS officer, R.K. Krishna Kumar (TAS 1963), then the Vice Chairman of Tata Tea, who was instrumental in persuading Ratan that the Tata Group was ready for an international play.

Tata Tea's leveraged buyout of the much larger Tetley Tea in 2000, for $450 million, was for several years the largest in Indian corporate history. Led by Krishna Kumar, the Tetley buyout catapulted Tata Tea from being merely a large Indian tea manufacturer to becoming the world's second-largest branded tea seller, just behind Lipton.

The Tetley buyout tested the Tata Group's ability to successfully integrate overseas acquisitions. Govind Sankaranarayanan (TAS 1992), who served early in his career as Krishna Kumar's Executive Assistant, and was among the first two executives (Abanti, his wife, also a TAS officer, being the other) sent to London (in Govind's case, as the Group Treasurer at Tetley), confesses, 'The going was initially tough. A few senior Tetley leaders proved to be difficult in their interactions with the new owners, and would push back hard on changes in strategy desired by Tatas.' The Tetley bosses could, at least for some time, resist executing those parts of the Tata strategy they disagreed with because of a covenant brought into place by the lenders to the transaction. Under it, the key management team would not be displaced until the debt that had been taken on was settled. Within three to four years of the acquisition, when the debt was substantially pared, stronger integration between the parent and subsidiary was indeed achieved.

Yet, the acquisition also established some ground rules for the way in which the Tata Group helmed by Ratan would approach subsequent acquisitions. There would be no firing or replacement of senior leaders. Due respect would be shown to the acquired entity and its people. Relatively few Tata managers from India would be laterally inducted into the acquired company's leadership team. And every effort would be made to retain the local ethos and heritage of the acquired company. In the case of Tetley, for instance, this meant holding on to the brand equity of the Tetley 'folk', the cartoon characters that were much loved in Great Britain, the home of Tetley. Honed at Tetley, this soft-touch approach became the model for several later Tata acquisitions, and by and large, served to establish Tatas as a responsible and respected acquirer. Above all, Tatas would be patient acquirers, prepared to grow companies in a consensual and evolutionary manner.

There was a downside to the Tata approach to integration, too. There was an assumption, perhaps, that somehow integration would take place in due course 'on its own'. In the case of the Tetley acquisition, for instance, there was no clear demonstration that it was Tata Tea that had acquired Tetley, and so immediate synergy benefits—that could have been derived in the first flush—were lost.

Bharat Wakhlu (TAS 1985) recollects that when he took over as President of Tata Inc. in New York, in 2003, the Tetley team in the US was operating without any alignment with Tata Tea, including the latter's Florida facility for making instant tea. It took some prodding from Bharat to get the Tata Tea leadership to take advantage of the opportunities they were missing, and to get the integration finally done in the US.

Bharat had a similar experience after the Corus acquisition by Tata Steel a few years later. On that occasion, however, he was able to ensure that the Tata Steel team in the US—despite significant push back both from the US-based managers and their superiors in Britain—were integrated in a proper and dignified manner with Corus's operations in the US, thereby deriving synergy benefits early on. The US was the first geography where the integration between Corus and Tata Steel happened neatly, with minimal loss of talent or heartburn.

The chutzpah of Krishna Kumar rubbed off on Ratan and other senior Tata Group managers. Krishna had already impressed Ratan some years earlier with his grit and ability to pull through an incredibly stressful situation when, as Managing Director of Tata Tea, he was accused of having illegal parlays with a banned extremist organization, the United Liberation Front of Assam (ULFA), in order to maintain peace in the tea plantations run by the company in Assam. Krishna, with strong backing from Ratan, took on the Assam state government. He stoutly defended his actions on the basis that they were undertaken with the full knowledge and the endorsement of central intelligence agencies; eventually, the cases lodged against him and the company would be withdrawn. Naturally, when looking for a tough administrator for the Indian Hotels Company to replace the redoubtable Ajit Kerkar, Krishna was Ratan's preferred choice.

With the successful acquisition of Tetley, Krishna became a trusted advisor to Ratan. He was appointed to the Board of Tata Sons—only the second TAS officer to be inducted on to the Board after Freddie Mehta (the first TAS officer)—and was also made a member of the GCC. Later, he would be appointed a Trustee of the Tata Trusts and would serve as a member of the Selection Committee to appoint Ratan Tata's successor. Krishna, somewhat unexpectedly in the eyes of many peers in the TAS, became the most powerful TAS officer in the post-JRD Tata era and continues to have an important voice in shaping the Group's future as a Trustee of the Tata Trusts, the principal shareholders of the Group's holding company, Tata Sons.

While the Tetley acquisition showed the way, giving additional confidence to the Group's plans for going global was the fact that many Tata companies were exhibiting significant performance improvement within the TBEM framework. As was seen with Tata Steel, the first winner of the JRD QV Award in 2000, managers across the Tata Group were beginning to benchmark their operating performance metrics with international peers and adopting global best practices.

A new ambition now drove a concerted move towards expanding the Tata Group's footprint around the world. This phase would see the Group's consolidated turnover increase ten-fold in a little over a decade, from $10 billion in the early 2000s to $100 billion in FY 2012!

Taking a cue from the success of the Tetley acquisition, much of the growth that took place through the early to mid-2000s was inorganic. In some cases, Tata companies were able to acquire assets and operating revenues that transformed the scale at which they were able to operate. In other cases, they also acquired brands that eased their entry into global markets.

In the string of acquisitions that took place, TAS officers played important roles at several companies. These included the purchase by Tata Communications (earlier VSNL) of the world's largest submarine cable fibre optic network built by Tyco, and its acquisition of the Canadian long-distance telecom operator, Teleglobe—these acquisitions were led N. Srinath (TAS 1986), the Executive Director at Tata Communications, assisted by his CFO, Govind Sankaranayanan. R. Mukundan (TAS 1990), soon to become Managing Director of the company, was closely involved in Tata Chemicals' acquisition of the US-based General Chemicals, the world's largest producer of soda ash, and the largest salt manufacturer in the UK, Brunner Mond. Likewise, Prakash Telang (TAS 1972), the soon-to-become Managing Director of Tata Motors, was closely involved in the acquisition of the truck business of Korean company, Daewoo Motors.

At the prodding of its Vice Chairman, R.K. Krishna Kumar, the Indian Hotels Company also undertook a series of overseas acquisitions. The acquisition of the iconic Pierre Hotel in New York in 2005 raised the visibility and the cachet of the Tata Group, and helped demonstrate to global investors and business leaders that it was much more than its IT arm, TCS, which at that time was internationally the better known Tata company.

The mid-2000s witnessed a period of easy liquidity in international markets and strong growth in emerging markets. With seemingly strong prospects, rising ambitions and backed by a booming stock market, Indian companies were welcomed in many developed markets as prospective buyers of assets and companies. The Tata acquisition binge eventually culminated in the largest-ever foreign buyouts by any Indian firms up to that point: the acquisitions of Corus Steel by Tata Steel (for $ 12.1 Bn) and Jaguar Land Rover (for $ 2.3 Bn) by Tata Motors.

In sync with the Tata Group's expanding international footprint, efforts were also made at this time to spread the TAS recruitment net in foreign universities like Harvard. However, these failed, on account of the relatively low salaries on offer, though some students from premier universities in the US did take up summer projects with the TAS to avail of the extraordinary learning the Group could offer. Bharat, who was in the US at the time, is of the view that the decision to recruit bright talent from there was taken hastily by a few executives at the Group Centre in Bombay House, without either fully understanding the cultural nuances of such an exercise or even the roles the new hires would play within the Tata ecosystem. Even the Tata executives who were sent to recruit officers were recent lateral entrants into the Group, without a sense of the ethos, the great and uplifting stories that brought alive the achievements of the Tatas, or the Group's deeper values.

Similar targeted recruitments from China were also made to employ talent in the Tata businesses in that country, which by the late 2000s had become the Group's largest overseas market. The recruitment programme, called the Tata China Management Programme, started off well, partly because it was clear that the new recruits would serve within China itself, albeit after a short induction within the Tata Group in India. But within a few years, this programme would lapse, partly in the wake of a general revisit of the internationalization agenda and the fact that several of the recruits did not live up to the high expectations that the Group had of them.

The TAS, sadly for a Group with the majority of its revenues earned in markets outside India, has not strengthened its ranks with the induction of non-Indian managers. It lacks an essential element of diversity for the kind of global management cadre it ought to have become by now.

24
Two Home-Grown Successes with Contrasting Tales

THE PERIOD OF FRENETIC INTERNATIONALIZATION AT THE TATAS ALSO saw two of the Group's most successful home-grown businesses coming into their own. These were TCS and Titan, and they were studies in contrast.

Where TCS was revelling in the international growth it was experiencing after the so-called Y2K projects it took on at the turn of the century, as also the new opportunities arising from business process outsourcing, Titan was licking its wounds from a failed international growth strategy and refocusing on the domestic market. And where TCS's growth was led by managers recruited largely from the computer sciences domain and Tier 1 and Tier 2 engineering schools across India, with very few TAS officers within its ranks, Titan was founded by a TAS officer and soon became a magnet for others, including some of the brightest marketing minds drawn from India's best business schools.

Common to both companies, however, was the long-term approach to managing business of their promoter, Tata Sons. This allowed these companies to become the twin jewels in the Tata crown today, enjoying the highest market capitalization within the Tata portfolio of companies. Their success over the decades has given confidence to Group managers, including many TAS officers, that they have the room to experiment, take risks and even stumble or fail, in their quest for eventual value-creation, delivery and success.

TCS started life in 1968 as a division housed first in Tata Power and later in Tata Sons. At every stage of its evolution, through the 1970s, 1980s, and even the early 1990s, as a small business, TCS could conceivably have been moved in directions very different from the one it eventually took. It could have been sold, shut down or moved into a joint venture with a global major, and it is unlikely that anybody in the Tata system outside TCS would have batted an eyelid.

But by the late 1990s, the subject of a TCS Initial Public Offering (IPO) began to be vigorously debated within Tata Sons. This was the period of the dotcom boom in the US, when all kinds of companies were being listed on NASDAQ at unbelievable valuations (and indeed, many would eventually come crashing back to terra firma during the subsequent dotcom bust!). Dr Mukund Rajan (TAS 1995), then the Executive Assistant to Ratan Tata, recalls a note at the time put up for Ratan by one of his key financial advisors. 'What was extraordinary in the note was the suggestion that if Tata Sons were to list TCS at that stage and dilute a small percentage of its equity, the proceeds would be sufficient to permit Tata Sons to buy out the public shareholding of every listed Tata company!' exclaims Mukund.

Taking each listed Tata Group company private would have more than fulfilled one of Ratan's stated objectives—that of completely securing the right to control and manage Tata companies by shoring up Tata Sons' equity stake in them. As we have noted earlier in the book, the Managing Agency system had allowed the Tatas to retain management control of many Tata companies with relatively low equity stakes; however, this privilege was increasingly likely to face challenge in the post-1991 era of liberalization, when the right to manage would have to be earned, and control exercised through significant ownership stakes could offer better insurance against hostile take-over threats. Despite this, Ratan, after some deliberation, turned down the advice he had received to list TCS. He felt that retail investors in an IPO taking place at a time when the markets were very frothy would subsequently feel short-changed when the markets declined. A Tata company, he felt, had a responsibility to its investors and ought not to take advantage of a short-term bubble to mislead them about its real value.

As a long-term participant in the Indian market, Ratan was clear in his mind that the Group had to always be conscious about the expectations of fair play that investors would have from it. 'This was a remarkable lesson in good corporate governance. That a leader should think about long-term repercussions, even sacrificing immediate short-term gains, in order to preserve an organization's reputation, was hugely inspiring,' shares Mukund in his measured voice.

Eventually, after the dotcom boom and bust were over, TCS was listed, in 2004. The most successful IPO in the Tata Group's history also translated, over time, into TCS becoming the highest market capitalization company within the Group.

Titan, meanwhile, was established almost twenty years after TCS in 1984, by a TAS officer, Xerxes Desai (TAS 1961). An Oxford graduate with a degree in politics, philosophy and economics, Xerxes was 'a totally different kind of CEO', according to Jamshed Daboo (TAS 1986), who worked under Xerxes for over a decade till the late 1990s. 'He combined a very high vision quotient with a very high emotional quotient, and deeply felt for people. The culture you see at Titan, which combines vision with inclusiveness, is what he put in place right at the beginning. When a housing colony had to be developed for employees, he was not content with just putting up some functional structure but happily commissioned a leading architect like Charles Correa to design it. With an amazing eye for detail, he [Xerxes] was superb to watch at work. He really led without leading, if you know what I mean', continues Jamshed.

Xerxes conceptualized a major watch production initiative while working at Tata Press. Vibha Paul Rishi (TAS 1982) was part of the core team set up by Xerxes. She remembers that time as an exciting one. 'We were trying to do something completely different,' she says. Watch production was reserved for public sector entities, and so Tatas opted to partner with the Tamil Nadu Industrial Development Corporation (TIDCO) for the watch project. The company that resulted from the joint venture was appropriately named Titan, the name being drawn from the initials in Tata Industries and Tamil Nadu.

Very swiftly, the new company displaced the decades' old public sector unit, Hindustan Machine Tools (HMT), as the market leader in watch manufacture and sales in India. Xerxes's strong sense of aesthetics drove Titan's watch and store designs. He focused on bringing world class watches in a wide range of designs and prices to the Indian customer, backed by the inherent trust enjoyed by the House of Tata.

Xerxes also put pressure on his team to create retail stores that conformed to international standards. Kalpana Kohli Kar (TAS 1984) was part of the team in Bangalore. 'We were a small team and as a result we did many things outside our core responsibility areas. We were all aware that what we were doing had the potential to change the watch market in India. We were young and full of enthusiasm and were excited to be part of this company,' remembers Kalpana.

Young art and design graduates hired from the National Institute of Design were given exposure at the international watch fair at Basel, Switzerland. They were encouraged to benchmark the look and feel of Titan's Indian stores with those of international watch companies in cities like Paris, Geneva and London. Xerxes's stamp was also left on the branding of Titan's watches with the unusual selection of a Western classical music piece to accompany the presentation of Titan's watches in advertisements—Mozart's 25th Symphony, which became Titan's signature tune.

Emboldened by the strong domestic customer acceptance of its well-designed new products, Titan decided to expand its sales footprint in the mid-1990s to advanced markets in Europe, including the UK, Germany, Austria, Denmark, France, Belgium, Netherlands,

Luxembourg, Italy, Greece, Spain and Portugal. This internationalization effort, however, with what was at the time a still vulnerable 'made in India' proposition, failed. With quality and delivery challenges, and having to build brand equity from scratch, the combination of high media expenses and difficulties in breaking into the distribution channels for high footfall watch brands ensured Titan remained a loss-making brand in Europe through the 1990s.

Thus, by the time the rest of the Tata Group came around to exploring international growth opportunities, Titan was already licking its wounds from its unsuccessful attempts to take its watch business international. Significant losses were racked up before the European operations were stopped in 2004 by Xerxes's successor, Bhaskar Bhat.

In an effort to find other avenues of growth that could leverage its design competencies and customer connect and earn scarce and much-needed foreign exchange, from exports, to fund its imports of watch movements, components, and technology, Titan started building a new domestic jewellery line of business in the mid-1990s, christened Tanishq. This business took significant losses in its early years, and following several critical business reviews at Tata Sons, Titan came within a hair's breadth of being forced to shut the business and take a write-off.

However, Xerxes offered a strong defence of the jewellery business. Nawshir Khurody (TAS 1960) recalls with feeling how Xerxes and he were the two most outspoken CEOs on the Tata Group Strategy Forum, an ad hoc body formed by Ratan to hear the views of Tata CEOs. Both were willing to air strong views on various subjects, even if it meant incurring Ratan's ire! Xerxes argued strongly that there was a compelling logic to leveraging all the connotations of trust that Titan had built up as a Tata company to make inroads into the Indian jewellery sector. The sector was dominated at the time by family jewellers with small-scale handmade jewellery units and was plagued by customer angst at unfair business practices, especially surrounding the purity of precious metals and stones used by the jewellers.

The company was given more time to stabilize the jewellery business. Shrugging off the departure of key senior executives of Titan who set up a competing business, aggressive marketing strategies crafted by a team led by Chief Operating Officer (COO) Jacob Kurien (TAS 1983) eventually saw Tanishq sales surge.

The Tanishq jewellery range was extended, and as its outlets shed their elitist persona, walk-in numbers climbed dramatically. Emphasizing its commitment to offering authentic and trust-worthy products, Titan installed so-called Karatmeters—spectroscopy machines to measure the purity of gold in less than 3 minutes—within the Tanishq stores to allow customers to assess the purity of the gold in the jewellery being sold to them. These expensive machines bolstered the company's claim of not ripping off its jewellery clients, unlike many other jewellers in India. Stories abound of customers coming with their family heirlooms, breaking down in tears after the Karatmeter showed them that their jewellery was fake!

Over the years, Tanishq grew from strength to strength. A business which could quite easily have been closed down in the early 2000s, Tanishq now accounts for around 80 per cent of Titan's turnover and the lion's share of its profitability. As a retail company with world-class design capabilities and powerful brands, Titan now accounts for the highest market capitalization within the Tata Group after TCS.

25

The Limited Benefits of Internationalization

As Titan had already discovered in the mid-1990s, overseas plays, unless done with a robust value proposition and a long-term orientation, can prove to be costly and value destructive. Sadly, for the Tata Group, a number of its investments in foreign entities during the phase of its internationalization have not yielded value.

Costly overseas acquisitions in the mid-2000s, significantly funded by debt, continue to impact the prospects of Tata companies such as Indian Hotels and Tata Steel. The timing of many acquisitions, just before the Global Financial Crisis struck in 2008, was unfortunate; rising interest rates and the denial of cheap credit by large lenders would take their toll.

Jehangir Ardeshir (TAS 1983) recollects that Europe-based Anglo-Dutch steel company Corus Steel, which became the target of the largest corporate buyout in Tata history in 2007, was under assessment during the last phase of Dr Irani's time as Managing Director at Tata Steel in 1999/early 2000. Based on the advice of its internal Strategy team, the company chose not to pursue a possible acquisition in those days due to concerns about the lack of efficiency and quality focus, coupled with very high operating costs of the company. Dr Irani's successor, B. Muthuraman, also originally shared concerns about the fit of the company with Tata

Steel. Some years later, however, the acquisition moved ahead anyway which, in hindsight, proved to be a mistake.

The acquisition of Corus Steel was bedevilled by the fact that the Brazilian steelmaker—one of the largest crude steel makers in Latin America—Companhia Siderúrgica Nacional (CSN) also made a simultaneous bid for the company. Corus Steel forced Tata Steel and CSN into an auction, maximizing its own shareholder gains, but making the acquisition more expensive for the acquirer.

Bharat Wakhlu (TAS 1985) remembers his conversation with Ratan Tata in the US, shortly after the successful acquisition. 'They were slow,' the Chairman said, with visible annoyance about the decision-makers in Tata Steel, while referring to the timing of the acquisition, and the high price that was eventually paid. 'I wish they had acted when I told them to. Now we are paying £6.08 per share, when we could have made the acquisition at less than £4 per share!'

For well over a decade after its acquisition by Tata Steel, Corus has struggled to deliver even operating profits in a European market that, ever since the Global Financial Crisis, has been functioning at capacities far below where they used to be in 2007.

Reflecting poor value creation, several Tata companies have, in recent years, been forced to shed overseas assets acquired during the period of internationalization. These span sectors such as steel, where Tata Steel has divested some assets across Europe and South-East Asia; hospitality, where Indian Hotels has unwound its acquisition of the erstwhile Ritz-Carlton Hotel in Boston; energy, where Tata Power has sold its stake in coal mining operations in Indonesia; chemicals, where Tata Chemicals has sold its majority interests in a Mozambique biofuel unit; communications, where Tata Communications has sold its South African business, Neotel; and many more. No grand overseas acquisitions have taken place at the Tata Group now for well over a decade.

The Tata brand, for a brief period of time, did acquire additional lustre as a result of its many international acquisitions. It seemed to represent a Corporate India that was coming of age and able to hold its own against international competitors. However, the subsequent struggles experienced by several of the overseas entities eroded some of the brand equity.

Dr Mukund Rajan (TAS 1995), appointed as the Group's first Brand Custodian in 2013, observes that while the Tata brand equity remains strong in India, absent a determination at the very highest levels in the Group to allocate a substantial war-chest for brand building in overseas markets, it is unlikely that the Tata brand overseas can come to enjoy the kind of resonance it has with stakeholders in India. Plans were made to leverage the occasion of the 150th anniversary of the Tata Group in 2018 to make a big splash in key international markets, including the UK, China and the US. However, these had to be abandoned in the wake of the messy shareholder spat at Tata Sons between Cyrus Mistry and Ratan Tata.

Mukund also points out, 'Creating a powerful brand requires, first and foremost, internal alignment among the employees, and achieving this takes time. For many overseas employees brought into the Tata fold via acquisitions, the Group was merely the latest in a long line of owners. This was brought home vividly for Mukund when employees on the shop-floor at the Jaguar Land Rover facility in Birmingham confessed that they viewed Tata Motors as just their latest owner, following from a string of previous owners like BMW and Ford. They had no real knowledge of their new parent's history or culture or value system.'

Mukund goes on, 'Thus, we began to make significant investments in communicating the Group's story to all the new employees and integrating them into the common systems and processes that had been put in place, such as the TBEM framework and cross-company functional platforms like the Brand and Corporate Communicators' Meets, to create a sense of unity and common purpose.'

Meanwhile, as some of the international acquisitions made by the Tatas began to flounder, some seeds planted in the mid-2000s in the domestic market began to sprout into major enterprises. These served as a reminder of the large scale of opportunities still available within India. Two, in particular, financial services and defence, bear mention.

Tata Capital was created in 2007, to fill the gap left when the Tata Group partially vacated the financial services sector following the closure of Tata Finance after a scandal in the company (see a subsequent chapter for details). A TAS officer with a unique skill set, Govind Sankaranarayanan (TAS 1992), was appointed the founding Chief Operating Officer and Chief Financial Officer of Tata Capital. Govind had been sent to Tetley in the UK as the Financial Controller after the successful acquisition by Tata Tea. While there, he also completed a Masters in Finance at the London Business School. He then served Tata Communications International as its Chief Financial Officer, based between New Jersey and Montreal in North America. His appointment at Tata Capital reflected the high regard in which his international experience across foreign markets, and his depth of experience in financial services, were held.

Alongside the CEO at Tata Capital (the erstwhile Tata Motors Chief Financial Officer, Praveen Kadle), Govind built out a wide array of financial product and service offerings to address the needs of a growing and poorly penetrated retail market and an underserved corporate market. Tata Capital has been able to leverage the Tata brand's reputation for trust and grow its book over the past decade to over $11 billion.

Defence and aerospace is another sector that is yielding rich dividends for the Tata Group, as the Indian government opens up opportunities to meet the needs of the Indian Armed Forces to the private sector. A series of joint ventures undertaken by Tata Advanced Systems, created in 2007, with global majors like Lockheed Martin, Boeing and Sikorsky, have resulted in major new streams of revenue for the Group. Some of these, like the joint venture with Sikorsky, were shepherded by Bharat from his vantage point in the US as President of Tata Inc. And as with new ventures in the past, several of the defence and aerospace entities have been staffed with capable TAS resources, such as Masood Husseiny (TAS 1999), who undertook a stint in Ratan Tata's office working alongside Sukaran Singh, before both moved to the rolls of Tata Advanced Systems, with Sukaran taking on the role of Managing Director.

Tata ventures in the defence and aerospace sector are now producing critical components for many different aircrafts. These include the floor beams for the Boeing 787 and the wings for the F-16 fighter aircraft. For a while, Tata Advanced Systems also made the main cabin aerostructure for the S92 Sikorsky helicopters (the same helicopter type that flies the President of the US, better known as Marine One). Tata Advanced Systems also manufactures the central wing boxes and empennage for Lockheed Martin's C130J airlifter and the fuselage for the AH-64 Apache combat helicopters of Boeing. Indeed, the Tata Group is now in a unique position to design and build a complete aircraft if it so desires!

26

Values on Test—Singur and the Tata Nano

WHILE NEW TATA BUSINESSES IN SECTORS LIKE DEFENCE AND AEROSPACE and financial services have flourished in the domestic market, established ones in sectors such as automobiles have encountered massive challenges, putting the values of the Group to test. This was the case when Tata Motors sought to establish a new manufacturing plant in Singur in the state of West Bengal for its proposed small car, the Tata Nano.

When Tata Motors designed the Nano, it projected that this could be retailed at a price of around Rs 1 lakh, which would make it the lowest-priced passenger car in the world. In designing the low-cost product, the Tata Motors team undertook a number of innovations and patented several of these. The use of composites to make the car lighter, the development of a low displacement engine that would meet the twin requirements of fuel efficiency and reasonable thrust, a new wheel architecture for the smaller frame and hundreds of additional innovations in the way normal cars are produced, all with the goal of getting the cost down and retaining essential functionalities, received applause from global peers and corporate leaders ranging from Carlos Ghosn of Nissan to Jeff Immelt of General Electric.

The Rs 1 lakh price point, it was expected, would incentivize millions of Indian two-wheeler owners to upgrade to their first self-owned four-wheel vehicle. The demand such an attractively priced vehicle would generate was conservatively expected to run into hundreds of thousands of unit sales every year. Based on this calculation, a major exercise to identify a location for Tata Motors' newest manufacturing plant was kicked off in 2005.

Prakash Telang (TAS 1972) was appointed by the then Managing Director of the company, Ravi Kant, to lead the team that would explore the best location to manufacture the new Tata Nano. A number of potential locations across India were inspected by Prakash and his team. State governments bent over backwards to attract the Tata Motors investment, which was expected to not only bring fresh employment with the new car plant, but also create a large vendor park and allied new manufacturing and services activities in the vicinity of the park.

A number of states, including Maharashtra, Karnataka, Himachal Pradesh, Uttarakhand, Punjab, Uttar Pradesh and West Bengal, laid out the red carpet. Eventually, West Bengal was selected in 2006, after significant input and counsel from Chairman Ratan Tata. Ratan felt that West Bengal, under Communist rule by then for three decades, had missed out on some mainstream developments that other states had experienced. Under a more progressive Communist Chief Minister, the state appeared inclined to undertake the necessary reforms to create a more hospitable environment for industry. Besides the attractive incentives being made available by the state government, locating the Nano plant in West Bengal would therefore also serve a larger national objective—that of supporting industrialization in the eastern part of India.

Prakash notes similarities in the personalities of Ratan and the then Communist Chief Minister of West Bengal, Buddhadeb Bhattacharyya. 'Both were soft-spoken, self-restrained individuals and got along well.' Prakash and his team were in favour of the location identified by the government at Singur as the site of the new Nano plant, close to the highway linking Kolkata with New Delhi. This was an important consideration, as goods would have to be moved in and out of the plant, and there would be easy access to other forms of cross-country transport. The West Bengal government took the responsibility of acquiring the identified land parcels on which the plant would be built.

Unfortunately, the Nano project became a pawn in a battle between the opposition parties and the ruling Communist Party in West Bengal. Allegations were made by the principal opposition party, the Trinamool Congress led by its firebrand leader Mamata Banerjee, that much of the land acquired in Singur for the Nano project was fertile agricultural land. She claimed that many innocent farmers, including sharecroppers whose livelihoods depended on this land, had been forcibly evicted with little or no compensation.

The dispute over land acquisition got violent, and the buildings and other installations being constructed on it became targets of arson and physical attacks. Vendors were forcibly prevented from entering the Tata Motors plant, and employees working at the plant were harassed and physically prevented from moving freely in the area.

Tata Motors was caught in a bind. When it became clear that any kind of rapprochement between the warring political parties looked unlikely, Ratan was forced to issue an ultimatum. He said that Tata Motors would pull out of the state if the violence and threats to the company's employees and vendors continued. Yet, the state government seemed unable to restore law and order in the area.

A last-ditch effort was made by the Governor of West Bengal to achieve conciliation between the three parties: the West Bengal Government, the Trinamool Congress and Tata Motors. Just when it was felt that a solution would almost certainly be found, and while the meeting of the parties was still going on, Mamata Banerjee derailed the talks by saying there would be no compromise. Attitudes hardened thereafter, and Tata Motors soon announced its decision to pull out of the state.

Ratan had reached the end of his tether. He saw allegations of Tata collusion with the state government as unfair and unwarrantedly hurting the Group's image and reputation. There was also a serious risk to the safety and well-being of Tata Motors employees and vendors because of the local violence. All this outweighed the importance of bringing the Nano plant on stream for production as soon as possible.

The pull-out from Singur had many significant consequences. It was a huge setback to the efforts of the Communist government and its reformist Chief Minister to promote industrialization in the state and, for many years after, big industrial investments in the state would prove elusive.

For Tata Motors, as Prakash recounts, 'There was no Plan B possible at this late stage.' Despite this, the employees of Tata Motors 'wholeheartedly supported the decision to pull out', as it was taken in their own best interests. A temporary makeshift location for manufacture of the Tata Nano at the company's plant in Uttarakhand was identified by Prakash.

The need to find a permanent home for the relocated Tata Nano plant yielded a unique invitation to host it from a Chief Minister in western India, who had smelt the whiff of a big opportunity here. That Chief Minister, Narendra Modi, succeeded in persuading Tata Motors to locate the plant in Sanand, Gujarat. He would leverage the Tata Motors investment commitment in 2008 to showcase his progressive policies in Gujarat, and this factor, among others, including an endorsement of his policies by Ratan, would eventually see him rise to the position of Prime Minister of India in 2014. In a prescient comment, as the Chief Guest at the Vibrant Gujarat Summit in January 2007, Ratan had already told industrialists, 'It is stupid if you are not in Gujarat.'

The Tata Motors employees welcomed the relocation of the Nano plant to Gujarat. Working with pride in the top leadership that had looked out for their interests, they tried to make up for lost time. Prakash and his team found the Gujarat government officers very responsive, delivering much-needed infrastructure like power connections for the Nano plant within days; clearly, they were adept at wooing and supporting the private sector, unlike their West Bengal counterparts.

Despite the best efforts of the management team, the loss of precious time to market during the relocation of the Nano plant cost Tata Motors dearly. The additional time allowed its competitors to find ways to counter the threat posed by the Nano, including through value for money equal monthly instalment schemes on their low-cost range of products. The Global Financial Crisis of 2008 inflicted a further blow to the company, which had taken on significant debt to finance its multibillion-dollar acquisition of Jaguar Land Rover. It took years for Tata Motors to begin its recovery from this combination of unfortunate events.

The delayed launch of the Tata Nano was coupled, unfortunately, with a marketing plan that backfired. Though it addressed an aspirational Indian consumer, it focused excessively on the 'cheap' price of the product rather than on its many attractive product features. This resulted in significant customer pushback. Over the years, dwindling sales of the Tata Nano eventually led to calls for its withdrawal from the product mix at Tata Motors, and the plant in Gujarat that was supposed to produce hundreds of thousands of units of the vehicle was eventually utilized to manufacture other products from the Tata Motors stable.

Notwithstanding the setbacks on the business side, the Singur episode clearly demonstrated how much the Tata Group's values meant to it. There was no effort to try and enter into backroom deals to sort out the problem at Singur. Tata Motors had clearly and proudly responded to the conundrum. When core values—in this case, concern for the firm's image, its brand reputation, and the safety and well-being of its employees and partners—faced a challenge, the firm did not allow short-term business considerations to triumph. This meant a costly and time-consuming relocation of the Nano plant and accepting the serious financial consequences of this move.

There is also another lesser-known fact about the Tata commitment to invest in West Bengal. Alongside the Singur plant investment, Ratan Tata had promised the state government that a high-quality cancer treatment facility would be set up in the capital city of Kolkata, and it would be funded by several Tata companies and the Tata Trusts. This would draw upon the expertise of India's premier cancer treatment facility, the Tata Memorial Hospital in Mumbai, and would address the needs of the local population, who at the time had poor access to specialized cancer treatment within the state.

When the Nano plant was relocated out of the state, some expected that the investments of the Tata Trusts and companies in the cancer centre in Kolkata would be terminated. However, Ratan Tata was very clear that the Group's problems were with the political dispensation, not with the people of West Bengal. He promised that the investments would continue and the centre would be built. The Tata Medical Centre was eventually inaugurated in 2011 and has lived up to the promise of being a world-class facility accessible to the people of the state.

27
Personalities and Clashes of Values

THE SINGUR EPISODE DEMONSTRATED THAT WHEN ETHICAL CHALLENGES presented themselves, support in favour of doing the right thing was available at the very highest levels of the Tata Group. There are scores of tales from TAS officers, like Prakash Telang (TAS 1972) who was at the centre of the Singur storm, on how they never felt pressure from within the Group to compromise on their values. Their pride comes through clearly about the way the Group earned the goodwill of governments while standing up for what was right.

Another illustration Prakash readily offers relates to the manufacture of environmentally-friendly CNG buses at Tata Motors' Lucknow plant in the state of Uttar Pradesh (UP). Some vested interests in the then administration sought to deny permission to produce these buses at the Lucknow plant on spurious grounds linked to allegedly inadequate pollution control measures in the plant. Tata Motors recognized the expectation of back-handers embedded in this pressure tactic and stood its ground. Prakash, with the backing of the company's leadership, threatened that Tata Motors would transfer the production of the buses to another plant at its facilities in Dharwad in the state of Karnataka if UP denied permission. The state government blinked in the face-off and gave its approval to Tata Motors.

Similarly, TAS officers like Prateek Pashine (TAS 1995), who early on in his journey at Tatas blew the whistle on the unethical goings-on at a Tata joint venture operation, found great support at the very top. Prateek personally experienced Group Chairman Ratan Tata's genuine commitment to get to the truth of the matter and his support for whistle-blowers (including Prateek) who were facing intense pressure within the joint venture company at the time. When the Tatas eventually exited the joint venture, Ratan would take personal interest in finding Prateek his next assignment within the Group.

Ironically, then, given the commitment at the very top to sound values, TAS officers observed that some of the gravest risks of inappropriate conduct or departure from the Group's values stemmed from certain individuals who managed to gain proximity to the leadership and the Chairman. This happened on more than one occasion through the 1990s and the 2000s. Among the several larger-than-life figures who exercised considerable influence within the Group, and had run-ins with TAS officers in which they would usually come off as winners, were people like Dilip Pendse, Niira Radia and C. Sivasankaran.

These three individuals, each of whom is discussed in more detail in the subsequent chapters, enjoyed very close relationships for significant periods of time with Ratan. As many in the TAS note, they were as different from Ratan as is chalk from cheese. By taking the risk of indulging these adventurous individuals with interesting and provocative ideas, Ratan probably felt he would spur the Group to bolder accomplishments. Unfortunately, his close association with each of these individuals would raise questions about his judgement of character and people, when some of their actions came to attract controversy within and outside the Group.

Dr Mukund Rajan (TAS 1995) worked closely with Ratan at the time. Mukund says, 'It is not as if Ratan Tata would refuse to act when presented with compelling evidence of unethical or improper conduct. Ratan Tata could make difficult calls, even terminating relationships of long standing with very powerful individuals if he felt they had abused his trust.' Mukund offers the example of a long-serving officer who had risen through the ranks to become an Executive Director on the Board of Tata Motors.

Ratan admired this Tata Motors veteran's ambition and steely determination to pull himself up from the shop floor to the Board Room. However, this Executive Director could also be a difficult boss and colleague.

Bharat Wakhlu (TAS 1985) remembers attending—as a Graduate Engineer, well before he joined the TAS—a number of meetings that this experienced veteran would convene with his direct reports and their colleagues every morning. 'The meetings', Bharat reminisces, 'were always a tense affair. The veteran would ask questions about targets and the reasons, if any, for slip-ups. If he didn't like the answers given—even if there were reasons that were beyond anyone's control—he would pounce on the poor person who had responded. He would reprimand his hapless victim in the presence of all the others with a sound and abusive tongue-lashing!' Meetings with this veteran, says Bharat, gave him enough ideas to create a diary that he would call 'How *Not* to Manage People'!

The Executive Director's thirst for control saw him manoeuvre the exit of peers on the Board of Tata Motors. He would also have periodic face-offs with another capable Tata Motors' officer who was overseeing operations at the main Pune plant, and who had played a key role in the production of the Indica. Ratan warned the Executive Director that he had to mend his relationship with the officer so that the organization could secure the best of both the men's capabilities.

When the altercations between the two Tata Motors officers did not cease, and instead the junior officer volunteered to resign, Ratan intervened. Determined not to tolerate a situation that he felt had been deliberately created in spite of his warnings, he secured the resignation of the senior of the two, the Executive Director. It did not bother him that the Executive Director was a very influential manager with over forty years of service in the company, and was well networked not only in the Tata Motors' system, but also within the Indian automotive vendor community. The next day the press reported that the gentleman had quit on health grounds and had proceeded on sick leave.

For Mukund, this case demonstrates that Ratan did not shy away from difficult decisions. Other TAS officers who served in Tata Motors at the time, however, point out that the problem was not the ultimate decision, but the delay in reaching this decision point. A lot of unnecessary damage was done by the Executive Director during the time he held office, with several TAS officers who were at the receiving end of his bullying and humiliation opting to quit the company.

There were also allegations of conflicts of interest, including some arising from business being undertaken by the Executive Director's own son, who had set up a company to produce automotive seating systems. A number of dealers also plucked up the courage to complain to the Chairman about the channel stuffing pressures they were encountering. Several TAS officers who were in the company at the time claim that they reported their concerns to Ratan, but no action was forthcoming until he personally experienced the Executive Director's insincerity.

Perhaps Ratan did not believe all the negative feedback he received. He may have felt some of the TAS officers had vested interests in ganging up against the Executive Director who they may have seen as being inadequately qualified for the position he held. Possibly he was looking for clear evidence and actionable data, which can often be difficult to find. Be that as it may, what this does underline is the need for good judgement—especially about people one may rely upon—at the very top, and a willingness of the top person to heed the notes of caution and be receptive to occasional dissent that advisors may strike.

28

Dilip Pendse and the Tata Finance Scandal

DILIP PENDSE WAS ONE OF THE MOST CONTROVERSIAL PERSONALITIES IN the Tata Group. Of humble beginnings, he was not the genteel South-Mumbai-raised manager that one would often find at Bombay House (the Tata headquarters). He had instead journeyed from the urban middle-class sprawl of Dombivali to the Tata offices in South Mumbai. His father was a small-time businessman, and Pendse had studied in a Marathi-medium school, graduating in commerce before qualifying as a Company Secretary and studying law.

Dilip's smart handling of various matters for Ajit Kerkar and his capacity for hard work had him quickly climbing the ranks of the company secretarial department at Indian Hotels. His resourcefulness in tackling problems caught Ratan Tata's eye, and he soon became one of his closest protégés.

Ratan inducted Dilip into Tata Industries, which he was reshaping into a new technologies vehicle for the Tata Group on the back of his 1983 Strategic Plan. As Vice President of Tata Industries, Dilip oversaw the creation of a series of joint ventures that followed with hallowed names like Honeywell, AT&T and IBM. At one time, Dilip would serve on the Boards of as many as eighteen Tata companies. With significant delegated powers, including the influence that inevitably came from the placement of his loyalists in various managerial positions, Dilip enjoyed huge influence within Tata Sons and the broader Tata ecosystem.

An example of the influence Dilip wielded was his role in recommending a candidate for the role of Chief Financial Officer at Tata Motors in the late 1990s. Dilip had worked closely with this candidate at Tata IBM. The level of trust he enjoyed with Ratan at the time was so high that his recommendation was promptly accepted for this critical role at Tata Motors.

Dr Mukund Rajan (TAS 1995) notes that soon after his entry into the Chairman's office, he became aware of some complaints made to Ratan about Dilip by Tata colleagues. There were rumours about the latter's role in some questionable transactions, including the way he managed sensitive property matters for some senior Tata executives. Ratan's response to the complaints he did receive, typically, was to demand concrete evidence of wrongdoing. If this was not forthcoming, as was often the case, he would let the matter drop.

Several TAS officers from the time, however, believe that Ratan should have heeded the concerns expressed about Dilip's integrity. They empathize with the challenges faced by those who carried such concerns to Ratan—it would have taken courage to carry complaints about somebody who was clearly trusted by the organization's leader. Dilip, for his part, would consistently drop Ratan's name to get his work done, and as a Board member of Tata Finance would later acknowledge, even Board Directors were in awe of him and lacked the courage to check back on his assertions of having cleared various issues with the Group Chairman.

It is unclear if the repeated allegations against Dilip created growing unease in Ratan's mind. Certainly, he seized with alacrity the opportunity to move Dilip out of Tata Industries into another Tata company, Tata Finance Ltd, when the top job there opened up in 1996. Whether done deliberately or not, this led to a significant decline in Dilip's proximity to Ratan and the associated influence that he wielded at the Group Centre.

Correspondingly, at Tata Finance, there were several departures from the Board once it became clear that the fortunes of the company were being entrusted to Dilip. Among those who would choose to opt out of the Tata Finance Board were well-regarded senior Tata executives with a reputation for integrity, including the then Finance Director of Tata Sons, Noshir Soonawala, and an old Tata hand, Subbaraman.

As it happened, the opening at Tata Finance occurred in the wake of the departure of the previous incumbent, a TAS officer from the 1975 batch, Partha Sarkar. Partha had worked closely with Ratan as his Executive Assistant in the past. However, some arguably poorly conceived investments in government securities at Tata Finance and alleged misinformation about these engineered by Dilip, led to Partha's resignation and exit from the Group.

Dilip thereafter embraced the opportunity to run his own shop with both hands. He had ambitions of building Tata Finance into India's most successful financial services company. Overnight, he injected new energy and a frenetic pace of growth into the business, inducting joint venture partners like American Express, Abbey National and T.D. Waterhouse. As events unfolded, however, Dilip would be found to have indulged in a series of unethical activities that eventually destroyed Tata Finance and hurt the reputation of Ratan and the Tata Group.

The Tata Finance scandal was first brought to light by a letter from an anonymous whistle-blower in 2001. The letter alleged that significant losses of hundreds of crores of rupees had been incurred by the company as a result of the speculative positions in the stock market taken on Dilip's instructions. The detailed nature of the disclosures made it incumbent on the Board to order a full inquiry, and in the course of the investigations, a number of skeletons came tumbling out.

These included the fact that some individuals, including Dilip, had made personal gains at the company's expense and transferred personal losses to the company's account. This was a time when risk-management protocols, audit trails and information systems were still relatively weak in the Indian market, and Dilip and his cronies could get away with hiding their activities for a while. However, the sudden collapse of key stocks in which they had been investing, including the infamous Ketan Parekh Stocks (named after a stock broker who was eventually jailed for market manipulation), left them exposed.

As the mess created by Dilip in the company assumed large proportions, he decided to leave Tata Finance. He secured a new assignment outside the Tata Group, as President of Global Telesystems in North America, and made plans to leave for the US. However, the Board of Tata Finance finally woke up to the disaster he would be leaving behind for them to manage, and after due consultations with Ratan, resolved to sack Dilip on his last day at work. In the subsequent investigations, a host of malpractices at Tata Finance were uncovered, including real estate transactions undertaken at inflated prices, self-dealing, and loans extended to undeserving subprime corporates and some auto dealers who were close to Dilip, which were then defaulted upon.

Eventually, criminal cases were filed against Dilip and others, and he did spend some years in jail. This hardworking and brilliant, albeit flawed individual, years later paid the ultimate price in his tragic life by committing suicide in 2017 while still fighting a number of cases in various courts against the Tata Group and different regulators.

Dilip's departure, along with several of his senior team who were also asked to leave, resulted in a leadership vacuum at the top. This was eventually filled by placing a TAS officer, Francis DaCunha (TAS 1971), as the Managing Director. Francis was plucked by Group's Finance Director, Ishaat Hussain, from Tata Special Steels Ltd, where he was the Joint Managing Director, prior to this company's merger with TISCO.

Francis undertook a wholesale clean-up of Tata Finance. On his arrival at the company, he immediately achieved a saving of Rs 1 crore by scrapping the practice of handing out expensive Diwali gifts that Dilip had started. The gifts were given to politicians, bureaucrats and regulators, among others!

Francis received full support from the Group in addressing all of Tata Finance's issues; in his words, the affair had become *izzat ki baat*, or an issue of reputation, for the Tata Group. Each and every depositor in the company was repaid in full. Tata Sons as the holding company pumped in some Rs 300 crores to allow depositors to be repaid, and other dues were squared off by selling the company's assets.

At the instance of Ratan, full disclosure of all misconduct by Tata Finance and its officers was made to the relevant regulators, including the Securities and Exchange Board of India (SEBI) and the Reserve Bank of India (RBI). How difficult a decision this must have been can be gauged from the fact that some cases filed by the regulators against Tata companies on the strength of these voluntary disclosures are still being prosecuted a decade and half later.

Francis oversaw the eventual closure of Tata Finance in 2005, which put paid to the Group's ambitions at the time of its becoming a major financial services player. This was a huge setback. Given the Group's reputation for good governance and for generally running clean businesses, it should have been possible to leverage the Tata brand to build an extremely powerful financial services vehicle. Instead, it would take several years before the Group once again plucked up the courage to re-enter the financial services space by launching a new company, Tata Capital.

In a demonstration of gracelessness, the Tata Group dragged its feet in appointing Francis to another senior role within the conglomerate after his stint at Tata Finance, and he chose instead to take premature retirement. His case is not unique—over the years, a number of Tata officers, hand-picked to serve as trouble-shooters for diverse Tata companies in difficult situations, have been left to fend for themselves after having effectively discharged their duties. This mercenary approach fuels the view that while talent in the Tata Group is indeed valued, many senior leaders have been unwilling to go that extra mile to ensure that good people are retained in the Group. Group HR, in a peculiar show of acquiescence, has invariably played along, instead of suggesting alternatives to retain experienced talent.

One of the major learnings from the Tata Finance episode was the need for, in the words of Francis, 'a powerful corporate audit function, and a strong risk team that reports to a strong audit committee without getting overawed by a powerful Managing Director.' The internal audit professional in Tata Finance had been very junior and was hardly likely to blow the whistle.

The Tata Finance episode also demonstrated the dangers of allowing CEOs of companies to stuff the Boards of subsidiary companies with favoured friends and those who reported directly to them. Some of Dilip's misconduct could have been caught in time if the Tata Finance subsidiaries had truly independent directors on their Boards who could have asked difficult questions without fear. The Group General Counsel, Bharat Vasani, who joined at the time of the Tata Finance scam, later circulated an advisory to all Tata companies, pointing out the need to ensure the independence of Boards and to monitor, at the parent Board level, the activities of subsidiary companies.

The Tata Finance scandal also underlined the attention that must be paid to whistle-blower complaints. In the years since, formal whistle-blower legislation has been enacted by the government, which makes it incumbent on companies to define a policy and create a process for consideration of such complaints, protecting the whistle-blowers' identities and safeguarding them from vindictive action.

Yet, too often, whistle-blower complaints continue to be made anonymously, for fear of retribution by influential managers whose conduct could come under the scanner as a result of the complaints. It is also the case that some anonymous whistle-blower allegations, unfortunately, prove to be unfounded and without merit, and are used to settle scores with rivals. Investigating them can result in the unfair humiliation and demoralization of those whom they seek to target.

It is therefore incumbent on ethics counsellors, senior leaders and the Board of Directors, especially the Audit Committee Chairmen to whom anonymous whistle-blower complaints are often addressed, to assess the nature of these accusations. Where there seems to be accurate and verifiable data, the complaints must definitely be probed, but where data are missing and the allegations seem motivated and subjective, no investigation may be necessary. To ensure no slip-ups, however, it helps for the organization to be vigilant.

The Board of Directors of Tata Finance had overseen the self-destruction of the company, and was clearly found wanting. Some of the Tata Finance Directors had established beneficial and intimate relationships with Dilip, including privileged access to share purchase offers he would syndicate. An otherwise respectable Director had even leased his apartment to Tata Finance, allegedly on an informal understanding that it would never actually be occupied, so as to retain it in pristine condition while still earning from it! With some prodding, the members of the Board were eventually persuaded to accept moral responsibility for the debacle and collectively resign.

The Tata Finance episode sank the reputation of Dr Freddie Mehta, the very first person to be appointed to the TAS, and the first TAS officer to also serve on the Board of Tata Sons. As the Chairman of Tata Finance, Freddie had overseen its decline under Dilip. As a recipient of daily Net Asset Value (NAV) statements of Tata Finance's exposure in the stock markets, he could not but have known about the predicament the company was facing, thanks to Dilip's speculative investments. Perhaps he did not realize the magnitude of the problem. He certainly treated Dilip with great consideration and affection in public, and one surmises, therefore, that he must have felt even more betrayed when the latter turned rogue.

Within the Tata Group, there were many lessons to be learnt from the Tata Finance scam. These included, perhaps most importantly, the need for Boards to oversee Tata companies and their subsidiaries better, putting in checks and balances to rein in overly powerful or adventurous chief executives, and preventing CEOs from stuffing Boards with their chosen favourites and yes-men. It also highlighted the risks embedded in having overly powerful personalities in any role, including that of the Group Chairman, without adequate checks and balances in place to mitigate errors of judgement.

29

Niira Radia and Vaishnavi Communications

THE TATA FINANCE EPISODE HAD ONE FAR-REACHING CONSEQUENCE. This was the introduction of a new construct within the Tata Group—a Group-wide public relations advisory mandate. The task of instituting this was entrusted to an organization, Vaishnavi Communications, created specifically to service the Tata account. Vaishnavi Communications was led by somebody who would herself acquire considerable notoriety in time—Niira Radia.

Niira came to command significant influence within the Tata Group. Her style of functioning and the manner in which she would navigate the corridors of power, however, would create unease in the minds of many Tata CEOs and TAS officers. After she became mired in the so-called 2G scandal, questions would—once again—be asked about the judgement of Ratan Tata who had allowed her unprecedented access within the Group. It is therefore important to understand why this came about.

The Tata Finance scandal had seen the Tata Group and Ratan's reputations smeared for a while. Dilip Pendse made allegations that he was merely a scapegoat for the troubles at the company. A leak to the media about the withdrawal of a sensitive (and tainted) forensic audit report also created confusion on whether the Tata Group was strong-arming the audit firm that prepared the report to withdraw it merely because its conclusions might be inconvenient. Dr Mukund Rajan (TAS 1995) has this to say: 'There were senior executives within the Group who saw the opportunity to feed the media with adverse information about their colleagues and revelled in their discomfiture.' The Tata Group was coming across as a house divided, and the episode underlined the need to establish and control a consistent narrative from within the Tata Group. This was where Niira stepped in.

Niira was originally an aviation industry specialist. Her father, an Indian settled in Kenya who later moved to Britain, had been close to a number of members of the Bharatiya Janata Party (BJP) whose coalition government, the National Democratic Alliance (NDA), was then in power in Delhi. Niira had spent several years in London, where she built up an aircraft leasing and consulting practice. After her marriage ended in divorce, she decided to pursue business opportunities in India in the early 1990s.

The gutsy and straight-talking woman quickly made a mark in Delhi circles, serving as an advisor for some time to the controversial Subroto Roy Sahara, who had launched his own domestic airline. She was first introduced to Ratan in the late 1990s when discussions were going on with the Government of India about possible acquisition of management control in Air India by the Tata Group.

Ratan was impressed by Niira's knowledge of the aviation sector and her insights on how the government and bureaucracy tended to operate in India. The specific trigger, however, that hastened her entry into the affairs of the Tata Group, was a sustained campaign through late 2002 by a financial daily, *The Financial Express,* against the Tata Group, on its handling of the Tata Finance matter.

The Financial Express would reproduce, a page at a time and almost on a daily basis, damning sections from the tainted report of the audit firm appointed to look into the Tata Finance scam. The Tata Group's desire to protect key witnesses privy to the manner in which the audit report had been compromised for unethical considerations, meant that it was unable to fully clarify its stance on the report. It was also unnerved by the hostile reception it encountered in response to an advertisement criticizing the campaign of vilification against it. The Group's response was coming across as directionless and flat-footed. Enter Niira.

Niira felt that the Tata Group simply did not leverage its many strengths in handling the media well. She believed that the Tata companies and their senior executives, for the most part, tended to be reluctant to engage with the media and were quite chary of building relationships with journalists who covered their areas of business. This meant that the media needed to find other avenues to secure information about the Group, including rival companies. She also felt that the Group was not leveraging its overall advertising spend in a cohesive and focused manner to secure better engagement and essential courtesies from the media. Each Tata company, moreover, had its own style and manner of corporate communication and media engagement, and there was no effort at coordination across companies.

Bharat Wakhlu (TAS 1985) points out that during JRD's time, Sharokh Sabavala, Jamshed Bhabha and a few others in Tata Sons played a key role in ensuring that the Tata Group's responses to issues were integrated and harmonized. They also ensured that the Group's concerns and challenges were regularly discussed with the corporate communications and public relations professionals of the larger Tata Group companies, ensuring alignment and cohesion across the Group. These actions ceased after Sharokh Sabavala retired, and the lack of cohesion had definitely emerged as an area of weakness in the Tata Group's external communications approach by the end of the 1990s.

To prevent further drift and to bring back a degree of cohesion in the Group's response to externally emanating communications challenges, Ratan used a heavy hand to do what he considered the appropriate thing for the Group. He persuaded his colleagues to appoint Niira and Vaishnavi Communications, the agency she had created to provide dedicated support for the Group's needs, as advisors on public relations and media management.

Initially, this appointment did not go down well with many of the CEOs who were prodded to take on the services of Vaishnavi and jettison agencies or public relations consultants they might have been working with for years. When a few senior Tata leaders asked R.K. Krishna Kumar (TAS 1963), by then on the Board of Tata Sons, the reasons for hiring a public relations firm for the entire Group, the cryptic response was, 'This is a fait accompli. It just has to be done.' Eventually, as in the case of Dilip Pendse, protests gradually became more muted, as the perception grew that the Group Chairman was in favour of the change.

Over time, Niira became familiar with the different leadership styles and personalities of the Tata CEOs and was able to win over several of them by supporting them through her significant networks and information gathering systems organized across New Delhi and other major cities. Some Tata CEOs who didn't agree with Niira's suggestions or methods were bluntly warned that she would complain to the Chairman about them and tell him that they were preventing the unfurling of the 'grand communications strategy' that she was trying to execute.

Over time, the personal equations Niira cultivated with most of the media, especially on the editorial side, her strong connects with the political establishment on both sides of the aisle and her enormous energy helped her to effectively communicate the Group's perspectives on various issues to the media, and also to proactively alert senior Tata executives to the significance of various government initiatives and policies.

Mukund recollects her valuable intervention in brokering peace for the Tata Group with Telecom Minister Pramod Mahajan in 2002. At the time, Mahajan was one of the most visible and voluble members of the Union Cabinet. The dispute with Mahajan arose from a decision by the then recently privatized VSNL, under Tata management, to invest in the equity of another Tata telecom enterprise, Tata Teleservices Ltd (TTSL). Mahajan, without the benefit of a detailed brief from the bureaucrats in his ministry who served on the VSNL Board, went public with his disapproval of the Board's action in approving a related-party transaction. He accused the Tatas of 'asset stripping'.

The ensuing controversy required Niira to reach out to Mahajan through various mutual friends and Ministers of the ruling NDA. She was eventually able to convince him about the merits of the VSNL Board decision and the importance of a rapprochement with Tatas.

Niira brought to Ratan a more nuanced understanding of the policy orientation of Ministers, the political class and the bureaucracy. Her access to Ratan and ability to move swiftly to act on insights she gleaned from Delhi made her quite effective in several situations. Ratan consequently grew to rely considerably on Niira's understanding of the complicated politics of the country and the workings of the bureaucracy. Her influence within the Tata Group correspondingly increased.

Niira was able to get things done in Tata companies through the CEOs who worried that if they did not cooperate with her, word would get back to Ratan about their lack of support. Several Tata CEOs also hit upon a stratagem of trying to use her as a conduit to have good things said about them to the Group Chairman!

Niira's capability was demonstrated vividly when, some years after her appointment at the Tata Group, another major Indian corporate house, Mukesh Ambani's Reliance Industries, also offered her a retainership. By creating an arm's-length relationship between Vaishnavi and a new company created to separately service the Reliance account, she was able to meet the expectations of two of India's most powerful corporate chieftains.

By the time the arrangement with Reliance was inked, Mukesh Ambani had temporarily withdrawn from the telecom industry as part of a family settlement reached with his brother, Anil Ambani. This limited the explicit conflict of interest between the Tatas' lines of businesses and those undertaken by the Mukesh Ambani-run Reliance to then relatively minor areas of business operations, like retail. However, there were many raised eyebrows within the Tata Group about the willingness to allow Vaishnavi's boss, who was now privy to some of the organization's most intimate secrets, to work with a long-standing competitor.

Niira became what might be described as an extra-constitutional authority, with accountability almost exclusively to Ratan. On paper, Vaishnavi's contract would be overseen by Tata Sons' Director responsible for Group Corporate Communications, R. Gopalakrishnan, but in practice it was the huge value that Ratan placed on her services and capabilities that counted.

Mukund observes that Ratan Tata would frequently identify extremely talented individuals from outside the Tata Group, often with some inbuilt angularities, personality quirks or sharp elbows, and thrust them upon professional managers in the companies. The strong reactions which such individuals would provoke were occasionally helpful in catalysing some of the changes needed within the Tata system. The downside to this was that these individuals were not accountable to the normal chain of command and their influence could lead to the erosion of well-established Group values. This could adversely impact the morale and professional work ethic of senior Tata executives. Indeed, it did in Niira's case when a huge controversy was stirred up over her role in the so-called 2G Scam.

Unbeknown to Niira, a government inquiry into the affairs of Vaishnavi had resulted in the tapping of her phones. The tapes and transcripts of many of her delicate and sensitive conversations found their way into the hands of a corporate rival of Tatas, and thence to the media. Among other things, these tapes suggested a role played by Niira in the so-called 2G Scam.

The 2G Scam essentially involved the sale by the Indian government in 2008 of mobile telecom licences supported by 2G spectrum on a first-come-first-serve basis to well-connected companies. The price of the 2G spectrum was linked to prices discovered in 2001, ostensibly to provide a level playing field for the new entrants with the incumbent operators. Several of the new licensees then proceeded to sell stakes in their companies at a significant profit.

In total, the Indian Telecom Ministry, led by Minister A. Raja, granted 122 telecom licences to various companies. In its 2010–11 audit report, the Comptroller and Auditor General (CAG) of India concluded that the allocation of these licences was characterized by policy gaps and irregularities in procedure. By not adopting market-based auction mechanisms, and instead administratively allocating licences at prices discovered in 2001 on the pretext of providing a level playing field with incumbent operators, there had been a massive loss of revenue to the government.

In the fracas that followed in Parliament, the government felt compelled to order an investigation by the Central Bureau of Investigation (CBI). Minister Raja was forced to resign from the Union Cabinet in November 2010. He and nine others were arrested in February 2011. Several corporate leaders from companies like Unitech, DB Realty, and the Anil Dhirubhai Ambani Group (ADAG) were also arrested.

The CBI filed a charge sheet in April 2011 against Raja and others for causing loss to the Exchequer in the allocation of telecom licences. They were tried under the Prevention of Corruption Act for criminal conspiracy, cheating, forgery, abusing official position, criminal misconduct by a public servant and taking bribes. In February 2012, the Supreme Court struck down the flawed first-come-first-serve spectrum allocation policy. It described the allocation of licences by Minister Raja as arbitrary and unconstitutional, and cancelled the 122 licences that had been issued during his time.

Within the 2G Scam, grave questions were raised about the propriety of a Tata Realty deal with Unitech, one of the real estate players that took telecom licences under Minister Raja's liberalized regime and quickly realized significant value by inducting a foreign partner, Telenor, at a handsome valuation. Bharat, then the Resident Director of the Tata Group in Delhi, recalls raising a red flag on the optics of the deal on several occasions, including through confidential notes and personal meetings with the Group Chairman and others. However, his words were not heeded in the face of strong pressure from Niira to get the deal with Tata Realty done.

The Tata Realty deal was alleged to have delivered the financing Unitech needed to secure the cost of its telecom licence, though the Tata Group vehemently denied any connection between the two transactions. Niira was alleged to have brokered the controversial transaction, with powerful support on the Tata Sons board from Tata Realty's Chairman, R.K. Krishna Kumar. A Tata Sons' Board member from the time discloses that the name of the counterparty (Unitech) was initially not shared with the Board, and the manner in which approval for the transaction was secured created misgivings amongst some Directors.

The 2G controversy took the sheen off Ratan's reputation and exposed him to significant criticism. A number of senior Tata leaders, including Ratan, the Managing Director of Tata Teleservices, Anil Sardana, and Krishna in his capacity as Chairman of Tata Realty, were summoned to answer questions by members of Parliament and the law enforcement agencies probing the 2G affair.

The revelations about Niira's delicate interactions with various politicians, including lobbying in support of some for specific ministerial berths and taped conversations that seemed to suggest that members of the media had been compromised in their pursuit of honest and accurate reporting made the continuance of her public relations mandate for the Tata Group untenable. In the midst of a public relations' disaster, and with several law enforcement agencies lining up to interrogate her, Niira felt compelled to withdraw from the Tata mandate. Vaishnavi, the organization she had set up to exclusively service Tata Group companies, was eventually closed down.

The harsh glare of the media upon her and the can of worms opened up by her involvement in the 2G controversy did not surprise some old Tata watchers and TAS officers. They would point to Ratan's mixed track record of selecting close advisors and say, 'I told you so!'

30

Sivasankaran and the Tatas' Tryst with Telecom

In an earlier chapter we have seen how the telecom sector was first opened up to private sector participation in the 1990s and quickly attracted a large number of TAS officers. These officers were drawn by a combination of factors, including the fast-paced growth of the sector, the rapidly evolving technology supporting this growth, the exciting array of services it was fuelling from education to banking, and the largest capital deployment in the Tata Group's history.

Telecom was seen as a sector where the natural draw of the Tata brand, with its commitment to protecting customer interests, should have worked well in building a strong national presence. Several TAS officers invested the prime years of their careers in the telecom sector, including S. Ramakrishnan (TAS 1972), Jehangir Ardeshir (TAS 1983), N. Srinath (TAS 1986), Harish Bhat (TAS 1987), Prateek Pashine (TAS 1995), and a number of others. It would not be an exaggeration to say that some of the best managerial talent in the Tata Group was made available to the telecom business.

Yet, in truth, the story of the Tatas' long dalliance with the sector is one of missed opportunities and inconsistent and unstable leadership. When the Indian telecom market was first opened for private sector investment, the Group delayed deploying the large sums of capital some of its competitors were willing to invest to gain first mover advantages. Smaller companies like Airtel and Aircel that were willing to commit fully and deploy large resources thus got off to a much better start.

On the technology front, the Group selected what seemed to be a better mobile technology in the form of Code Division Multiple Access (CDMA) technology, only to give it up in favour of Global System for Mobile (GSM) technology after some years. It became a large retailer of devices, given its early dependency on CDMA handsets that worked exclusively on its network, but then abandoned what could have become a profitable national electronic retail footprint after the launch of its GSM services.

The Group undertook significant optical fibre build-out that could support broadband services (whose critical relevance has become particularly visible during the COVID crisis), only to slow down investment later in order to preserve capital for participation in the expensive auction of 3G spectrum and the subsequent launch of wireless 3G services. It signed on a world-class partner in the form of NTT Docomo, the pioneers of 3G services in Japan and the world, but lost them after a spate of litigation in India led to their losing interest in the Indian market.

The Tatas successfully bid in 2002 to acquire majority ownership and management control of the government-owned VSNL, a large and very profitable business, principally engaged in long-distance voice and data carriage and enterprise business support, and the pioneer of internet services in India. But the Group, as we saw in the previous chapter, soon got embroiled in a spat with its partner, the central government, over misunderstandings linked to investments that VSNL sought to make in TTSL.

Even as VSNL sought to resolve its issues with the government, the newly created regulator appointed by the government, the Telecom Regulatory Authority of India (TRAI), focused significant attention on busting all relics of the earlier monopoly environment in which the company used to thrive. VSNL also failed to take advantage of its reputation as the pioneer of internet services in India and made a slow start in upgrading its network capabilities and data-throughput speeds to enable broadband services. It made some calamitous efforts to partner with local cable operators to secure access to customer homes, with terrible customer service to boot, effectively dooming its retail play in India. On the other hand, it made little effort to collaborate with the Group's software services company, TCS, to offer convergent enterprise voice and data services.

Worst of all, during a critical and formative time span of six years, the Tata Group changed as many as seven leaders at the sister telecom companies offering mobile services, TTSL and TTSL (Maharashtra). As a result of the frequent leadership changes, consistent strategies were not followed at these companies.

Dr Mukund Rajan (TAS 1995), then a member of the Board of TTSL, opines that 'these companies were not well served by many of the Board Directors' lack of deep technological insight and their unwillingness or inability to think really big and commit resources in pursuit of such ambition.' He recollects one instance when the Board members seriously debated whether or not the company should become a pure play fixed wireless company on the back of the traction it had been experiencing with fixed wireless phones that were called 'Walkies'. It took significant dialogue and the threat of dissent on Mukund's part for the move to be dropped. Mukund points out, 'Had such a call been taken at the time, TTSL would have missed out on much of the mobile telephony revolution in India! My dissent was viewed constructively by the Chairman of the Company, Dr Jamshed Irani, and the move to abandon mobility was fortunately dropped.'

It was in this milieu that an exasperated Ratan Tata brought into the business C. Sivasankaran, known to his associates as Siva. Siva happened to meet Ratan on one of his trips to the US and deeply impressed him with his knowledge of telecom and his vision of how the sector was likely to evolve in India. Having established a successful telecom play, Aircel, in South India, Siva had built an intimate understanding of the key drivers of success in this sector. He offered Ratan help.

Mukund, then part of the Group Chairman's office, coordinated many of Siva's interactions with the Tata telecom executives. He observes that they quickly learnt to respect Siva's formidable knowledge of the telecom sector and his lateral thinking. Short, stocky, swarthy in complexion and with a fiery temper, this only son of a schoolteacher had bet the shirt on his back to become a successful entrepreneur. He would closely track his competitors and was a fount of knowledge about the corners that were being cut by entrepreneurs to achieve success within the system.

Those who mistook Siva's claims for mere braggadocio would be in for a shock when they found out that they had miscalculated his native intelligence, his capacity to bend the system to his will and, most importantly, his ability to put in a great deal of hard work to analyse all aspects of any situation and then negotiate ruthlessly to improve his interests. A media house described the Tamil entrepreneur as 'the Southern Ambani'.

Over a few briefings delivered by TAS officers like S. Ramakrishnan, then the Managing Director of TTSL, and N. Srinath, the Executive Director of VSNL, Siva gained a comprehensive understanding of the situation the Tatas were facing in telecom. He did not mince any words in giving his feedback to Ratan. His assessment, in a nutshell, was that VSNL was swiftly losing its market dominance, thanks to a failure to build out its hitherto-dominant infrastructure and services play in data carriage. Meanwhile, TTSL was suffering from limited vision and capacity to compete at scale with large players like Reliance and Bharti as well as with the early and more adventurous entrants in the wireless mobility space.

Siva encouraged VSNL to build its own Chennai–Singapore submarine cable to compete with the infrastructure that was being created by its rival, Bharti. This infrastructural addition was complemented by VSNL's acquisition of the Tyco Global Network from Tyco International in 2004. The Tyco acquisition for a few cents on the dollar, part of the overall strategy of internationalization then being pursued by the Tata Group, made VSNL the world's largest submarine cable network operator. Siva also identified Vinod Kumar, then a senior executive with Asia Netcom, as a useful resource to manage the company's growing network. Vinod would eventually become VSNL's Managing Director.

On the TTSL front, Siva understood how vital it was to get costs down. He volunteered to negotiate ambitious and lucrative deals with vendors for the Tatas. Mukund vouches that he did a splendid job of this. He negotiated critical CDMA handset delivery contracts and telecom network infrastructure contracts for TTSL at prices dramatically lower than anything that had been delivered till that point of time.

Siva realized substantial commercial benefits from the relationships he built with Ratan and the Tata Group. He was able to sell his internet access company, Dishnet DSL, to VSNL for a good price. Subsequently, he landed large contracts with TTSL to manage the company's network infrastructure rollout. The icing on the cake for him would have been securing shares of TTSL at a modest entry price and on very favourable transaction terms, where, as has been publicly reported, Tata Group entities even extended inter-corporate loans to him to facilitate his acquisition of the Tata shares!

Years later, several of Siva's transactions became embroiled in significant controversy in the midst of the Ratan Tata–Cyrus Mistry spat. A loan he was provided by Tata Capital against the pledge of TTSL shares was not repaid, leaving the company holding papers that by then had depreciated considerably in value. Siva also refused to compensate the Tatas for his portion of a pre-committed shareholder buyback of NTT Docomo's shares by TTSL, and this matter eventually headed towards litigation. Once again, Ratan Tata's critics had a stick to beat him with, saying that his mixed track record in selecting advisors eventually hurt him and the Group.

Jehangir Ardeshir (TAS 1983) gained a ringside view of the constant churn taking place in the telecom business at Tata for nearly four years. In late 2004, towards the end of his tenure as CEO of TQMS, Jehangir was asked to meet the Group Chairman at his office in Bombay House. He said to Jehangir, 'TTSL is a company in crisis. Are you prepared to throw your hat in the ring?' Jehangir's former TISCO senior, Firdose Vandrevala, was the then Chairman of TTSL, and with the then TISCO Managing Director B. Muthuraman's approval, Jehangir answered the call of duty and happily moved to TTSL (rather than back to TISCO after his stint at TQMS, as had originally been envisaged).

Jehangir was initially appointed President of Customer Care at TTSL. Later he became the President of Business Improvement and also handled Branded Retail. What he discovered in TTSL was 'a complete mess'. With frequent management and leadership changes, myriad mistakes being made, ten Presidents and no Managing Director for too long a time, and as a very late strategic entrant into the industry, the company had arrived at a place from which it simply could not be successful, a view he formed soon after joining and which deepened as the months progressed. He would share this perspective with the Group Chairman in 2007, when he was called in for discussions about the future direction of the company, after the departure of an expatriate CEO, Darryl Green.

Jehangir recalls sharing his belief with the Group Chairman that TTSL did not have the capability to hold its own in the very tough and unscrupulous telecom market place. He suggested that the Group cut its losses and exit the business, and in response, he was told that the Group was in telecom for the long game. At the time, the business had already racked up accumulated losses of over Rs 3,500 crore, and while large, this quantum of losses must be compared with the subsequent write-offs, of some twenty times this amount, taken by the Group after a further decade had elapsed.

Jehangir later heard from two Tata Group seniors that he had since been perceived as too negative, and he eventually chose to leave TTSL and the Tata Group around a year or so after that last conversation. He was, by then, also deeply disillusioned about some of the tactics he witnessed being adopted in the telecom business, including what he felt was an unnecessary reliance on external advisors who did not seem to share the Group's values.

Jaspreet Bindra (TAS 1994), another TAS officer who spent over half a decade with the Tatas' telecom business during its formative period, offers an interesting insight. He singles out 'smart regulatory interface' as the key success factor for doing well in the industry. This impacted a host of issues, ranging from licence fee payments, to spectrum allocation for mobility operations, to permissible new product offerings in the market. He believes that a values-driven group like Tatas should have quickly understood that it was not cut out for success in a business where so much depended on regulatory favour and support. He agrees with Jehangir that the Group should have pulled the plug on the telecom business much sooner than it eventually did.

31

The Imperative of Checks and Balances

IN ANY ORGANIZATION, THERE IS A NEED FOR ADEQUATE CHECKS AND balances to ensure abuses of power do not occur; but if they do, they are swiftly curbed, and there is accountability for decisions and actions taken by senior leaders. It could be argued that poor advice from his inner circle and inadequate checks and balances on the power of the Tata Group Chairman yielded situations in which individuals like Dilip Pendse, Niira Radia and Siva were able to leverage their proximity to Ratan Tata and exercise considerable power and influence within the Tata Group. But what of the role of senior TAS officers who may have been able to blow the whistle on the wrongs they may have seen being committed, or the strategies they may have disagreed with?

It does appear that there were relatively few senior TAS officers who had sufficient visibility of what was happening in the spheres controlled by Dilip, Niira and Siva, be it the affairs of Tata Finance, or the building of relationships with the media, or the execution of the Group's telecom strategy. Conversations with those who did have some visibility suggest that some of them did take their concerns to Ratan, but they did not get a very receptive hearing.

In a few cases, there was perhaps a degree of awe in the presence of the Group Chairman and a reluctance to challenge decisions that seemed to have his blessings. By the time individuals like Niira and Siva arrived on the scene, Ratan had become a strong, self-confident leader with a stature that was growing into that of a global corporate statesman. It would require a brave soul who would want to discuss or debate controversial questions with him, especially those on which he was judged to have a strong point of view.

Several TAS officers did record their concerns with the next level of leadership, including members of the GCC and Tata Sons' Board, but came away without any meaningful action resulting from their disclosures. All this points to excessive powers being wielded by the office of the Tata Group Chairman, and the overwhelming control and dominance of whoever occupies the chair.

Dr Mukund Rajan (TAS 1995) notes that it is lonely at the top, and Ratan's growing isolation over the decades made him lose the spontaneous mirth and sense of fun he used to display in the early years of his leadership. Looking at the almost permanent frown that had developed on his brow, Mukund would even comment in his farewell essay when Ratan was stepping down in 2012, 'If I had to give only one message to Mr Tata, it would be this—you have done your duty, now I wish the frowns and burdens vanish from your forehead, and the smile comes back permanently to your handsome face.'

As Ratan neared the end of his final term as Chairman, with over $100 billion worth revenues clocked in 2012, the Tata Group was achieving heights no other Indian business group had touched. But in an ironic twist of fate, its brand reputation was taking a serious beating at the exact same time: thanks to the 2G Scam and a variety of allegations made against the Tata Group and Ratan Tata.

32

A New Chairman

Echoing the 'After Nehru, who?' concern about the successor to India's first Prime Minister, the question on everyone's lips towards the end of Ratan Tata's tenure as Group Chairman was, 'After Ratan, who?'

Ratan Tata's age, stature, dominant personality and the manner in which he had completely stamped his authority over the Tata Group meant that there would be few individuals within the Group who could fit into the large shoes he was wearing. An extended search, significantly shrouded in secrecy, seemed to throw up very few names from within the Group. None of these were from the TAS—a significant commentary on the manner in which the service had been managed over the decades and the linked departure of a number of potential leaders who, instead, went on to make their mark in other organizations.

Several names that purportedly received serious consideration were those of foreign corporate leaders who had very little in-depth knowledge of the Tata Group, and probably even less cultural sensitivity around how business is conducted in India. The names included Sir John Rose of Rolls Royce and Indra Nooyi of Pepsico. Finally, in a bewildering u-turn, the name that the search process finally yielded was that of a member of the Search Committee itself, and a significant shareholder in the holding company Tata Sons: Cyrus Mistry from the Pallonji Mistry family. What apparently turned the Committee's mind to consider one of their own was a very informed and persuasive presentation made by Cyrus on the key challenges the Tata Group would face in future and some of the qualities its leader must possess to navigate these.

Bharat Wakhlu (TAS 1985) laughs as he's reminded of an interaction he had with senior leaders of the Tata Workers' Union (TWU) in Jamshedpur, who were visiting New Delhi, and had dropped into his office to chit-chat. '*Humko yeh samajh mein nahi ata hai,*' the President of the TWU said in chaste Hindi, '*ki jo aadmi examiner tha, woh candidate kaise bana?*' ('We can't understand: How did the examiner became the candidate?').

Cyrus had served on the Board of Tata Sons since 1996. He had, however, never played an executive role within any Tata company, and to that extent, could be expected to bring in a fresh and objective perspective. His first priority was to create a new generation of leadership in the Tata Group, following the retirement of almost all of Ratan Tata's earlier colleagues.

Cyrus wanted a 'Brains Trust' around him that would act as his sounding board when making critical decisions for Tata Sons and for the Group companies. This resulted in his nomination of a five-member Group Executive Council (GEC). Cyrus was clear that he wanted a change from Ratan's system of appointing insiders on the Board of Tata Sons. He wanted to keep the GEC separate from the Tata Sons Board and preferred to have independent professionals with a reputation for integrity and strong business instincts appointed to the Board.

In the GEC, very similar to the manner in which Ratan had years earlier created the GEO with talent drawn from both within and outside the Tata Group, Cyrus sought a mix of insiders and lateral hires so that balanced perspectives could emerge on all issues in future. The appointees to the GEC were Dr Nirmalya Kumar (strategy); Dr N.S. Rajan (HR); Madhu Kannan (business development and public affairs); Harish Bhat (portfolio—retail); and Dr Mukund Rajan (brand, ethics and Corporate Social Responsibility [CSR]).

Among the three lateral entrants to the Tata Group, Dr Nirmalya Kumar was a Professor at the London Business School and one of the most cited Marketing Professors in the world; Dr N.S. Rajan led the leadership practice at Ernst & Young for many years and had consulted with most of India's leading corporates; and Madhu Kannan was a former Managing Director of the Bombay Stock Exchange, having earlier interacted as an officer of the New York Stock Exchange with many of India's leading corporates when they were considering a possible foreign listing on that exchange. From within the 'old hands' of the Tatas, in a reflection of the still-considerable cachet that the TAS commanded in the Tata Group, Cyrus selected two TAS officers, Harish Bhat (TAS 1987) and Dr Mukund Rajan (TAS 1995).

Both Harish and Mukund were Tata 'lifers', having spent their entire working career in the Group and moved across different Tata companies. Harish had spent a number of years in companies like Tata Tea, Tata Coffee, TTSL and Titan, and had served in senior positions such as President of TTSL, Managing Director of Tata Coffee and Chief Operating Officer of Titan, before moving to the GEC. Mukund had been Ratan Tata's Chief of Staff for twelve years, before moving to TTSL (Maharashtra) as the Managing Director, and then setting up the Tata Capital flagship private equity fund, the Tata Opportunities Fund as the Founding Managing Partner, and overseeing the private equity business at Tata Capital.

Since there was no template for the GEC, which was a new construct in the Tata Group, the members collectively proceeded to invent things as they went along. They created a Group Policy and Strategy Forum, comprising the CEOs of the Group's largest companies, to act as a sounding board for the GEC. In a departure from the Ratan Tata days of an overly powerful corporate centre, the GEC was especially conscious that good corporate governance meant that Group companies could not be mandated or instructed to toe a particular central line. Instead, it needed to win their confidence and allow time for the individual processes of engagement with and between the CEOs, Boards and shareholders to deliver the outcomes it was keen to see.

There are very few parallels to the Tata Group's structure anywhere in the world, with an unlisted holding company—which in turn is principally owned by charities—controlling significant stakes in large listed enterprises. Fundamental questions about the appropriate roles of owners and managers across different entities, such as the Tata Trusts, Tata Sons and the Tata Group companies, could confuse even the brightest of lawyers. At the GEC, Mukund indicates, 'We put our heads down and focused on what we could do well, leaving it to Cyrus to work out the mechanics of engagement between the Tata Trusts, Tata Sons and the Tata companies.' Sadly, as events would turn out, achieving a working arrangement on this proved beyond Cyrus's reach.

The GEC took some time to find its feet. The lateral hires from outside the Tata Group were perceived to be arrogant and lacking in civility by some of the TAS officers who interacted with them. They were also seen to be quite inadequate in their own operating experience. One TAS officer tartly comments that these hires did not appear to have gone through any serious check on their values orientation and certainly did not have to jump the kinds of hoops a TAS officer would have had to before being selected.

Mukund admits that mistakes were made by the GEC. However, he believes that through extensive engagement with Tata people across the Group, the GEC was able to make good progress in developing a fairly accurate understanding of organizational needs and was able to secure broad endorsement of the mission and vision the Group had embarked upon under Cyrus's leadership.

Mukund observes that there was a high degree of continuity that Cyrus sought to maintain with the past, particularly in preserving the Tata Group's strong values and reputation for good corporate citizenship. This was reflected in the role that Mukund himself was assigned within the GEC, that of serving as the first Tata Brand Custodian. As Mukund puts it,

'This entailed responsibility for the Tata corporate brand owned by Tata Sons as well as oversight of corporate communications at the Tata Group. In Cyrus Mistry's view, the Tata brand had been built on the twin pillars of commitment to giving back to society and good corporate governance, and so he additionally tasked me as the Brand Custodian to serve as Chairman of the Tata Global Sustainability Council, with oversight of Group CSR activities, and as the Chief Ethics Officer of the Group.'

Cyrus's creation of the role of Brand Custodian, and the responsibilities he entrusted under the ambit of this role to a TAS officer, was forward-looking. Today, as corporations are increasingly tasked to focus on Environment, Social and Governance (ESG) issues, there are valuable lessons they can take away from the Tata experiment.

33
Continuing the Legacy of Caring

Cyrus Mistry's GEC re-enunciated the Group's mission, or core purpose, as follows: 'To improve the quality of life of the communities we serve globally through long-term stakeholder value-creation, based on leadership with trust.' This amplified the historical connection between the Group's brand and its reputation for giving back to society. As the Brand Custodian, Dr Mukund Rajan (TAS 1995) says that he saw his role as reinforcing the connection each Tata colleague felt with this mission.

To enable Tata colleagues to have first-hand experience of the joy of giving so that they could make the connection for themselves between the work they did and how communities ultimately benefit from this, a major new Tata volunteering programme, Tata Engage, was announced. This was launched on 3 March 2014, the 175th birth anniversary of the Founder of the Tata Group, Jamsetji Tata, alongside the first Tata Volunteering Week. Tens of thousands of Tata colleagues around the world took officially sanctioned time off work, for a half day to a full day, to spend with non-profits of their choice. Eventually, the GEC settled on organizing two Tata Volunteering Weeks every year, one coinciding with the Founder's birthday and the other kicking off with the International Day of Charity in the first week of September.

This carried forward a tradition in the larger companies in the Tata fold, such as Tata Steel, Tata Motors, Tata Chemicals and Tata Power, and those such as Titan that were located in places where the employees lived in close proximity to the factories, where volunteering was already a part of life. Employees contributed substantially to improving the quality of life of people, helping NGOs and a variety of civil society organizations with resources and their time. During disasters, these Tata companies were always in the forefront of galvanizing their employees to be of assistance in delivering relief and securing the well-being of those affected.

Tata Volunteering Weeks were gradually extended to become volunteering months as Tata companies sought more time to be able to ensure that more volunteers were able to contribute. Volunteering initiatives encompass a wide variety of activities, such as energy-conservation drives, blood donation, medical camps, road safety campaigns, beach cleaning, visits to orphanages and old age homes, and career counselling sessions for youth. Over time, not only Tata employees but also their family members and retired Tata colleagues, joined the volunteering efforts.

As the sign-ups for the first Tata Volunteering Weeks quickly crossed 100,000 employees, a second flavour of volunteering, ProEngage, was launched. With ProEngage, Tata employees could deploy their individual skill sets to undertake pro bono projects to support non-profits. These projects were curated by the Tata Sustainability Group (TSG), the newly created in-house sustainability centre of excellence, and matched with the volunteer skills on offer. Thousands of projects have been delivered to non-profits under ProEngage, in areas ranging from the creation of management information systems to website design, development of marketing campaigns, creation of vocational skill curricula and pedagogy, and coaching and mentoring of non-profits.

Within two years of its launch, Tata Engage was delivering over a million hours of volunteering support each year to non-profits across India, and had become India's largest corporate volunteering programme. Surveys of Tata volunteers showed that an overwhelming 99 per cent were happy to spend time undertaking some volunteering activity. This demonstrated that they were achieving a level of self-actualization in what they were doing and that volunteering appealed to their inner social instincts to help others.

Importantly, for many of the younger Tata employees, the Volunteering Weeks and the pro bono projects persuaded them that they were working with a truly enlightened employer. Mukund says that his team also discovered a truth about millennials—'They are looking to work with employers who demonstrate a social conscience. Volunteering programmes, consequently, can prove to be talent-attraction tools in addition to the good they do.' Mukund adds, 'corporate volunteering is an idea whose time has come in India.'

Relief and rehabilitation following natural disasters were another area of consistent activity for the Tata Group during Cyrus Mistry's regime. Group responses were mounted to address a series of disasters, including the floods of 2013 in Uttarakhand, which killed over 5,000 people; the unprecedented floods of 2014 and 2015 in Jammu and Kashmir and Tamil Nadu, respectively; the Hudhud cyclone in Andhra Pradesh in 2014; and the earthquake of 2015 in Nepal, which killed over 9,000 people. TAS officers, including new hires, were roped in to play valuable roles in the relief efforts.

These involved systematic and calibrated support for communities, beginning with supplying essential relief material like clean drinking water and water purification devices, solar lamps, tents and medicines; followed by sending volunteers to the disaster sites, including a number of Tata medical practitioners, to help with the distribution of relief material and to attend to injured individuals or those in trauma; and finally, the work of long-term reconstruction and rehabilitation of the affected communities—be it by creating self-help groups and livelihood training for widows who had lost their menfolk in the Uttarakhand floods, the rebuilding of community shelters and schools, or investing in trauma counselling for children affected by the Nepal earthquake. Millions of individuals have benefited from these relief efforts in recent years.

Alongside the volunteering activity and relief work being undertaken at the Tata Group, the traditional CSR activities of many Tata companies were also continued. For decades, the major Tata manufacturing companies had been undertaking CSR activities in the neighbourhood of their plant operations. Tata Steel, for instance, with significant manufacturing facilities in the state of Jharkhand, had created the largest community services department in the Tatas, and employed hundreds dedicated to working with the mostly tribal communities in the state. Dhruva Dey, a TAS officer of the 1962 batch, oversaw Family Welfare and Community Relations at Tata Steel in the 1970s, and guided the creation of the Tribal Culture Society and the Tata Steel Rural Development Society (TSRDS). Likewise, Tata Chemicals had been sponsoring significant water conservation efforts in the arid area of Mithapur in Gujarat where the company operated its soda ash plant, and Tata Motors had been supporting education, skill-building and local mobile healthcare projects around its plants in Pune and Jamshedpur.

During the administration of Prime Minister Narasimha Rao in the early 1990s, there had, in fact, been a move by the government to impress upon Corporate India—through industry associations such as the Confederation of Indian Industry (CII), the Federation of Indian Chambers of Commerce & Industry (FICCI) and Associated Chambers of Commerce and Industry of India (ASSOCHAM)—that businesses should deploy at least 1 per cent of their profits for socially impactful projects. When the Tata Group companies put their social and community welfare expenditure together, the total was way above 3.5 per cent of profits at that time! The sentiment of successive governments that businesses had to 'do more for society' received a fillip with the new legislation on CSR introduced in 2013 as part of the amendments to the Companies Act in India. The CSR rules require companies that meet a size and scale test to contribute at least 2 per cent of their net profits for CSR activities. In addition, such companies need to create a CSR committee of the Board, with at least one Independent Director as a member, and make appropriate disclosures in their annual reports about how their CSR funds are being spent.

Common threads within the CSR programmes of individual Tata companies were identified during Cyrus Mistry's tenure and expanded to enhance the Group's impact. The most significant initiative of this kind was a skills development programme that was christened Tata STRIVE. Under this programme, a three-pillar network of skill development centres was created—some owned by Tata companies, some managed by non-profits and the remaining from the Industrial Training Institutes (ITIs) established by the central and state governments. The Group's ambition was to develop the capacity across this network to skill over a million young people each year. The Tata Sustainability Group also drove a number of initiatives to mainstream thinking on sustainability and integrate its principles into all the Tata businesses. Significant investments were made in capacity-building and training at all levels across the organization. Over 150 C-Suite executives experienced the well-regarded Cambridge Sustainability Leadership programme, and over 500 carbon and energy champions, 180 water champions, fifty disaster management project managers and thirty natural capital champions were trained.

The month of June, during which the World Environment Day is celebrated, was designated as the Tata Sustainability Month each year. During this month, numerous campaigns would be conducted on subjects like climate change and global and Tata best practices in sustainable development. Annual Tata Sustainability Conclaves were organized, which were addressed by renowned experts like Nobel Laureate Prof. Muhammad Yunus. A number of industry first publications were produced, including a compilation of case studies on the Tata Group's efforts to deliver the United Nations Sustainable Development Goals (SDGs), titled 'We Dream of a Better World—The Tata Group and the SDGs'. In recognition of the Group's sustainability commitment, Globescan rated it Asia's Sustainability Leader in 2016.

Mukund underlines how the focus on sustainability was in sync with the growing consciousness in recent years about the environmental challenges India faces. Extreme climatic events caused by global warming are expected to take a major toll on India—with its long coastline, the country is vulnerable to sea level rise, and intense heat waves and weather changes will take their toll on human and agricultural productivity. As India's largest industrial group, the Tatas will naturally be expected to lead the industry response to these sustainability challenges. Indeed, the Group is itself a significant contributor to some of these problems—the greenhouse gas emissions of companies such as Tata Steel, Tata Power, Tata Chemicals and Tata Motors in aggregate terms exceed those of a number of small European countries.

It is also increasingly clear that some of the solutions to the sustainability challenges India faces can only be found in the long term. Corporates will require courage to set aside short-term advantage in favour of long-term solutions, and will need to invest considerable resources in educating their investors and other stakeholders on the strategic choices they make.

The emerging new focus within the corporate world will need to be on an appropriate model for sustainable growth, one that values the various forms of capital, including social and natural capital, embraces the circular economy, and encourages collective action through partnerships and collaborations. As Mukund puts it, 'This offers the perfect context for the Tata Group, with its stated mission of improving the quality of life of the communities it serves, to demonstrate its sustainability leadership.'

34
Carrying Forward the Ethical Torch

In 2013, the Indian government amended the Companies Act. Some clauses in the Tata Code of Conduct, like those relating to the promise of preferential treatment of Tata companies towards each other, could have been violative of provisions of the new Act, which required material related-party transactions to be approved by the minority shareholders of listed Tata companies. Rather than do a knee-jerk tweaking of clauses, the GEC authorized Chief Ethics Officer Dr Mukund Rajan (TAS 1995) to embark on a comprehensive review and recast of the Code.

A cross-company effort to benchmark the Code with global best practices, and accordingly revise it, followed. What emerged from this exercise in 2015 was essentially a new code. This was simpler to understand and more informal and easier to embrace, especially for the much younger demographic that now constituted the majority of the Tata Group's employee base. It was conversational in tone, with many illustrations of the typical kinds of ethical dilemmas Tata colleagues might encounter. And it was organized by stakeholder category so that colleagues and other stakeholders could quickly contextualize and grasp what was required of them.

The Code was also made relevant to the truly global organization that Tatas had now become. Illustrating this, Mukund refers to the way in which the whistle-blower clause had to be carefully phrased. He says, 'We learnt that we had to appeal to employees, particularly in Europe, to blow the whistle on violations of the Code in such a way that they did not feel we were encouraging them to unfairly tattle on their colleagues. We had to respect the tragic history of countries like France and Germany, where Tatas had sizeable operations, and acknowledge that our well-meaning desire to encourage whistle-blowing could have significant negative connotations in the light of the experience of those societies, dating back to the Second World War, with informers who were in the pay of the hated Nazis.'

Once the recast Code was ready, a determined effort followed to deploy a number of tools to cascade to the rank and file the understanding of the Code, including basic self-study e-modules for employees, advanced modules for trainers and three-day masterclass programmes for ethics counsellors. Where earlier a lot of faith was placed on self-declaration by Tata companies of their compliance with the Code of Conduct, a new, streamlined annual compliance reporting format was rolled out.

Mukund shares, 'The old adage of "what gets measured, gets improved" is as true in the corporate governance space as in any other. We assessed and benchmarked the performance of Group companies against each other and against global standards, and provided feedback to them. The feedback was structured across four criteria—Leadership, Compliance Structure, Communication and Training, and Measurement of Effectiveness.' At the Group Chairman's behest, feedback reports were not only shared with the CEOs of Group companies but also with the Chairpersons of the companies so that they could be discussed within each of the Boards.

Another unique initiative was to hold half-day seminars for the Board and Audit Committee Chairmen and CEOs across the Tata Group companies, to explain the main tenets of the new Tata Code of Conduct, share the best practices, explain the new legislation that was emerging in areas such as sexual harassment, and discuss the typical dilemmas faced by many Group companies. The highlight of these seminars were candid question-and-answer sessions for the audience with the Group Chairman.

Mukund reflects on his experience as the Chief Ethics Officer and emphasizes, 'Open, transparent and sincere dialogue with key stakeholders will be critically important if the Tata reputation for good corporate governance is to be sustained and enhanced.'

35
Enhancing Group Performance

The Ratan Tata years had bequeathed to Cyrus Mistry and his GEC a Tata Group that had grown hugely in size. However, top line growth was not matched by bottom-line performance, and significant restructuring of the Group's portfolio of companies based on performance was called for.

One of the most critical challenges in this respect was the awkward perception that gained ground, that the need for restructuring was driven in significant measure by the poor performance of several flagship projects and acquisitions undertaken when Ratan Tata was the Group Chairman. These included the Tata Nano project at Tata Motors, the Corus acquisition by Tata Steel, and high value property acquisitions made by the Indian Hotels Company. Media commentary on the complicated legacy left by Ratan would annoy him and create further friction with his successor, Cyrus.

Cyrus and the GEC needed to create alignment within the Group around the key expectations from Group companies for the future. Towards this end, Cyrus initiated the practice of organizing the Annual Group Leadership Conference (AGLC) on 29 July, JRD Tata's birthday. Invitees for the half-day conference included the entire senior leadership of the Tata Group and representatives of key functions, including human resources, finance, technology, corporate communications, marketing, ethics, and so on. Cyrus also made it a practice to invite young employees, including the new entrants to the TAS.

The first step at the very first AGLC in 2014 was to articulate a compelling vision of where the Group could head. The new Vision announced was, 'By 2025, a quarter of the world's population will experience the Tata commitment to improving the quality of life of customers and communities. As a result, Tata will be among the twenty-five most admired corporate and employer brands globally, with a market capitalization comparable to the twenty-five most valuable companies in the world.' Thereafter, at multiple platforms, this inspiring Vision and the changes the GEC were trying to introduce in the Tata Group were cascaded. These platforms included the Group HR Conclave, the Group Ethics Conclave, the Brand and Corporate Communicators Meet, the CTO Conclave, the annual Tata Business Excellence Model Conclave, and Tata Innovista.

Tata Innovista, the Group-wide programme organized by the Tata Innovation Forum, was particularly relevant to the objectives of encouraging innovation and creating a culture of intelligent risk-taking within the Tata Group. These were crucial if the Group was to achieve competitive success at the global level and emerge among the most valuable companies in the world. Four categories of awards were given for innovation: 'Promising Innovations' for those that had been successfully implemented during the year and had accrued benefits to a company; 'Leading Edge Technologies' for global/industry first technologies that were under development and promised to deliver significant benefits after implementation; 'Dare To Try', which recognized courageous and determined attempts at creating global-first technologies, products and services that did not achieve the desired results but had potential for success; and 'Design Honour', which sought to promote the focus of Tata companies on design thinking.

The financial benefits from innovations in the Tata Group were estimated at about $1 billion on a recurring annual basis. Significant progress was also made across Group companies like TCS, Tata Steel, Tata Motors and Jaguar Land Rover in filing for the largest number of patents in Corporate India; the Tata Group, in fact, doubled its published patents within two years, from about 3,500 at the end of calendar year 2013 to about 7,000 at the end of 2015. Around 2.7 per cent of the Group's turnover was being invested in R&D, against India's R&D to GDP ratio of 0.7 per cent.

Cyrus also re-articulated the Tata values to embed the culture of innovation and pioneering firmly in the Tata Group. The value of 'pioneering' was incorporated, alongside four existing values of 'integrity', 'excellence', 'unity' and 'responsibility'. This new value was rooted in the proposition that the Tatas will 'be bold and agile, courageously taking on challenges, using deep customer insight to develop innovative solutions'. This linked directly to the DNA of the Tata Group, and was well reflected in many inspiring endeavours—from Jamsetji Tata's plan to build Asia's first integrated steel plant to JRD Tata's establishment of India's first airline and Ratan Tata's leadership in building India's first indigenously developed passenger car, the Tata Indica.

Other areas of focus for the GEC included the modernization of the Tata Business Excellence Model programme, and a greater thrust on digitization with the dramatic growth in digital opportunities across spaces like retail and finance. New growth engines for the Group were identified, including retail, financial services, infrastructure and realty, and defence and aerospace. Companies like Titan, Trent, Tata Capital, Tata Housing, Tata Realty and Infrastructure, and Tata Advanced Systems consequently featured more prominently in the Group's communication to the markets.

In terms of enhancing the financial performance of the Group's portfolio, the GEC saw its role as a combination of nurturing companies, orchestrating greater synergies and optimizing the portfolio. Strategies were customized for the different kinds of companies in the Group's portfolio, with well-established listed companies obviously requiring a much lighter touch than newly created unlisted subsidiaries.

Tata companies were evaluated by the GEC on the 'RESPect' model, predicated on Returns, Excellence, Scale and Prospect. These parameters were used to determine whether a company was delivering the expected returns; whether it was globally competitive or at least an India champion in its business; whether its scale justified its existence in the Group portfolio; and whether it had potential for future growth. Businesses that did not meet these tests were divested, including the Tata logistics business, DIESL; the communications company in South Africa, Neotel; Tata Communications' data-centre business; and Tata Chemicals' fertilizer business.

At the larger Tata businesses, there was a clear focus on growth, reflected, for instance, in the commissioning of the new Kalinga Nagar steel plant of Tata Steel, and the launch of several attractive new passenger vehicles from the Tata Motors stable. In the loss-making telecom business and in the loss-making European steel operations of Tata Steel, consolidation opportunities were pursued. And where required, top leadership changes were effected at a number of Tata companies, including Tata Steel, Tata Motors, Indian Hotels, Tata AIG and Tata AIA, yielding perceptible changes in terms of result orientation and better performance. Young TAS officers were also tested in key leadership roles, like Ashutosh Pandey (TAS 1998) who was made the founding CEO of Tata CLiQ, the digital commerce venture of the Tata Group established in 2014, and Nirav Khambati (TAS 1997), who succeeded another TAS officer, Sanjaya Sharma (TAS 1980), as CEO at Tata ClassEdge and Tata Interactive Systems, the custom e-learning venture promoted by Tata Industries.

Through the Cyrus Mistry period, the Tata Group's market capitalization growth significantly outperformed the Bombay Stock Exchange Sensitive Index (or the Sensex, which consists of thirty blue-chip stocks). Importantly, this outperformance held true even without including the performance of the Group's largest company by market capitalization, TCS.

Sadly, despite the progress being made, the friction between Cyrus and his predecessor mounted. An impression seemed to gain ground in some circles that Cyrus somehow stood to benefit from belittling Ratan's contributions. Dr Mukund Rajan (TAS 1995), however, is emphatic on this point—'Never, at any stage, did Cyrus Mistry seek to downplay the enormous contribution Ratan Tata had made to the Group. On the contrary, he went out of his way to appreciate and applaud Ratan Tata's achievements. This is a matter of public record and the evidence can be seen plainly, whether in the form of Cyrus Mistry's New Year messages to Tata employees, or other forms of communication collateral that were distributed within the Group and outside.'

Writing in *The Economic Times* in 2016 on twenty-five years of Indian economic reforms, Cyrus acknowledged Ratan's contributions, saying, 'Isaac Newton had said, "If I have seen further, it is by standing on the shoulders of giants." Today, as we celebrate twenty-five years of economic reform, we in the Tatas salute the vision of Ratan Tata, who recognized the need to embrace open markets and prepared us well to face the challenges and address the opportunities which the next twenty-five years will present.'

36
Cyrus Mistry Exits

On 24 October 2016, just before a Tata Sons Board meeting, Cyrus Mistry received an unexpected visit from his predecessor, Ratan Tata. Ratan was accompanied by a Board member, the then Harvard Business School Dean, Nitin Nohria. Just a few months earlier, the Nominations and Remuneration Committee of the Board had given Cyrus an outstanding performance appraisal. On this day, however, the two visitors conveyed to him that the Tata Trusts, the principal shareholders of the company, had lost confidence in his leadership, and requested him to step down.

Cyrus, aware that his fixed-term contract had several more months to run, had questions on his mind about what might have motivated the move. He had been raising questions of corporate governance, including the appropriate role of the Tata Trusts in guiding the strategy of Tata Sons and was conscious of the growing tension this was creating with Ratan. He refused to resign and sought a discussion with the full Board. What transpired at the Board, where he was essentially fired, and the aftermath of it, have been the subjects of legal dispute. Suffice it to say that Cyrus did not go quietly into the night but fought back against what he alleged was the whimsical decision of essentially one individual at the Tata Trusts, Ratan.

Had the relationship between Ratan and Cyrus not broken down, the latter could have contemplated a long tenure at the Tata Group. He was only the sixth Group Chairman at the helm of affairs in over 145 years—the others before him being the founder, Jamsetji Tata; his son, Dorabji Tata; Nowroji Saklatwala; then JRD Tata; and finally, Ratan. The two Group Chairmen immediately preceding Cyrus had, between them, occupied the Chair for over seventy-four years. Cyrus, appointed Chairman at age forty-four, could possibly have had three decades in the job.

There is a profound impact of consistency on long-term policy that emerges when an organization has stable leadership at the top. A special risk-taking ability is nurtured when it is clear to managers across all levels that the future is not going to be defined by worries about a few bets going south in the short term, but by the ambition to ensure the long-term success of some really big bets.

Two superb examples of how the Tatas benefit from their long-term orientation towards business development, as we saw earlier in the book, have been the successes of TCS and Titan. The Group's long-term orientation has been critical in making the Tatas who they are and has helped enormously in strengthening the Group's bonds with communities and diverse stakeholders.

Lenders aware of the Tatas' long history of not defaulting on loans tend to offer them finer interest rates and long-tenor debt. Non-profits aware of the Tatas' long history of supporting local communities tend to give them a fair chance to explain any actions that might seem to conflict with their reputation for caring for the public. Employees in a company that is being acquired by the Tatas, when made aware of their history of working collaboratively with the existing management teams of acquired companies, tend to welcome them as the new owners. Corrupt officials in the government, aware of the Tatas' history of rejecting demands for gratification even at the cost of losing business, tend to avoid sweating them for a bribe.

One can thus see that the history of the Tatas and their long-term orientation have played an essential role in the Group's evolution over the past few decades. So, losing Cyrus even before he had completed what should have been his first five-year term as the Group Chairman was a setback in the narrative of the Tatas' long-term oriented leadership.

After a volley of accusations had been traded by both Cyrus's as well as Ratan's supporters, it seemed as if most of the Tata seniors chose to wash their hands off the matter. They seemed inclined to watch the proceedings from the side lines rather than try and mediate between the two.

The GEC constituted by Cyrus was disbanded, and the employment of the three lateral entrants to the Group, Dr Nirmalya Kumar, Madhu Kannan and Dr N.S. Rajan, was terminated without any notice. The only wrong they had apparently committed was to develop a close association with Cyrus. This action was most unexpected from an institution that prides itself on its core value of unity and its treatment of its people with 'dignity and respect'.

The three GEC members were professionals who had contributed their best to the organization and had each been appreciated for their contributions. Dr Mukund Rajan (TAS 1995) mentions how some Tata leaders reached out to him and mentioned the contrast they saw between the action against his GEC colleagues and the way in which, for instance, Dr Jamshed Irani treated Russi Mody acolytes at Tata Steel two decades earlier, after the Ratan–Russi spat. Russi's favourites were not treated vindictively and were given every opportunity to adapt to the post-Russi dispensation; some even went on to hold the highest positions in the organization.

When queried about his own stand on the Ratan–Cyrus spat, Mukund, as someone who worked intimately with both the individuals, responds, 'I owed my loyalty to the institution of the Tatas, not to the individuals concerned. My values were aligned with those of the Group and not with specific personalities. So long as I was an officer of the Group, I would abide by the reasonable orders I might receive from the Tata Sons Board and the Group Chairman. But I would not go beyond this and take a position on the spat, unless I had compelling evidence that such a position was justified. Sadly, in the mud-slinging that took place at the time, it was difficult to ascertain where the truth really lay about each of the opposing sides' perspectives on the issues that divided them.'

Mukund reveals that he was asked by one of the Trustees of the Tata Trusts whether he would consider representing their position on national television. He says, 'I responded that I would not do this unless I was personally convinced about the merits of the Trusts' position on the matter. No effort was made to share evidence with me to back up the charges that were being bandied about at the time, and I stayed out of the fracas.'

Mukund and Harish Bhat (TAS 1987), both TAS officers, were the two members of the GEC who were retained in the Group after Cyrus's exit. They were re-assigned senior roles within the Group, with Harish taking on a somewhat pruned role of Brand Custodian (without charge of Corporate Communications, ethics or CSR); and Mukund continuing to serve as Chief Ethics Officer and Chairman of the Tata Global Sustainability Council, and taking on additional oversight of the Tata Sons' international offices. For most TAS officers at this time, the period ahead would be one of uncertainty and confusion in the midst of swirling allegations, media commentary and many unsavoury revelations about the nature of corporate governance within the Tata Group.

Under Cyrus's leadership, a number of younger TAS officers had felt encouraged by his support of their leadership of new businesses. These included individuals like Brotin Banerjee (TAS 1998) at Tata Housing, Ashutosh Pandey (TAS 1998) at Tata Cliq, and Nirav Khambati (TAS 1997) at Tata ClassEdge and Tata Interactive Systems. Within two years of the leadership change at Tata Sons, they all had left the Tata Group.

Given the spectrum of reforms required in the Tata Group, however, one aspect which saw little change was the amount of focus the TAS received as an important instrument available to champion new approaches. In this respect, there was relatively little differentiation from the attitudes of the Group HR Heads of the preceding two decades, and few investments were made in training TAS officers or ensuring they acquired the skills necessary to be successful in the future.

Two years into Cyrus's regime, some preliminary efforts commenced in 2015 to more comprehensively monitor the TAS programme. A commitment was also made at the time to track the careers of TAS officers for at least twenty years. Even these modest efforts have seemingly been abandoned after Cyrus's exit.

For a brief period after the exit, Ratan Tata assumed the interim Chairmanship of Tata Sons. Then, in 2017, N. Chandrasekaran, the CEO of TCS, was appointed the new Chairman. The uncertainty at the very top was rekindled a couple of years later when the National Company Law Appellate Tribunal overturned an earlier National Company Law Tribunal decision and ordered that Cyrus be reinstated as Group Chairman. This decision was promptly appealed by Tata Sons, and the case moved to the Supreme Court, which eventually closed in its favour in 2021.

Chandrasekaran is the first professional CEO at Tata to become the Chairman of the Group. A non-TAS officer himself, he has been open in his disapproval of any special treatment of TAS officers. He has significantly centralized authority at Tata Sons over Group companies, and sought to place many of his trusted comrades from TCS in key positions across the Group. A TAS officer wryly suggests, 'TCS is the new TAS'.

Former TCS officers now head Group HR, help to oversee Group Communications and direct the Group's digital strategy. They have also been appointed to head several new businesses the Group is trying to build in online retail and medical devices, as well as established Tata companies like Tata Communications. Many observers speculate that the TAS as a vehicle for building the Tata Group's leadership pipeline while sustaining the Group's values—even while the Group itself changes in complexion—may be headed for oblivion.

During the writing of this book, the Tata Group lost its first woman TAS officer, Khorshed Jhaveri. A contemporary of Khorshed, Nawshir Khurody (TAS 1960) took it upon himself to inform the Head of Group HR about this loss. Maybe it is a reflection of the times, but he received a terse two-line message in response, which read:

'I am sorry to hear this sad news. May her soul rest in peace.'

Part III

Leaders for the Future

37

The Mixed Success of the TAS Experiment

The TAS, as we have seen through this book, was created by the longest-serving Chairman of the Tata Group, JRD Tata. The purpose was to find officers who would serve as a general management cadre and provide leadership talent for Tata companies. Besides their intellectual abilities, officers of this cadre were chosen for their integrity and moral compass. They were expected to champion cohesion and unity within the diversified Tata Group, and carry forward its values. As leaders, they were expected to be decisive and ethical in their decision-making, and able to handle power and authority while remaining grounded and humble.

For many years, certainly till around the mid-1990s, the TAS succeeded in consistently attracting outstanding talent. The brightest students from the best educational institutes vied to get into the TAS. The selection of these individuals took place, for the most part, in an era when India was still a protected economy, attractive job opportunities were relatively limited, and the TAS itself was hiring very few officers, typically in single digits each year. Many of those selected during this period, like Dr Freddie Mehta, Nawshir Khurody, R.K. Krishna Kumar, Camellia Panjabi, Arun Maira and Prakash Telang would make a mark in the Group, while a number of others, like T.K. Balaji, Kris Ramachandran,

Siddharth Kak, Navtej Sarna, Vir Chopra, Raghuram Rajan, Patu Keswani and Srikumar Misra would leave to go on to build highly respected careers in the corporate world or as entrepreneurs, as well as in other realms such as public policy, the arts and culture.

As the Indian market opened up in the post-liberalization era, however, a variety of exciting new opportunities became available to India's best and brightest. The TAS had, as we have seen in the preceding chapters, traditionally been behind the curve on offering market standard compensation. The effects of this became visible as it began to struggle to attract the best students from B-School campuses. Instead of the TAS, many of the brightest students increasingly opted for lucrative careers in international banks and management consultancies. "Modest TAS salaries aside, these students could spot only a few senior TAS officers leading large companies. By the late 1990s, the TAS had been in existence for just under fifty years; but it could not showcase a large bench of Managing Directors and CEOs who had started their careers as TAS officers. In contrast, the international banks and management consultancies, and indeed, many multinational companies, offered clear and well-defined career paths for their management cadres.

The TAS did, however, continue to earn respect for its meticulous and thorough selection procedure, with candidates being assessed on a host of exacting dimensions of management and leadership. The Bharat Darshan, offering exposure across the country to the Group's many different establishments, excited the imagination of young budding general managers. Yet, a fundamental and continuing failure through the decades was the inability of those tasked to supervise the operation of the TAS to develop a structured training programme that could carry candidates beyond their entry year.

Many TAS alumni today regret that the Group made few efforts to invest in their growth and development after they had been selected. And while there is something to be said for the expectation that the officers would be self-starters and take the initiative to find learning opportunities on their own, the fact is that even modest-sized multinational enterprises have far superior training programmes for their managers, as compared to anything the TAS ever put together.

In a world where there is growing sophistication of skills in every functional domain, even general management skills that TAS officers are expected to have need to be honed and sharpened continuously with formal inputs. Gone are the days when well-meaning young managers like Xerxes Desai, armed only with degrees in subjects like history, politics and philosophy, could flourish simply because of their intuition and people management skills. In the changed business world, especially after 1991, specialization or knowledge of a particular domain has become almost de rigueur for any leader. Alongside a waning commitment at the very top to nurture and grow these skills in TAS officers, it is increasingly the case that leaders across Tata companies are being hired laterally for their perceived domain skills and managerial capabilities rather than groomed internally.

Be it a Sunil D'Souza from Whirlpool who replaced Ajoy Misra (TAS 1980) as the Managing Director of Tata Consumer Products, a Sanjay Dutt from Ascendas who replaced Brotin Banerjee (TAS 1998) as the Managing Director of Tata Housing Development Company, or the induction of Saurabh Agarwal, formerly from the Aditya Birla Group, as the Group CFO, lateral hires seem to be getting preferred for many top-level vacancies in the Tata Group now. As a proportion, far fewer active senior leaders across the Group today have emerged from the ranks of the TAS than ever used to be the case in the past.

In trying to assess the achievements of the TAS thus far, then, let us evaluate delivery against expectations. TAS officers were to be selected in significant measure for their ethics and values orientation. We have seen in this book that there were indeed some aberrations through the decades—not all TAS officers were paragons of virtue, unfortunately. There are a few hairy stories TAS alumni still whisper about, including the alignment of a few TAS officers with the nefarious activities of some Tata satraps that went far beyond the call of duty. But it is also true that the vast majority of TAS officers seem to have been untainted by familiar

Indian allegations of corruption. Broadly speaking, many TAS officers did justifiably earn respect for their integrity and the positive examples they set for others both within their companies and outside.

The TAS, at its inception, took a lead in the Indian corporate world by actively recruiting women in the cadre. Khorshed Jhaveri, the first woman TAS officer, was recruited in 1958 when women in management were quite the exception. For the next ten years, women continued to be part of the new batches. One of those early recruits, Camellia Panjabi, in fact went on to earn accolades, not only in the Tata Group, but as an internationally respected restaurateur and hospitality industry veteran. And then, inexplicably, the TAS stopped recruiting women. It even stopped accepting applications from women from the late 1960s onwards. This changed only in 1982 when three women were recruited, among them Vibha Paul Rishi, who played a role in the creation of Titan, and went on to a successful career in the multinational, Pepsi.

The fact that a number of women TAS officers are known more for their work outside the Group tells a story in itself. While attrition has been a problem within the cadre as a whole, it is the attrition among the women TAS officers that is startling. The women clearly identified as high-potential managers by Tata companies still found it easier to achieve their career aspirations outside the Group rather than within. Even today, it is difficult for most people to name a handful of women, TAS or non-TAS, in senior leadership roles within the Tata Group, let alone any Tata company that is headed by a woman.

Another important yardstick for evaluating the success of the TAS would be the achievements of the cadre in championing the unity of the Tata Group. Here, it has to be said that while the idea of a strong and cohesive Tata was one that appealed to most TAS officers, too few of them were actually able to play any meaningful role in delivering on this concept. Many TAS officers tended to build senior careers within single Tata companies and had little role to play in shaping the fortunes of the conglomerate, especially during the years when it dramatically expanded under Ratan Tata's stewardship.

Very few TAS officers enjoyed the access or were able to command the clout to influence the Group Centre. A far greater role in preserving the Group's unity was played by two personalities who occupied the position of Tata Group Chairman, first JRD Tata, and then his successor, Ratan Tata.

A third measure of success could be how many TAS officers were able to distinguish themselves in any significant manner for their business genius or their entrepreneurial flair. Many have certainly been admired managers and played important, sometimes vital, roles in the growth of a number of Tata businesses; several continue to do so today. However, as we have seen in the preceding chapters, during the post-liberalization years when the first crop of TAS officers came into their own as Heads of companies, and younger hires began to make their mark, relatively few created a long-lasting positive impact.

These few would include Xerxes Desai (TAS 1961), who created Titan as one of India's best-known brands and most successful retail enterprises, and R.K. Krishna Kumar (TAS 1963), who championed Tata Tea's growth into a global enterprise. Several potential future leaders of the Group were unfortunately lost due to the significant number of exits of senior TAS officers from companies like Tata Motors and Indian Hotels in the wake of the change of guard at the top, when Ratan Tata displaced the satraps.

In evaluating the legacy of the TAS, it can be said that it attracted good talent and produced a great many well-respected managers, but it did not substantially deliver on its mission to become the mobile superglue of outstanding leaders who could hold the Group together and take it to ever greater heights. Across large Tata businesses, managers from outside the TAS, such as Dr Jamshed Irani at Tata Steel, S. Ramadorai at TCS, Prasad Menon at Tata Chemicals and Tata Power, and Ravi Kant at Tata Motors, would enjoy significantly more influence in shaping the fortunes of these companies. Very few TAS officers would ever come to rub shoulders with the Chairman of Tata Sons.

Seen through the lens of its officers, for all the hype around the TAS, there was grossly inadequate focus on training and development, especially in the early years of an officer's career. Successive commitments of HR Heads at the Group Centre to monitor and support the career progression of the officers were largely honoured in their breach.

Many TAS officers, after being tested in the early part of their careers within a particular industry, and having learnt how to navigate office politics that is so common in every organization, preferred to simply carry on within those organizations. This did not imply any lack of ambition. It was simply a safe choice to make. However, it did mean that the idea of cross-company mobility with the corresponding transfer of values and best practices from one Tata company to another via TAS officers was defeated. Instead, the roll-out of the Tata Business Excellence Model, which admittedly saw a major and successful thrust under the leadership of TAS officers like Jamshed Daboo (TAS 1986) and Jehangir Ardeshir (TAS 1983), played a bigger role in the transfer of best practices across the Tata Group.

Some TAS officers did embrace Group mobility, and had successful careers that flourished largely because of their own drive and initiative. However, at the very apex of the Tata Group, senior TAS executives encountered the dominating personality of the Tata Sons Chairman Ratan Tata—it ultimately mattered little what they were trying to champion if it did not converge with his plans for the Group. Grand successes such as the launch of India's first indigenously developed passenger car, the Tata Indica, as well as debacles such as the Tata Nano and the European steel operations, were envisioned by Group Chairman Ratan Tata and the team around him with relatively modest contributions of TAS officers beyond the execution, for the most part.

It therefore appears plain that the TAS has not been able to fully live up to the early expectations of senior Tata leaders like JRD Tata. Does that, however, detract from the relevance of the TAS vis-a-vis the role it was expected to play? Is there still a role for the TAS as a protector of Group values, an agent of greater cohesion and synergy within the Tata Group, and a driver of competitive outperformance by Tata companies? In the sections that follow, we argue that there is indeed still a vital role for the TAS, provided there is an inclination within the Tata Group at the very highest levels to allow the institution to flourish. We also argue that there are important lessons in the evolution of the TAS, and not just for the Tata Group, but also for corporations anywhere in the world. The key leadership competencies that TAS officers have traditionally exhibited are now more relevant than ever before for the successful and sustainable conduct of values-driven businesses.

38
The Creation of Wholesome Value

Across the globe, economic growth is still measured in terms of gross domestic product (GDP). It is well known that GDP exhibits a strong, positive correlation with the extent of exploitation of natural resources and the levels of consumption. To show that economies are growing, and to demonstrate that GDP figures are 'healthy', nations around the globe are overusing our fragile planet's resources and jeopardizing its capacity to recharge its ecosystems.

In the process, Human Development Indices—across the world—are showing an alarming decline; and large number of people are increasingly finding that their quality of life is characterized by deprivation, disease, hunger, poverty and despondency. The coronavirus pandemic has brought these hidden facts out in the open, much to the horror of many people who seemed to have no clue that the benefits of prosperity have not been shared equitably over the past century.

Had Jamsetji Tata been alive today, he would have been greatly saddened by the wanton destruction of the environment and the extent of neglect that millions of men and women—who have the skills and the ability to work—are experiencing at the hands of their employers. Jamsetji believed that businesses need to be a transformative force for good. Human decisions and actions should not leave us all collectively, including other living beings, worse off than before businesses begin to operate. These extraordinary values, which we find deeply inspiring, have still not been 'mainstreamed' in most companies across the world. Investors are still hankering for rates of return on their investments that are completely out-of-whack with what our planet can sustain. There is an urgent need, therefore, to reframe economics and the metrics which measure the creation of true value, including the net impact of our actions on our fragile ecosystems and the environment, along with the health and happiness of people, and the equitable distribution of wealth.

If these changes are not made without further delay, we would be staring at a bleak future for ourselves, as well as for many other living beings. We need to appreciate that it would be dangerous to all if we were to continue on the current path of development, and not adapt to sustainable methods of improving the indices of Human Well-Being (HWB), a term which includes holistic health and happiness). It is imperative that we change the way we live, the way we produce food, create services and goods, and the manner in which we consume them.

One would have expected the political and business leaders of today to demonstrate more awareness of the pressing issues affecting our environment, and the adverse impact that changes in air, water and land are having on our own lives. Sadly, this is not in evidence. For most leaders, there is neither maturity, nor wisdom that is discernible. Instead, it is business as usual and a continuation of the very same behaviours that have brought the many crises of our times upon us.

The Edelman Trust Barometer Survey of 2021 corroborates this. As in the previous years, 2020 also saw more than 55 per cent of people surveyed across the globe, who believe that neither business leaders nor governments can be trusted to tell the truth—about anything. Furthermore, business leaders, globally, are still driven by a need to maximize shareholder wealth, even if the consequences of such actions erode value for all other stakeholders, and people, in general.

An overemphasis on the interests of shareholders, at the cost of other stakeholders, creates conditions where profiteering, exploitation and, in extreme cases, serfdom seem to be 'normal'. One of the primary changes in the metrics related to assessing businesses, therefore, would be to balance the interests of all stakeholders at the heart of every business, and ensure that it is not the enrichment of shareholders alone that drives the wheels of business.

For most businesses worldwide, financial performance is still determined on the basis of current accounting practices which do not incentivize businesses for being concerned about 'non-financial' parameters in their balance sheets. Accounting practices, as well as the manner in which profits are determined, will need to be transformed suitably. Organizations will need to capture the impact of the externalities of their business actions, and assign a dollar figure to whatever may be the positive and negative impacts even outside the traditional boundaries of their businesses. The gross profits of an enterprise, in such circumstances, would factor in all the actual costs of ameliorating the adverse externalities of the enterprise; or if those were unlikely to be incurred in the short-term, then financial provisions would need to be made for damages done to the environment which would require reparations from the firm or the promise of a clean-up in the future.

This important change will require the involvement and acceptance of key regulators globally. It will call for international advocacy and a concerted engagement with investors and business leaders, among others.

For the Tata Group, given the manner in which the ownership of Tata Sons was conceived during the chairmanship of Dorabji Tata, it is much easier for managers to recognize that the whole community is a beneficiary of what each of the Tata companies achieves. As we have shared earlier in this book, two-thirds of Tata Sons is owned by the Tata Trusts. The mandate of the Trusts is to serve the diverse needs of society in an efficient manner, whereby long-term benefits accrue to people. Therefore, dividends and other incomes that accrue to Tata Sons, comprise the net worth that the Trusts use for the betterment of the community in value-adding ways.

Many people who may intuitively understand the benefits of moving away from shareholder primacy to a more comprehensive set of metrics to measure business performance often wish to know how the functioning of the business itself will change. Fortunately, many progressive companies have adopted workable templates of what it means to operationalize a more conscious, multi-stakeholder-oriented approach to business. These templates endeavour to factor the legitimate aspirations of all stakeholders into business decisions, while actively encouraging managers and business leaders to engage with all stakeholders, thereby determining their concerns and needs. When an enterprise wilfully engages with its diverse stakeholders and demonstrates a desire to accommodate their aspirations and apprehensions, a mapping of what all stakeholders expect, forms the nucleus of a more committed organization. It is around this nucleus—of caring—that the processes and systems of the enterprise are designed and arranged. A balanced approach to the management of all stakeholder interests ensures that the right metrics are incorporated in business reviews, so that the performance of the enterprise is comprehensively assessed.

There is another important aspect that also needs to change, internally, within the enterprise for the change to be 'hard-wired'. This is the organization's Performance Management System (PMS)—the metrics and methods used to encourage managerial action, and incentivize the right kinds of behaviour by senior leaders, the decisions they take and the outcomes they deliver. Typically, managers, especially those who are accountable for key business results, will function in ways so as to maximize those outcomes against which their performance is measured. If the metrics and the deliverables—as a part of the organization's PMS—are aligned with the expectations of all stakeholders, and not just shareholders, it makes a material difference to the manner in which decisions are taken, results achieved and how the business may determine a critical tie-breaker if one or more stakeholders have important, but conflicting, expectations.

As a result of upholding a multi-stakeholder focus, and a clear orientation that all stakeholders are important, progressive companies gently goad managers to perform in ways that harmonize the diverse expectations of stakeholders (including by treating Planet Earth as a stakeholder) even as the organization produces goods and services for its chosen customer base.

The pandemic and the attendant disruptions in business have altered the balance of power between employers and employees in a way that is reminiscent of the exploitative era of industrialization. Therefore, if we do not wish to lapse into a phase where we treat people callously and display the uncaring and insensitive manner of handling employees that appalled Jamsetji Tata in the nineteenth century, we will have to plumb the depths of our spirit and draw copiously from the fount of compassion, awareness and gratitude.

Not just nations, but even businesses would have to wilfully and consciously change the manner in which they collectively measure economic growth and HWB. Newer metrics have got to be used to gauge true economic value-creation. Linear measures will have to be discarded, and these need to be replaced by multi-dimensional metrics and circular economic models that emphasize not just the creation of surpluses, but also the simultaneous enhancement of ecological capital, as well as the augmentation of societal well-being, equity, social justice, happiness and peace. Our collective endeavour, then, has to ensure that as we progress, we create an environmentally sustainable, socially prosperous and just society, while also ensuring overall happiness and spiritual fulfilment—not only for humans, but all living creatures as well.

This will not be easy. UNCTAD's Technology and Innovation Report, 2021 notes that every spurt of technological and economic progress has sharpened inequalities within and between countries. Inequalities tend to get worse over time, because the speed at which people and communities change and adapt to new technologies and ways of doing business are slower than the relentless pace at which new technologies are introduced. If we don't stem the divergence in wealth between people now, the matter can only get graver and more intractable to resolve as time goes by.

It is our view, therefore, that business leaders, supported by key stakeholders, including institutional investors and agencies responsible for the regulation of enterprises, will need to evolve new, sustainable, socially just and equitable methods of the creation of wealth, that stimulate widespread opportunities and the reduction of existing and potential inequalities. Such approaches call for conscious, compassionate leaders whose understanding of life and of the interconnectedness of all living things is deep and lucid; and who are rooted in this awareness as they manage the technologies, organizations and enterprises of the future.

39
Businesses as a Positive Force for Change

Businesses play a critical and beneficial role in the economy. Not only do they serve as the engines that enable the creation and delivery of value to society, but well-governed enterprises, led by principled, compassionate leaders can also be a force of benign and constructive transformation for humanity. The Tata Group, in its long and storied history of over 150 years, has demonstrated this. The strategic initiatives that the Tatas took in creating enterprises, also strengthened India's industrial prowess, and the country's ability to create jobs and bring millions of families out of poverty.

In the light of the rapid pace of technological advancement that is in evidence currently, companies need to consciously ensure that access to technologies, and the benefits therefrom, are widespread, affordable and sufficiently 'close' to all people for them to be benefitted. The many aspects of our lives that we take for granted—from healthcare to mobility, from nutrition to communications, and from security to entertainment—are all the results of many scientific advances, technological and process innovations that businesses have smartly converted into affordable products and services that are today within the reach of many. Furthermore, it is the power of enterprise alone that serves as a potent magnet which attracts technologies, novel ideas, talent, capital, and design innovations, and then harnesses them all for the benefit of humanity.

Yet, as the United Nations Conference on Trade and Development (UNCTAD) Technology and Innovation Report, 2021 shows, the inequality between nations, and also within nations, is rising, and this can only get worse as frontier technologies of the Internet of Things (IoT), Artificial Intelligence, robotics, automation, blockchain, 5G-Long-Term Evolution (LTE), gene-splicing, electric and autonomous vehicles, 3D printing, nanotechnologies, drones, and solar power transform the manner in which business is conducted and the value benefits get delivered to society.

It is our view that businesses led by conscious leaders will have to play a critical role in the expansion of the global economy and in bringing about significant improvements in the quality of life of humankind. Businesses can do this by working collaboratively with other stakeholders, including national governments, regulators, policy-framers, the investor community and funding agencies, to develop innovative ways of creating value for all, and becoming potent engines of transformative change.

But this will also require changes within business corporations. Leaders of enterprises will need to possess a set of competencies that is aligned with the values of integrated and wholesome development for all. Their business models can no longer consider the boundaries of their factories to be the 'arena' within which they operate—disregarding anything outside of the boundaries as being 'external' to the firm, and therefore, not of their concern. Conscious leaders know that there is no 'outside', since we are all interconnected, and wherever we look, everything is but an integral part of Planet Earth. Even the effluents we discard are still circulating within the aquifers of our planet, adversely impacting flora, fauna, and humans in faraway parts of the globe. Sensitive, caring and compassionate leaders are therefore aware and cognizant of the impact of their operations on the environment, on people and all other stakeholders. They ensure that they address all externalities with due attention and compassion—in a manner that is lasting, wholesome, ethical and desirable for all.

It is our view that businesses need to take the lead in putting in place small but purposeful steps to reframe and remodel the ways in which we produce and consume food, as well as goods and services, and the manner in which we measure our economic efficacy. We believe that an enlightened public and informed civil society would only accept a sustainable and optimum use of natural resources. Inequity and other social injustices rankle the values and broader sense of fairness and propriety of people everywhere, especially the younger generation, and hence would need to be urgently addressed and permanently minimized. Progressive leaders and future-oriented businesses would welcome such developments in their pursuit of social legitimacy and longevity.

40
Core Leadership Competencies of TAS Officers

If the world has to evolve on a different and more beneficial development trajectory, the one component that needs to change in all realms of human endeavour is the quality of leaders and their styles of leadership. Leadership is the one potent ingredient that can make an impactful difference in transforming the world, and make it more wholesome, happy and peaceful for all. It was this vital characteristic of leadership that stimulated the creation of the TAS.

Meaningful change in the world occurs only when inspiring, visionary leaders are able to galvanize people to contribute and jointly co-create a brighter future that will benefit all. Systems and processes that may be in place today, and which may have outlived their utility or may no longer be practical or useful, will only change when leaders decide that the time for renewal has come, and wilfully attract and engage with others who resonate with their constructive and benign vision.

We believe that officers of the TAS have traditionally been selected for possessing a set of core leadership competencies that are essential not just for effective leadership in the present, but also for being able to stimulate and usher in transformative changes into the future. Organizations that are keen to develop leadership talent that can help co-create a future that is wholesome will do well to hire people with the core competencies that TAS officers have typically possessed.

As has been mentioned earlier in this book, the cadre of TAS officers was envisioned to serve as torchbearers of the values of the Tata Group, and as the 'gyroscopes' who would ensure that the human side of business—the compassionate, Tata way—was ever in focus. This was a critical role of the TAS, and while TAS officers were supportive of the legitimate business growth aspirations of their companies, they were not afraid to temper the efforts of some Tata leaders whose single-minded quest for customer loyalty, business growth and profits often overshadowed their companies' commitments to other stakeholders.

Those who know that TAS officers were more than staid bureaucrats within the Tata Group have posed the question: Were TAS officers meant to be 'managers' or 'leaders'? Managers are supposed to maintain the 'status quo' and not unsettle the applecart. Leaders, on the contrary, are capable of envisioning a new future, enlisting others and galvanizing a holistic involvement of all in transformative and beneficial change.

We believe that TAS officers were to be a blend of both, and were selected with both capabilities, so that they could be managers when needed as well as leaders when necessary, initiating and making a lasting change for the better.

The TAS officers who made the cut were well-rounded individuals whose commitment to people and principles stood out. They were academically bright, as well as clear-headed and articulate. Furthermore, they all had the ability to put their thoughts into words that were caring, polite, impactful and convincing.

We believe that the following ten core leadership competencies, which were consciously sought in TAS officers as a part of the assessment and selection processes, have helped the Tata Group. Besides, these competencies are also central to the process of co-creating a wholesome future for humanity.

Self-Awareness

Leaders are often categorized into two groups: those who are inclined to act swiftly based on the information that they receive and, at the other end of the continuum, those who reflect deeply on any situation and act thoughtfully based on an assessment of the pros and cons and the expected outcomes of each possible avenue. Sometimes leaders act hastily and brashly, jeopardizing a situation for want of reflection. Similarly, those who are reflective might miss out on opportunities because they take too much time to think and get into a situation of analysis paralysis. Obviously, neither of the extremes are desirable, and effective leaders are sufficiently self-aware to know that different situations demand different styles of functioning. Such leaders have the ability to work in the most appropriate style required in a situation.

Effective leadership requires self-awareness and flexibility across a number of continua. Whether to be autocratic (as the Chief Pilot of a large jetliner needs to be when the starboard engine is on fire) or democratic is one such continuum. TAS officers are expected to have the ability to diagnose situations carefully and swiftly, and then be sufficiently self-aware and flexible to be able to cognitively 'move' to the most appropriate spot on the desired continuum.

Spine and Moral Courage

TAS officers are expected to have moral courage and the nerve to be able to speak up to one and all, including their superiors, if they think that the decisions the latter are taking violate the Tata values and the Group's guiding principles.

As we have mentioned in some of the earlier chapters, many from the TAS did raise red flags to give their senior Tata leaders sufficient warning about taking certain courses of action. On occasion, they were overruled and the advice given to their superiors was not heeded. Nevertheless, demonstrating 'spine' and speaking up when essential were and remain to this day a critical leadership competency for the TAS.

Assertiveness

The ability to think clearly and present one's thoughts and ideas lucidly, both in writing and while speaking is a set of competencies that has been sought in those aspiring to join the TAS. As Earl Nightingale, the influential American radio-host of the sixties said, 'Everything begins with an idea.' The TAS selectors, much like Earl, knew this to be true, and considered it to be a prerequisite for business success as well.

However, they also knew that keeping an idea to oneself, either because one is too shy to speak up or because one is intimidated by people in positions of authority, would not serve the best interests of the enterprise. Those with ideas not only had to think them through, but they also had to have the ability to rationally and unambiguously present them to others, so that more people could be enlisted and aligned in support of such ideas.

Speaking to senior leaders in authority, and presenting new, fresh ideas to them, politely and assuredly, has therefore been an essential qualification. Being assertive, and speaking in a way that maintains the self-esteem and dignity of all parties has been a trait actively sought in TAS talent.

Empathy

One of the selection methods used by TAS recruiters to assess sensitivity and empathy for others has been the 'Chairman's Situation'. In this role play, each candidate is made to play the role of the Chairman of a Board or a governing committee of an organization and given a brief narration of a certain case. The other candidates are made members of the 'Committee', but have no clue about the case, and therefore, are oblivious about the situation and what they are to discuss. The person playing the Chairman knows the entire case-brief, and cannot share what is in the narration, but nevertheless has to carry the entire group along; and eventually he has to move towards a reasonable and effective decision related to the scenario.

The manner in which the Chair handles the interactions with the other members, and the way the others are heard and then aligned with the best interests of the organization, indicate the awareness of the candidate about the overall situation, and the candidate's empathy, listening ability and goal-orientation. Often the role plays also present ethical dilemmas—two equally appropriate and desirable options—for the committee to choose from, which would be difficult to resolve without demonstrating empathy.

Ability to Wield Authority Comfortably

It is well known that many people lose their heads with power and authority. Since TAS officers were expected to be in positions of power from an early age and many would be responsible for critical decisions related to people, resources and investments, it was imperative that those chosen were 'grounded' young men and women. The expectation was that even as the candidates let their ideas soar, they would have their feet firmly planted on the ground, showing evidence of the humility they would need to prevent them from becoming intoxicated with power, or developing bloated egos.

As has been mentioned elsewhere in the book, the high-handedness of a few powerful Tata leaders, and their attendant lapses of judgement, contributed to their companies and the leaders themselves getting adversely affected. For TAS officers, thus, being able to 'keep one's head' and stay humble, even when entrusted with much power and authority are essential capabilities.

Foresight with Long-term Thinking

The Tata Group, dating back to 1868, is one of the oldest business groups in India, and many of the actions taken by its leaders decades earlier have yielded benefits and contributed to its growth in subsequent decades. Being part of such a group therefore requires that its leaders think ahead and have the patience and staying power to see investments and actions taken to completion, even if they take many years. TAS officers are supposed to be committed to creating long-term value and should thus demonstrate the diligence and endurance to stay on course despite set-backs.

Execution-Orientation

Having all the above capabilities, but not having the boldness, the discipline or the daring to execute projects, while carrying the entire team along, would not make for a complete leader. TAS officers are therefore required to have the ability to organize the resources and the people to execute projects, and take decisions and actions at the right time. People who are effective at getting things done and driving results without compromising on the values and principles that define their enterprise are always an asset to have. TAS officers with a bias for action and delivering results are always in demand.

Willingness to be a Lifelong Learner

The diverse backgrounds of those chosen to be a part of the TAS have undoubtedly been a strength that has benefited the Tata Group. Within a few years of joining the Group, depending on their expertise and their passion, the officers would gravitate to positions that were best suited to their skills-sets and their overall aptitude. However, growth required being mobile—both upwardly and laterally, including across Tata companies—and that necessitated that TAS officers who were keen to grow to their full potential, had to be lifelong learners. There was no way that they could grow in the many diverse businesses of the Tatas if they didn't have the ability and the humility to be open to new learning.

Constructive Interpersonal Skills

TAS officers are expected to have excellent and constructive interpersonal skills that would enable them to work closely and collaboratively with diverse people—both within the Tata Group and with outside stakeholders. This capability was essential if the TAS was to act as the Group's 'superglue' binding disparate parts of the wide Tata organization in ways that were value-creating and beneficial for all.

These capabilities were assessed quite carefully by the selectors, because they knew that TAS officers would be effective in their roles only if they could give their best and draw out the best from others as well without being obtrusive, high-handed or obnoxious.

Authenticity

Finally, TAS officers are expected to be comfortable in their skins, open, transparent and at ease with themselves. These are essential elements of leadership that enable the creation of trust while engaging with others.

Together, the above ten core competencies have defined TAS officers over the years. They form the arsenal of leadership capabilities that have enabled them to perform the many diverse roles they have occupied in Tata companies operating in different industries.

Would TAS officers with the specified competencies have been able to guide the future strategies of the Tata Group or any large enterprise? Our view is that the above competencies definitely enable officers to guide the fortunes of any large business Group, provided their performance, the results that they deliver and their adherence to values are consistently monitored by their Group's HR function. Had these important parameters been systematically monitored within the Tata Group, and used as a basis for the further refinement of the capabilities of the TAS officers and their subsequent placement in senior positions, many more capable leaders with the ten core competencies discussed here would have charted myriad, novel, value-creating and compassionate pathways for the Tata Group.

41
Grooming Talent for Greatness

THE FUTURE WILL REQUIRE THE BEST AND THE MOST 'CENTRED' OF leaders to guide organizations. Yet, the selection of the right talent is just the first step in the creation of managers and leaders who will spearhead the process of delivering lasting value. The rigorous TAS selection process ensured that the Tata Group was able to draw in the right kind of talent and provided a supply of capable officers who could be deployed where the Group would most need them.

Good talent needs to be guided, empowered, developed further, and groomed for specific positions if the best is to be drawn out of them. The HR function whose primary goal is to ensure the continuous rejuvenation, retention, and development of human capital in an organization has to consciously work on an effective PMS to create a culture that reinforces the values and behaviours the organization needs. We think that on both these counts much was expected from the Tata Group HR, but its delivery was seriously questionable.

Most TAS officers who were assigned to Tata companies benefited from the elaborate HR policies of those organizations. However, at the Group level, the attention given to the TAS was modest. There were a few sporadic group-learning interventions, wherein some officers were brought along with other Tata managers to the TMTC in Pune, and together with facilitators and trainers from the Harvard Business School or other reputed academic institutions, they would spend up to a week deliberating subjects such as strategy, appropriate leadership styles and the challenges of the future.

However, for the most part, Group HR believed in a laissez-faire approach to the TAS. Its engagement with officers assigned to different Tata companies was minimal, and no attempt was ever made to institutionalize the induction, the development and the systematic growth of TAS officers. Many of the officers who were not finding their 'sweet spot' in the Tata companies that they were assigned to, rather than reaching out to Group HR, would simply choose to quit. The indifference of Group HR was often a key factor that prompted TAS officers to look outside the Tata Group at their first brush with some internal dissonance.

From the latter part of the 1990s, for many senior leadership vacancies that arose within Tata companies, Group HR would prefer to look beyond the TAS, often to talent outside the Tata Group. For several decades, the Group HR Head himself was selected from outside the Tata Group!

Even on the task of culture-building and monitoring the performance of TAS officers, Group HR was found lacking. TAS officers were left to fend for themselves, being dropped into the deep end and then expected to swim and deliver, or just sink and be forgotten! There was little feedback, if ever, about their performance and how they might grow within the Group.

The apathy and indifference of the Group HR towards the TAS has been mentioned elsewhere. The key point is that even the most thoughtfully chosen and qualified people need constant attention, objective feedback, guidance, personal development opportunities, and avenues for growth. In the absence of these, even the best of people with many desirable competencies will be lost to the organizations that hire them.

42
Creating Lasting Value for All

One of JRD Tata's quotes that may have seemed especially maudlin when he first said it in the fifties reflects the current mantra for the future of leadership: 'To be a leader, you have to lead human beings with affection.' It is a prompt for conscious and compassionate leadership because the underlying sentiment is love.

We can hear some of you exclaiming: 'Affection? Love, in leadership? Seriously?!'

The truth is that the only way for businesses to become a force for good is to be led by conscious and compassionate leaders, who not only understand that we are all a part of the mysterious web of life, but who also know that it is love, care and kindness that sustain this beautiful and intricate web! We know that the frontier technologies mentioned earlier would, in the next five years or so, dominate the processes of value-creation across the world. It is also a fact that many of the new technologies have already made inroads into the traditional value-creating arenas of agriculture, industry and services. This is forcing businesses and the organizations that regulate them to change their internal systems and processes at a rapid pace. Another change that is evident is that domain expertise and specialized knowledge are now in greater demand than before. The craftsperson era of the Middle Ages has reappeared in a way—demanding deep knowledge of specific aspects of technology.

While specialists are likely to be in great demand, there would be a need for generalists in the mould of TAS officers within the Tata Group, who would serve as a bridge between the changing, and essential needs of the 'web of life', while ensuring its continued vitality and exuberance. Such generalists would work closely with domain experts, specialists and others, to ensure that the overall process of value-creation is wholesome and benefits all.

Specialists and generalists will have to work closely together, ensuring that the needs of life, people and the planet are not sacrificed in the quest for 'perfecting' technologies that can become a source of atrocity.

JRD's conviction that he would like people to be happy points to the fact that he understood that the mere acquisition of 'things' can never be a source of happiness. Stimulating the ownership of goods—which is the basis of business activity—may also need to undergo a change. Newer models of business, which move away from the linear economic model of extraction (of natural resources), conversion (by using energy and people), utilization (by customers and users), and finally, dumping of used goods, cannot provide a sustainable way to create value and enhance the quality of life of all. Instead, the circular economic model of creating value, which emphasizes the Three Rs, Reduce, Reuse and Recycle, would need to be brought into effect.

The obvious starting locus for changes in all future leaders resides in our minds. The need, therefore, is for us to create a 'new mindset' that is necessary for each one of us to make decisions that enhance value, create wealth and expand happiness without limiting or eroding the ability of other people and living things to do the same.

Creating the right, compassionate mindset is all the more critical since the human brain, having evolved over millennia, does have a part that is useful to our survival as a species, but which yields to emotions and the feelings we experience. Most matters that elicit our emotions are likely to be decided at the gut level, without much effort and thought because it is hard-wired and therefore stimulates an automatic way of responding. But such thinking can actually erode value, and therefore, there is a need for a more rational mode of decision-making. The rational thinking mode which relies on data, facts and information is processed by the neocortex of our brains. Intelligent thinking is also at the heart of consciously moving away from ingrained human tendencies such as tribalism and in-group favouritism.

Values and decisions that would ensure the health of Planet Earth, environmental sustainability, and social justice, as also the overall development of all people and communities, as articulated by Jamsetji Tata, would remain front and centre in all businesses that seek success and longevity. Climate change and the myriad environmental crises that we have referred to and experienced in the last few years will need businesses and investors to demand growth that is sustainable and aligned with life itself.

43
Additional Competencies for Leaders

WE BELIEVE THERE ARE TWO ADDITIONAL AND DISTINCT COMPETENCIES that current and future leaders need to possess, over and above the ten core competencies that we have indicated earlier, especially if they wish to steer their businesses towards value-creation instead of eroding it. These are outlined below.

A Unity-with-Life Mindset

Current and future leaders have to consciously cultivate a mindset that enables them to 'see' and understand their interconnectedness with life itself. Creating such an orientation requires leaders to reflect deeply on the delicate balance between all life-forms; thereby realizing how the well-being of humanity rests upon the sustained health and vitality of life on land, and in the vast oceans of our planet. Leaders also need to realize that the notion that 'we can do whatever we wish' without any concern for anyone else is unethical. If pursued, the outcomes are fraught with many possibilities of eroding value for others, even as one may create value and surpluses for oneself.

A Unity-with-Life mindset also requires mulling on the fundamental nature of one's business, the goals that are being pursued, and the people or organizations that are being benefited. Often, people become part of organizations without truly knowing what purpose or mission drives the enterprise. Leaders need to reflect on this and understand whether the activities of the business are adding value, or eroding it for some or all groups.

Fixating On Net Value Creation, Not Just CSR Spending

American philosopher John B. Rawls (1921–2002) famously propounded the notion that each member of society lives behind a 'veil of ignorance'. This veil prevents each one of us from making sound ethical decisions since we have no idea about what's best for society. Consciously using our intelligence and rational thinking capabilities to tear down the veil of ignorance is essential to ensuring that the value created by businesses provides a net benefit rather than an erosion of value.

This is a vital point in the context of CSR. Many business owners hold the erroneous view that they can run their businesses as they please, as long as they share some of the surpluses generated with 'worthy causes'. In the Indian Companies Act of 2013, Section 135 stipulates that all companies meeting a size and scale test will have a CSR Committee which will ensure that 2 per cent of the net profits are spent on socially and environmentally relevant activities specified in Schedule VII of the Act.

While on paper this might seem reasonable, there is a danger that all need to be conscious of the fact that the actions of business themselves must create net value rather than eroding it, and in that sense, the CSR spending as advised by the Act needs to be an 'add on' to the value that the enterprise is creating. If philanthropy or CSR spending is done to compensate for net value creation that is negative, then the very idea of the spending is mis-directed.

In this context, it is worthwhile to go back to an example from the late 1800s. Andrew Carnegie (1835–1919), a contemporary of Jamsetji

Tata, was a successful American business tycoon who made much of his money in steel and railroads. Like Jamsetji, he, too, was considered a very wealthy businessman in his time. Towards the later years of his life, he gave away almost 90 per cent of his wealth to charity, creating the Carnegie Endowment for International Peace, Carnegie Hall, the Carnegie Foundation, the Carnegie Institute of Technology (now part of Carnegie Mellon University), and more than 2,500 libraries. Carnegie shared the reasoning behind his philanthropic decision-making: he believed that people should give their money away while they are alive and that more value is created by donating to the broader community than by leaving money to heirs. There is no denying that in the process, Andrew Carnegie created enormous value for communities across America. However, this is only a part of the entire situation, and this is where the similarities with the founder of the House of Tata cease.

In his book, *Better, Not Perfect*, Professor Max H. Bazerman mentions further that Andrew Carnegie, who created so much value through his philanthropy, also destroyed value by engaging in miserly, ineffective and potentially criminal behaviour as a business leader. Carnegie was very tough on his employees. In an attempt to bust the union at his Pennsylvania steel mill, Carnegie authorized his company, the Carnegie Steel Company, to institute massive pay cuts. When the labour union rejected the new contract, the mill managers locked out the workers and brought in hundreds of bouncers to guard the facilities. A battle broke out between the workers and the bouncers and sixteen people were killed. In the end, the union was destroyed and many workers lost their jobs, if not lives.

If company managers think that by doling out money as per the CSR Act, they can be absolved of value destruction, then the spirit of CSR will be lost, and it will do the nation, our planet and people enormous harm. Instead, if all the processes of a company are first evaluated on the basis of their value-creating potential and ecological sustainability, and only then is the two per cent amount spent in a way to uphold social justice, sustainability, and sharing of wealth, then that would be lastingly beneficial. Future leaders need to be fixated on this.

The two additional competencies spelled out above, together with the ten core competencies that have been the basis of selecting TAS offices, provide a framework for leadership capabilities and characteristics that will be essential for the future. Without these essential competencies, leaders would lack the resilience needed to manage the many conflicting expectations of stakeholders in a rapidly evolving world.

It is our view that the twelve competencies listed here need to be part of the toolkit of all future leaders. That is what will create compassionate leaders who run wholesome businesses, which in turn create net value and benefit all people and our planet.

The TAS cadre may have been created to keep such values at the heart of the Tata Group, but it is time that the same values and capabilities become a wholesome template for doing business in every enterprise anywhere in the world.

44

Whither the TAS?

In an India where environmental destruction, governance failings and corporate malfeasance have all taken a heavy toll on economic growth, values-driven businesses committed to improving their Environmental, Social and Governance (ESG) performance can see a new lease of life and create disproportionate impact. This should be hugely suited to Tatas' strengths. However, for reasons covered in earlier chapters, the Tata Group has not been able to adequately leverage such a business ecosystem to its advantage. Yet, we believe that the Tata Group has a rich legacy, on which it can build for the future to address the growing challenges of growth, good governance and community and stakeholder engagement. At their heart, all of these are really challenges of values-based leadership, exactly what the TAS was created to offer the Tata Group, and as reflected in the leadership competencies outlined earlier.

The TAS, as it is today, is not appropriately structured and supported to deliver the leadership that the Tata Group requires. But with modest tweaks, it could yet become an instrument for the revitalization of the Group, assuming that the Tatas are ready for such a transformation. The qualifier is crucial. The Group's recent past has owed much to the individual passion and drive of an individual like Ratan Tata, but the future will need acknowledgement from his successors that times have changed and leadership will need to be more distributed if a diversified group like Tata is to deliver sustainable, profitable growth.

Efforts by individuals to try and mould the Tata Group as Ratan Tata once tried and succeeded, are more than likely in future to instead diminish the Group and pave the way for shedding many of its businesses. The writing already seems to be on the wall for proud businesses like telecom, thermal power, European steel, and traditional passenger mobility.

Assuming there is a commitment at the very top, across Tata Sons shareholders and the Board of Tata Sons, to sustain and grow the broad multi-geography, multi-business portfolio of the Tata Group, the relevance of the TAS and the role it can play becomes vivid. However, this will need critical changes from the past in the way this cadre operates and functions. Alongside testing for values orientation, the Tata Group has to select TAS officers for diversity, invest substantially in their training both at the time of recruitment and then through their careers, compensate them fairly, and nurture and reward innovation and entrepreneurial flair.

The strategy of picking up young individuals below the age of twenty-seven for the TAS is a good one, allowing these managers to be moulded to suit the Group's needs and inculcating values in them that make them Group loyalists first and foremost, before they become set in their ways. The efficacy of the selection process has been demonstrated throughout the history of the TAS. TAS officers have delivered consistently as and when they have been given responsibilities within the Group. This ability of TAS officers to deliver results is seen even in the officers who left the Group. Rajeev Dubey, Navtej Sarna, Siddharth Kak, V.S. Krishnan, B.V.R. Subbu, Raghuram Rajan, Arun Shourie, Vibha Paul Rishi, Srikumar Misra and Abanti Sankaranarayan are just a few examples of officers who left the Group as they believed that they could fulfil their potential elsewhere.

However, the Tata Group needs more women, in general, and the TAS needs more women within its cadre, in particular. The lack of women in senior leadership positions combined with the consistent departure of TAS women officers within ten years of joining needs to ring alarm bells within the Group. The Group employs over seven hundred thousand people across the world; yet, there are only a handful of women leading Tata businesses in any country.

It is also a sad commentary on the past that the number of women TAS CEOs across five decades is still only in single digits. The same issues that plague Corporate India on retention and development of women managers have also impacted the Tata Group—from inadequate support through maternity and life stages, to various forms of discrimination and harassment—and need to be addressed on priority.

The 2014 commitment of the Tata Group to triple the number of women CXOs and double the percentage of women in the workforce by 2020 has been missed by a long margin. As a first step, these must be delivered at the earliest. Learnings from the pandemic period experiences of women working from home and being highly productive must be leveraged to ensure Tata companies are offering their women employees every support to ensure they see no reason to drop out of the workforce even temporarily.

Besides gender diversity, the TAS needs to recruit more nationalities to support the multinational enterprise that the Tatas have become. The Tata Group's many business verticals across multiple countries will then offer the perfect platform for further grooming TAS officers as general managers and future leaders of the Group.

The endeavour to make the TAS more inclusive, by offering the best managers within the Tata Group the opportunity to apply for entry, must continue. This will increase the acceptability of the TAS to Tata companies and make some of the privileges the cadre enjoys more palatable to the rest of the Group. Elements of accelerated leadership programmes at companies like Tata Motors could be merged down the line with the TAS programme, and TAS selections could be used as a common talent attraction programme to be leveraged by all Tata companies.

The TAS must also increase its sourcing universe, which has largely been confined to the IIMs. It needs to locate talent across more universities in India and overseas, and more academic domains, especially the liberal arts. Some of the most respected leaders from the TAS, like Nawshir Khurody, Xerxes Desai, R.K. Krishna Kumar and Camelia Panjabi never acquired management degrees but had a high propensity for creativity and innovation.

The lessons from the Tata Group's short-lived Tata China Management Programme need to be fully understood and targeted programmes re-launched as part of the TAS selection scheme. As a Group with an international footprint, key geographies of importance to the current Tata businesses should be targeted, including China, Europe and the US, as well as geographies of future importance in Africa. The starting compensation packages for offers made in some geographies will inevitably need to be linked to the cost of living in those geographies; hence, a US manager will be paid far more than an Indian manager. Through the course of officers' careers, the compensation can be progressively calibrated to accommodate the business and geography they serve.

Talent attraction in today's environment is not an inexpensive exercise. The right incentives need to be created to attract and retain talent in the TAS. One of the proposals that could be considered in this regard is the concept of a Long-Term Incentive Plan (LTIP) that stretches across, say, two decades, and rewards TAS officers for staying in the Group, subject to certain defined thresholds of minimum performance delivery. To the extent that the ultimate custodian of the Tata brand is Tata Sons, and Tata Sons has the greatest interest in deploying high quality managers to lead operations of companies across the Group, TAS officers could also be retained permanently on the rolls of Tata Sons and sent on deputation to individual companies, as required. The combination of an LTIP scheme and retaining TAS officers on the rolls of Tata Sons would help solve the challenge TAS officers face when deployed in struggling companies that are unable to pay market standard salaries, and eliminate the disincentive for officers to move to smaller and less visible Tata operations.

In the past, in its compensation philosophy, the Tata Group tried to maintain a balance between the need to attract good talent and the desire to fairly reward loyalty as well as performance. In a country that is home to the largest number of poor people in the world, Tata leaders tended to be sensitive to the issues of income inequality and job security. Consequently, Tata employees were aware of and welcomed the fact that while the Group was not the best paymaster, it endeavoured to retain employees in the workforce for as long as possible, often for their entire working careers. One of the reasons so many Tata managers were happy 'lifers' in the Group, dedicating their entire careers to the Group and adjusting to lower-than-market-standard compensation packages, was because of their identification with the higher purpose the Group serves.

With 'lifers' now retiring en masse, replaced in a number of cases by possibly more short-term-oriented managers from outside the Group with better-than market-standard compensation packages, questions are inevitably being asked about the kind of culture that will develop within the Group, and whether the sense of higher purpose will continue to motivate Tata leaders. Furthermore, the Tata Group stands depleted since much of the valuable tacit knowledge of lifers is lost without being transferred to subsequent generations of leaders.

Careers for life are no longer being advised as the norm, and senior executive compensation, in many cases, is several hundred times more than the median compensation of employees. These trends sit awkwardly with the Tata Group's reputation for balancing stakeholder interests and investing in its people. The large-scale redundancies declared at Tata businesses in recent years, including in telecoms, have left bitterness and disappointment in their wake.

In future, with growing competitive pressures, the easy option would be to declare wholesale redundancies and jettison a large section of the Tata workforce to improve operating ratios and the returns profiles of Tata companies. The tougher option, and the real test of a 'Tata way' of dealing with competitive pressures and creating 'One Tata', will be if people deemed surplus in some Tata businesses can be redeployed elsewhere within the Tata Group, or if businesses can be turned around and scaled up so that the challenge now shifts from one of resource excess to talent scarcity. Officers of the TAS must play a vital role in navigating such considerations.

A critical area of training and nurturing within the TAS will need to be directed towards fostering innovation and the spirit of entrepreneurship. Many more TAS officers need to emerge with entrepreneurial instincts of the kind that allowed Xerxes Desai to create and build Titan. The fact is that too few Indian corporations invest any significant amount in R&D and in creating a culture that rewards meaningful and reasonable risk taking. At media briefings on the Group's innovation platform, Tata Innovista, the Group has admitted to spending inadequately on R&D, at under 3 per cent of revenues (a number which also includes some debatable spends that could be classified as conventional capex rather than R&D investments). While the Tata spend has been much larger than the Indian economy's R&D spend of around 0.7 per cent of its GDP, it pales in comparison to the vast sums dedicated by many peers and multinational companies. Blue-blooded innovators like Apple, with an R&D spend of 6 per cent of total net sales, and Google, whose R&D spend runs into double-digit percentages annually, are far ahead.

If the Tatas are to retain an edge in business that is to be derived from sustainable competitive advantage, it has to come from being ahead of the curve on market trends. A number of Tata businesses have achieved scale without commensurate profitability and without a strong pipeline of innovative products and services. In an Indian market emerging from decades of protection, the Tatas did well to sustain their leadership in different businesses. However, many Tata companies have remained pygmies in comparison to their global peers who have grown enormously and have not been able to distinguish themselves sufficiently even in the Indian market they once dominated. Be it retail, financial services or information technology, there have been relatively few transformational innovations or ideas from the Tatas that have captured the imagination of stakeholders.

In a sector like information technology, where TCS and other Indian companies have done rather well over the past two decades through business process outsourcing, we are yet to hear of any dramatic initiatives or product developments in areas like artificial intelligence. As one of the pioneers of the IT industry in India, Infosys Founder N.R. Narayana Murthy put it in 2018: 'The biggest challenge that the Indian IT industry has faced in the last forty years and has still not solved is the inability to move from being "reactive problem solvers" to "proactive problem definers and solvers". Our customers used to tell me that our youngsters were sincere in doing whatever the customers asked them to do rather than suggesting solutions to customers' problems proactively. That was the situation in 1980, and it is the same today! This is a huge cultural issue in India. Huge investment in training by companies and a lot of hard work by employees are needed to overcome these cultural challenges.'

TAS officers must be given exposure to some of the best institutions focused on innovation around the world. An 'innovation trek' during their Bharat Darshan, across facilities of universities like Stanford and MIT and research organizations like NASA, with visits to campuses of global innovation leaders like Apple, Facebook and Google, could serve to inspire them, as could projects undertaken in collaboration with accelerators that support start-ups. Assigning TAS officers across all levels the task of developing innovation projects with cross-functional teams across Tata companies could also be a worthwhile initiative that would serve multiple purposes, including greater integration of managers across the Group and identification of novel ideas and new businesses for the Group.

It has often been queried, for instance, why the Tata Group has not developed a strong footprint across rural India and played a major role in stimulating agri-business opportunities, despite the powerful starting point it has had with companies like Rallis and Tata Chemicals in agri-inputs and fertilizers, Tata Motors in light commercial vehicles, TTSL with mobility services, and Tata Steel with its Agrico division. Perhaps a series of exercises to identify new and emerging rural opportunities could be among the innovation projects identified for TAS officers to pursue.

With the right training and developmental inputs, and as an organization with a strong values orientation, the TAS may yet become relevant to the future of the Tata Group. The Group has played an enormously important role in the past in India's industrialization and emergence as an economy of global significance. With leadership drawn from the ranks of the TAS that is values-driven and committed to the Group's revitalization along ESG parameters, perhaps there is a new chapter in the evolution of the TAS and the Tata Group that is yet to be written! And perhaps the time has even come to rechristen the TAS as the Tata Leadership Service (TLS)!

Appendix

TAS Officers Referred to in the Manuscript

1. Abanti Sankaranarayanan (TAS 1992)
2. Ajoy Misra (TAS 1980)
3. Arun Kumar (TAS 1973)
4. Arun Maira (TAS 1965)
5. Arun Wakhlu (TAS 1980)
6. Ashok Mehta (TAS 1966)
7. Ashutosh Pandey (TAS 1998)
8. Bharat Wakhlu (TAS 1985)
9. Brotin Banerjee (TAS 1998)
10. Camellia Panjabi (TAS 1963)
11. Debjani Biswas (TAS 1983)
12. Dhruva Dey (TAS 1962)
13. Dr Ashish Nanda (TAS 1983)
14. Dr Freddie A. Mehta (TAS 1956)
15. Dr Mukund Rajan (TAS 1995)
16. Dr Sunil Vacchani (TAS 1976)
17. Eric Vas (TAS 1991)

18. Francis DaCunha (TAS 1971)
19. Govind Sankaranarayanan (TAS 1992)
20. Harish Bhat (TAS 1987)
21. Harpal Singh (TAS 1974)
22. Harsh Chitale (TAS 1993)
23. Hasnen Varawala (TAS 1988)
24. Indira Pant (TAS 1984)
25. Jacob Kurien (TAS 1983)
26. Jamshed Daboo (TAS 1986)
27. Jaspreet Bindra (TAS 1994)
28. Jehangir Ardeshir (TAS 1983)
29. Kalpana Kohli Kar (TAS 1984)
30. Khorshed Jhaveri (TAS 1958)
31. Kris Ramachandran (TAS 1974)
32. Masood Husseiny (TAS 1999)
33. N. Srinath (TAS 1986)
34. Navtej Sarna (TAS 1980)
35. Nawshir Khurody (TAS 1960)
36. Nirav Khambati (TAS 1997)
37. P. Balaji (TAS 1990)
38. Partha Sarkar (TAS 1975)
39. Patanjali 'Patu' Keswani (TAS 1983)
40. Percy Siganporia (TAS 1974)
41. Prakash Telang (TAS 1972)
42. Prashanth Nayak (TAS 1995)
43. Prateek Pashine (TAS 1995)
44. R. Mukundan (TAS 1990)
45. R.K. Krishna Kumar (TAS 1963)
46. Raghuram Rajan (TAS 1987)
47. Rajeev Dubey (TAS 1975)
48. Rajendra 'Raju' Bhinge (TAS 1975)
49. Rajiv Dube (TAS 1990)
50. Rajvir Kadan (TAS 1971)

51. S. Ramakrishnan (TAS 1972)
52. Sanjay Johri (TAS 1975)
53. Sanjaya Sharma (TAS 1980)
54. Shayesth Desai (TAS 1990)
55. Silloo Surti (TAS 1962)
56. Siddharth Kak (TAS 1971)
57. Sonu Bhasin (TAS 1987)
58. Srikumar Misra (TAS 2001)
59. Steve Godinho (TAS 1986)
60. Suneel Bandhu (TAS 1989)
61. Surya Sethi (TAS 1975)
62. TK Balaji (TAS 1970)
63. V.S. Krishnan (TAS 1972)
64. V.S. Mahesh (TAS 1971)
65. Vibha Paul Rishi (TAS 1982)
66. Vijay Rai (TAS 1971)
67. Vinay Pande (TAS 1979)
68. Vipul Jain (TAS 1980)
69. Vir Chopra (TAS 1971)
70. Visty Banaji (TAS 1973)
71. Xerxes Desai (TAS 1961)

Acknowledgements

A book of this kind could not have been written without the support, guidance, insights, stories and anecdotes of all those men and women who have been a part of the prestigious TAS cadre over the past decades. We are, therefore, deeply appreciative and grateful to all those from the TAS who willingly opened up to us and unhesitatingly shared their unique and uplifting experiences. Thanks to them, we obtained stories and anecdotes aplenty. The full list of all those TAS officers who have, during their years with the Tatas, contributed to the Group's growth and success, and whom we spoke to, is given below. Our immense gratitude to each of them. We would also like to thank all those whom we may not have spoken to, but who have contributed to the visibility and the global impact of the TAS.

The TAS is a valued and renowned cadre on account of the fact that it is an integral part of an extraordinary Indian multinational, the Tata Group. All three of us have served the Tatas with devotion and joy for decades, and we feel proud to have been a part of many of the storied companies that comprise the Tata Group. It is heartening that the Tatas have always kept the interests of the nation, its customers, as also those of its diverse stakeholders, front and centre of all the Group's processes and long-term objectives. Our gratitude to the many wonderful leaders that we have had the privilege of working with, and whose guidance and mentorship have shaped our values and commitment to the greater good.

HarperCollins India and their team, led by Udayan Mitra were prompt in providing us their support when we broached the idea of writing a book on the TAS. Our commissioning editor Sachin Sharma provided valuable insights on the manuscript early in the process, and ensured that the book was launched as he'd promised, within weeks after the final copy-editing was completed. Our copy-editor Anju Christine was thorough in tightening the language and making the book an easy read. Our immense thanks to all of them.

We must admit that we were a little apprehensive when we started writing this book. Some of us had co-authored books with others, and we knew that collaborative writing does bring its own challenges. As if that were not enough, through much of the writing phase, we were stymied by our inability to travel on account of the lockdowns in place during the COVID-19 pandemic. Despite that, the three of us made sure that we met online frequently to plan the structure of the book and then discuss the finer aspects of the portions that we had written. We are grateful to one another for the patience that each one showed. We had our share of disagreements, but those were handled with the maturity expected of TAS officers! Our combined effort and commitment to see the project through in time has enabled the book to attain this final form.

Finally, our thanks to our respective spouses, namely Juggi (Bhasin), Soumya (Rajan) and Savita (Wakhlu) for their unstinted support throughout the writing of this book. Writing is a lonely, solo activity, and each one of us took time, away from our families, to focus on interviewing our colleagues and writing our chapters. We appreciate the loving support and understanding of our respective spouses and hope they find this book worth the effort that was put into it!

Sonu Bhasin
Mukund Rajan
Bharat Wakhlu

List of TAS Officers Interviewed (In Alphabetical Order)

Abanti Sankaranarayan, Aftab Ahmad, Arun Kumar, Arun Maira, Arun Wakhlu, Ashok Mehta, Aubrey Rebello, Avinash Kirpal, Camellia Panjabi, David Rebello, Deepak Dheer, Debjani Biswas, Eric Vas, Francis DaCunha, Geeta Prakash, Govind Sankaranarayanan, Harpal Singh, Indira Pant, Jamshed Daboo, Jaspreet Bindra, Jehangir Ardeshir, Kalpana Kohli Kar, Khorshed Javeri, Navtej Sarna, Nawshir Khurody, Nirav Khambati, P. Balaji, Prakash Telang, Prashanth Nayak, Prateek Pashine, Rajeev Dubey, Rajendra 'Raju' Bhinge, Rajiv Dube, Rustom Vesavevala, Sanjay Bhargava, Sanjay Johri, Sanjaya Sharma, Sanjeev Mohoni, Siddharth Kak, Steve Godinho, Surya Suraj Sethi, V S Krishnan, Vibha Paul Rishi, Vijay Rai, Vipul Jain, Vir Chopra, Visty Banaji.

Abbreviations

ADAG: Anil Dhirubhai Ambani Group

AGLC: Annual Group Leadership Conference

ASSOCHAM: Associated Chambers of Commerce and Industry of India

BCG: Boston Consulting Group

BJP: Bharatiya Janata Party

CAG: Comptroller and Auditor General

CBI: Central Bureau of Investigation

CDMA: Code Division Multiple Access

CII: Confederation of Indian Industry

CMIE: Centre for Monitoring Indian Economy

COO: Chief Operating Officer

CRY: Child Rights for You

CSN: Companhia Siderúrgica Nacional

CSR: Corporate Social Responsibility

ERC: Engineering Research Centre

ESG: Environment, Social and Governance

FERA: Foreign Exchange Regulation Act

FICCI: Federation of Indian Commerce and Industry

FMS: Faculty of Management Studies

GCC: Group Corporate Centre

GEC: Group Executive Council

GEO: Group Executive Office

GSM: Global System for Mobile

HMT: Hindustan Machine Tools

HWB: Human Well-Being

IAS: Indian Administrative Service

ICS: Imperial Civil Service

IIM: Indian Institute of Management

IIM-A: IIM-Ahmedabad

IoT: Internet of Things

IPO: Initial Public Offering

IT: Information Technology

ITIs: Industrial Training Institutes

JUSE: Union of Japanese Scientists and Engineers

LTE: Long-Term Evolution

LTIP: Long-Term Incentive Plan

MRTP: Monopolies and Restrictive Trade Practices

NAV: Net Asset Value

NDA: National Democratic Alliance

PMS: Performance Management System

RBI: Reserve Bank of India

SAIL: Steel Authority of India Ltd

SCIP: Second Career Internship Programme

SDGs: Sustainable Development Goals

SEBI: Securities and Exchange Board of India

SPJIMR: S.P. Jain Institute of Management Research

TACO: Tata Auto Components Ltd

TAS: Tata Administrative Service

TBEM: Tata Business Excellence Model

TCS: Tata Consultancy Services

TELCO: Tata Engineering and Locomotive Company

TIS: Tata Interactive Systems

TISCO: Tata Iron and Steel Company

TLS: Tata Leadership Service

TMTC: Tata Management Training Centre

TNIDCO: Tamil Nadu Industrial Development Corporation

TOI: Total Operation Improvement

TOMCO: Tata Oil Mills Company Ltd

TQM: Tata Quality Management

TQMS: Tata Quality Management Services

TRAI: Telecom Regulatory Authority of India

TSG: Tata Sustainability Group

TSRDS: Tribal Steel Rural Development Society

TTSL: Tata Teleservices Ltd

TWO: Tata Workers' Union

ULFA: United Liberation Front of Assam

UNDP: UN Development Programme

UP: Uttar Pradesh

VSNL: Videsh Sanchar Nigam Ltd

WEF: World Economic Forum

XLRI: Xavier Labour Relations Institute (now known as Xavier School of Management)

Index

About the Authors

Bharat Wakhlu

Bharat Wakhlu is a thought-leader, a futurist, a leadership coach, keynote speaker and the bestselling author of four books—covering Performance Excellence, Personal Growth, Ethics and Governance—and a novel. With over three decades of global corporate experience within the Tata Group and with Sikorsky Aircraft Corporation, he offers a slew of unique capabilities to help leaders across diverse organizations deliver lasting, wholesome value. He is the cofounder of the Foundation for Peace and Compassionate Leadership, a not-for-profit that's committed to a new paradigm of leadership. An avid drone hobbyist and golfer, Bharat is fluent in six languages.

Mukund Rajan

In a career spanning twenty-three years with the Tatas, Dr Mukund Rajan served as the Group's first Brand Custodian, Chief Ethics Officer, Chairman of the Tata Global Sustainability Council and Member of the Group Executive Council. A graduate from the Indian Institute of Technology (IIT) Delhi, he completed a Doctorate in International Relations on a Rhodes Scholarship at Oxford University. His previous books include *Global Environmental Politics* (1996), *The Brand Custodian* (2019) and *Outlast: How ESG Can Benefit Your Business* (2021).

Sonu Bhasin

Sonu Bhasin is one of the early and senior women professionals in the industry. Besides being a TAS officer for thirteen years, she has been President, Axis Bank and Group President, Yes Bank, among other senior leadership roles. Sonu is an Independent Director on the boards of well-known and reputed domestic and multinational companies.

She is a family business historian and is the Editor-in-Chief of *Families & Business* magazine. Sonu is a business author and her previous books include *The Inheritors* (2017), *Unstoppable: Kuldip Singh Dhingra and the Rise of Berger Paints* (2019) and *Gujarmal Modi: The Resolute Industrialist* (2022).

Sonu has a degree in B.Sc. (Hons) Mathematics from St. Stephen's College, Delhi University and an MBA from Faculty of Management Studies, Delhi University.